# Lincoln in the Atlantic World

This original and wide-ranging work reveals how Abraham Lincoln responded to prompts from around the globe to shape his personal appearance, political appeal, and presidential policies. Throughout his life, he learned lessons about slavery, American politics, and international relations from sources centered in Africa, Britain, and the European continent. Answering questions that previous scholars have not thought to ask, the book opens the vision of Lincoln as a global republican. Thanks to its new stories and compelling analyses, this book provides a provocative and stimulating read that will generate debate at both high and popular levels.

A professor of history and American studies at Franklin & Marshall College in Lancaster, Pennsylvania, Louise L. Stevenson writes about nineteenth-century American cultural and intellectual life in its transatlantic context. *Lincoln in the Atlantic World* follows her *Scholarly Means to Evangelical Ends: The New Haven Scholars and the Transformation of Higher Learning in America, 1830–1890* (Johns Hopkins, 1986), *The Victorian Homefront: American Thought and Culture, 1860–1880* (1991, new ed. Cornell, 2001), and articles on books and reading in everyday life, from the best sellers of Britain and America in the eighteenth-century through those of the twenty-first century, including Harry Potter. In 2015, the Abraham Lincoln Presidential Library and Museum selected her essay "The Global Meaning of the Gettysburg Address" for inclusion in *Gettysburg Replies: The World Responds to Abraham Lincoln's Gettysburg Address*.

# Lincoln in the Atlantic World

**LOUISE L. STEVENSON**

*Franklin & Marshall College*

CAMBRIDGE
UNIVERSITY PRESS

# CAMBRIDGE
## UNIVERSITY PRESS

University Printing House, Cambridge CB2 8BS, United Kingdom

One Liberty Plaza, 20th Floor, New York, NY 10006, USA

477 Williamstown Road, Port Melbourne, VIC 3207, Australia

314-321, 3rd Floor, Plot 3, Splendor Forum, Jasola District Centre, New Delhi - 110025, India

79 Anson Road, #06-04/06, Singapore 079906

Cambridge University Press is part of the University of Cambridge.

It furthers the University's mission by disseminating knowledge in the pursuit of education, learning and research at the highest international levels of excellence.

www.cambridge.org
Information on this title: www.cambridge.org/9781107524231

© Louise L. Stevenson 2015

First published 2015

*A catalogue record for this publication is available from the British Library*

*Library of Congress Cataloging in Publication data*
Stevenson, Louise L.
Lincoln in the Atlantic World / Louise Stevenson, Franklin & Marshall College.
pages cm
Includes bibliographical references and index.
ISBN 978-1-107-10964-3 (hardback) – ISBN 978-1-107-52423-1 (paperback)
1. Lincoln, Abraham, 1809–1865 – Philosophy.  2. Lincoln, Abraham, 1809–1865 – Knowledge and learning.  3. Lincoln, Abraham, 1809–1865 – Political and social views.  I. Title.
E457.2.S85  2015
973.7092–dc23    2015014702

ISBN  978-1-107-10964-3  Hardback
ISBN  978-1-107-52423-1  Paperback

*To Lila and Katie,*
*With love.*

# Contents

# Acknowledgments

The term "acknowledgments" insufficiently conveys the deep gratitude and appreciation that I wish to express to many generous colleagues and friends. Without their advice and encouragement, this book would not exist.

James Cornelius and Irwin F. Gellman backed this project from its inception. While their careful and perceptive comments added to the clarity and accuracy of successive drafts, their encouragement offered emotional sustenance at crucial moments. They were a small, but mighty cheerleading squad.

Deploying their inexhaustible knowledge of all things Lincoln, Matthew Pinsker and James Cornelius smoothed my passage into the realm of Lincoln scholarship. My husband Philip Zimmerman helped to polish the manuscript with his incredible ability to spot infelicities of expression. I also thank him for never complaining during the past five years about my single-minded devotion of time and mental energy to another man.

At a variety of research libraries and archives, the deep knowledge of archivists, curators, and other professionals provided invaluable assistance. With profound appreciation to: William Allman, at the White House; Susan Haake, at the Lincoln Home National Historic Site; Margaret Kieckhefer, Michelle Krowl, and Cheryl Regan at the Library of Congress; Cornelia King and Nicole Joniec at The Library Company of Philadelphia; David Langbart, at the National Archives, College Park, MD; and others whom I acknowledge as the text progresses.

At Franklin & Marshall College and in Lancaster, I am fortunate to labor among so many generous colleagues. Interdisciplinary projects become less daunting and increasingly fruitful with the contributions of their specialized knowledge: Douglas Anthony on Africa, Lynn Brooks on theater history, John Haddad on the U.S. in the world, Alison Kibler on American popular culture, Ben McRee on British history, Maria Mitchell and Guillaume de Syon on European history, David Schuyler on American history, Grier Stephenson on the Constitution, and Hoda Yousef on the Barbary pirates. Cecile Zorach and Karen Campbell offered translations of German-language sources, and Lisa Gasbarrone smoothed my translations from French documents.

The librarians and professional staff of the college provided crucial assistance in securing books and research materials and assisting with electronic preparation of the manuscript. Special thanks go to Tim Brixius for his efforts, and to Ann Wagoner for her skill with digital reproduction and her patience with my many requests. With appreciation to Jenn Buch, Mike Horn, Jared Julius, Tom Karel, Meghan Kelly, Carol Kornhauser, Louise Kulp, Meg Massey, Christopher Raab, Nikki Rearich, Lisa Stillwell, Rick Thompson, Sue Wood, and Scott Vine. A special shout-out goes to Mike Lear, whose mastery of the digital scanner produced so many of the illustrations in this volume.

Franklin & Marshall College students also made vital contributions to this book's production. Through the Hackman Scholars Program, I was able to benefit from the assistance of Kristina Montville and Rick Thoben. Philip Ehrig checked names and dates for accuracy. He both provided background on the histories of Austria and Hungary and asked provocative questions. Considering the answer to one of those, the significance of *Our American Cousin* in the nineteenth-century Atlantic world became apparent. In 2015, Emily Hawk ably assisted with indexing and checking page proofs.

Advanced history and American Studies students read successive versions of this book. Over the last several years, Lincoln taught both them and me how to make careful distinctions and to produce more powerful prose. I also hope that he taught them a good deal about leadership. For the comments and questions that prompted me to clarify ideas and to make explanations complete, I extend appreciation to: Kara Bacile, Leslie Bacile, Carson Bowes, Daniel Burke, Molly Cadwell, Stephanie Cespedes, D. Cicchiello, Andrew DeMaio, Brendon Denver, Joey Finnegan, Paul Giulio, Matthew Haller, James Hamilton, Mark Harmon-Vaught, Emily Hawk, Maxwell Hoffacker, Czarina Hutchins, Daniel Jacobs, Emilie Johnson, Xinyu Liu, Michael Lovisa, Patrick Musselman, Julia Philips, Maxwell Polans, Kelsey Prakken, Sheldon Ruby, and Kevin Stewart.

Time for composing the book and funds to help cover its research costs were provided by Franklin & Marshall College. May it continue and strengthen its practice of support for both teaching and scholarship. The production of this book proves how they can enrich one another.

Finally, I am dedicating this book to my daughters, Lila and Katie. The knowledge that they always will be there for me gives me strength.

# Introduction

## *My Lincoln Lessons*

In his speeches, President Lincoln frequently placed the United States in a global context. Readers often take these mentions as rhetorical flourishes that he used to surround his words with an aura of consequence. Consider his speech at Gettysburg, Pennsylvania, on November 19, 1863. Standing on a platform beside the new national cemetery, the president orated phrases that continue to resonate and define the basis of republicanism in the United States: "that government of the people, by the people, for the people, shall not perish from the earth."

Before the platform on that sunny day, 15,000 people stood near and among the newly shoveled graves of Union soldiers. Collected from the battlefield by gravediggers, many of whom were free African Americans, the soldiers' remains now rested in burial plots forming concentric semicircles. At the focal point, a monument with the statue "Genius of Liberty" on a towering pedestal would be placed in 1869. The orderliness of cemetery design had replaced the chaos and carnage of war. Mortally wounded during the great battle of the previous July, the soldiers had fallen in gruesome postures that defaced the town – its streets, house yards, and farm fields. To dedicate the cemetery, President Lincoln's address now transformed the corpses interred in their symmetrically arranged mounds into the "honored dead" whose sacrifice called for increased devotion to a great cause.

In his salient concluding sentence, the president explained that cause. The loss of each of the approximately 3,200 Union soldiers had mattered to the United States and to the world. They "had died that that nation might live."

In the present day, readers of Lincoln's well-known speech tend to emphasize his three prepositional phrases that sum up the central propositions of republican government: that governments depend on the consent of the governed and that they exist to serve those whom they govern. Readers then move quickly to the end of the sentence while overlooking why the president said that republican government, and in particular the republican government of the United States, possessed global importance. U.S. soldiers had died so that their national government should not perish, and even more, so that republican government should "not perish from the earth." For Abraham Lincoln, the outcome of the Civil War would determine the fate of republicanism both nationally and globally, in 1865 and for all time. If the Union prevailed, the United States would survive and the world would retain a model of republican government that other countries could emulate. As he had written to both houses of Congress in his annual message almost a year previously, the United States, the Union, was "the last best, hope of earth."

This book demonstrates that Lincoln meant what he said. It reveals the lessons of his early life and presidency that he drew from the Atlantic world. They taught him to think and to act globally as a politician and then as president.

This book had its beginning when my father gave me his father's volumes of Roy P. Basler's *Collected Works of Abraham Lincoln*. After spending a summer reading every volume and being suitably impressed with Lincoln's powers of analysis, I began offering students at Franklin & Marshall College a seminar on the president. While teaching that class a few years ago, attendance at a lecture about the French revolutions of the 1830s and 1848 moved me into a new and lightly charted area. During the discussion of European revolutions, my mind drifted from France to the United States of the 1830s and 1840s. The college semester was beginning, and the students in the current "Lincoln" seminar were considering the president's early life and how it had shaped his political career.

As the young Lincoln began to appear in a transatlantic context, questions naturally arose. To what extent had he resembled so many young Americans of those years; how had European revolutionaries inspired him with their vision of their countries' futures? After all, from Lincoln's teen years and through his early years in the politics of Illinois, he matured in an Atlantic world of democratic revolution.

Lincoln had grown up imagining his country as a member of the world community of nations. In 1823, President James Monroe issued the proclamation now known as the Monroe Doctrine to counter, at least in diplomatic prose, European threats to overturn the revolutions of Latin America. A few years previously, the Greeks' decade-long uprising against the Ottoman Empire had aroused great sympathy in the United States. In Congress, Henry Clay, then a representative from Kentucky, spoke in favor of a resolution, which went down to defeat, that would have sent an official emissary to Greece to observe their uprising. In his speech, Clay offered "good wishes" for Greek independence from his country – "almost the sole, the last, the greatest depository of human hope and human freedom."[1]

Given the momentous international events of Abraham Lincoln's teens and twenties, little wonder exists that he should have appreciated his country's membership in a global community. Even though the Lincoln family lived in rural Indiana, its curious and intellectually gifted son had borrowed books and newspapers from William Wood, a neighbor. The reading material brought international events to the attention of the young reader and pushed him to imagine his country's place in world history. The newspaper owner later reported that in 1829 he had read an essay by his neighbor. It claimed that the United States government was "the best form of Government in the world" and "ought to be Kept sound & preserved forever."[2]

More than revolutions in Greece and Latin America inspired Lincoln as he grew from a gawky teenager to adulthood. Before the 1850s, monarchies and social systems based on unfree labor had dominated the countries of the Atlantic world. In the recent past, the rise of reformers across western Europe and the political turmoil of the late 1840s had promised that the days of unlimited monarchy would end. Then, the forces of political reaction had taken over. The intervention of the Russian army into Hungary had quashed the chance for its independence. Soon, the victory of monarchical forces also had ended hopes for a unification of the Italian states and the German states. In France, Louis-Bonaparte Napoleon, President of the Second Republic, overthrew it in 1851, established the Second Empire, and proclaimed himself its emperor, Napoleon III.

In England, reformers had fared better. In 1832, the British Parliament extended representation in the national legislature to the country's burgeoning industrial cities and expanded the right to vote to an increased number of landholders and renters, thus enlarging the electorate by about 60 percent to include about 20 percent of adult males. Later in the same year, similar reforms were enacted in Scotland and Ireland. In the next decade, Parliament repealed the Corn Laws, which had benefited landowners while raising the cost of food. Agitation for public education promised that England soon might have an educated electorate.

Additionally, Parliament's end of slavery in almost all lands of the British Empire in 1834 and Alexander II's ending of serfdom of Russia in 1861 seemed to predict that all forms of unfree labor would end. Working people and reformers throughout Europe and former colonies in South America saw history ordaining that slavery, serfdom, and autocratic monarchies would disappear. The ideal government would be known as republican, and it would rest on the consent of the governed with free labor as the foundation of its economy. Ideally, citizens would be equal before the law, and the rule of law would prevail. Holding these ideals made one a republican no matter where one lived, although implementation of them differed in European and American countries.

Lincoln learned of these republican hopes through newspaper reading, conversation, and his everyday experiences. They confirmed that his country belonged to the Atlantic world both economically and politically. When nineteen years old, in 1828, he traveled some 750 miles to New Orleans. Transporting cargo to Louisiana on a flatboat, he learned of the commercial route that ran from the Midwest via the Mississippi River and its tributaries.

The trip taught him more than geography. As Lincoln and his rafting partner exchanged their goods at stops along the river, they learned how engaging in consecutive transactions offered the possibility of increasing the value of the merchandise that they were transporting. At the route's end, in New Orleans, they witnessed numerous commodities being transferred from riverboats and rafts to oceangoing ships. These vessels sailed to ports in the Caribbean Sea, the Mediterranean Sea, and islands off the African coast, eventually returning to the United States with manufactured items, minerals scarce in the Americas, or agricultural products.

Having made two trips to New Orleans by 1831, he probably had a good look at the polyglot people of the Atlantic world's economy. To a young man from the Midwest, the French- and Spanish-inspired architecture of New Orleans as well as the appearance and languages of the city's residents must have appeared exotic. Whereas the population of Illinois and Indiana in 1830 included less than 1 percent of free or enslaved African Americans, that of Louisiana had more than 58 percent. As a former possession of Spain and then of France, New Orleans was home to many Americans with ancestors from those countries. As an international port, the city inevitably brought Lincoln into contact with non-English-speaking sailors.

After the Lincoln family moved to Illinois in 1830, he, along with many Midwesterners, had the opportunity to learn about political ideas then percolating, especially those in Europe. Into their cultural and political baggage, immigrants, especially those from the German states, had packed a commitment to republicanism. Further, many had voted with their feet for a republican political system when they embarked from their homelands for the United States.

Starting in the 1830s and gaining momentum through the 1840s and 1850s, German immigration to Illinois increased significantly, until German Americans became the most numerous group of non-native-born residents of the state, amounting to about 9 percent of its foreign-born population, and 4.5 percent of its total population. The presence of these émigrés and their dedication to the European revolutions of the late 1840s eventually encouraged the politically active Lincoln to participate in community meetings in Springfield. There, he composed resolutions proclaiming sympathy with the Hungarian, Irish, French, and German people in their efforts "to establish free governments, based upon the principles of true religious and civil liberty."[3]

My reading Basler's collection combined with this thinking to create a novel understanding of Lincoln. It built on my previous research and publications, which had dealt with European influences on American culture from 1830 to 1880, whether in higher education or Victorian domestic life. Encouragement for this sort of analysis also arrived from myriads of recent books. In the first decade of the twenty-first century, history writers began to see the United States situated within a world community, or as Thomas Bender succinctly said, *A Nation among Nations*.[4]

Clearly, discovery of how the international events of the prewar decades intersected with the life of the young Lincoln would offer a new and fuller perspective. Subtracting world events from reconstruction of Lincoln's mental world leaves our understanding of him, both his thought and actions, incomplete and diminished. If global events help reveal in full resolution presidents of the twentieth and twenty-first centuries, the same should be true of earlier presidents, especially one who stands among the greatest of them all.

In 2007, Michael Oren's *Power, Faith, and Fantasy: America in the Mideast, 1776 to the Present*, a Christmas gift from my daughter, provided further encouragement for investigation of Lincoln's interactions with the world. On its title page, its author had written "to a fellow lover of Civil War history." Not until Oren's chapter 8 did I grasp why a domestic conflict in the United States would compel the attention of a historian of the Middle East.

Oren relates how a confrontation in Tangier, Morocco, had incited an international incident with France during the second year of the Lincoln presidency. The overly ambitious U.S. consul had encouraged local authorities in Tangier to apprehend two Confederates – a naval officer and a diplomat – whom the Navy then transported to Boston, Massachusetts, for imprisonment. Because France was a neutral power in the American war, its diplomats protested. Since the Confederates had journeyed to the African port on a vessel bearing the French flag, its diplomats argued that the United States had violated international law, according to which a ship carried the status of its home country, in this case neutral status. The Lincoln administration soon defused the crisis by releasing the Confederates. Additionally, Oren claimed that the young Lincoln's reading about African pirates in *Sufferings in Africa*, a well-known steady seller of the prewar years, a book mentioned prominently in the Republican candidate's 1860 campaign biography, and the subject of chapter 2, had played a major role in shaping the future president's attitude toward human slavery.[5]

To discover more about the lessons that Lincoln learned from around the globe, I began to reread the works by notable Lincoln biographers, who had taught me so much about his early life and domestic political accomplishments. They touch briefly on the revolts and revolutions that had roiled the Atlantic world during the 1820s through the 1840s. For example, David Donald's *Lincoln* summarizes the young Lincoln's sympathies "for liberal movements abroad" in several lines.[6]

When moving forward from Lincoln's Illinois days to his presidential years, most biographers focus on domestic events and justify their decision by relying on comments from the president's first months in office. For instance, in the spring of 1861, he expressed his misgivings about Queen Victoria's declaration that her country would recognize a state of belligerency between the United States and the seceded states. At that time, the president confided to his friend and political adviser Carl Schurz, an émigré from Prussia whom he later appointed as minister to Spain, that he deplored having to rely on others for foreign affairs and intended "to study up" on the topic. Donald set the pattern for his successors by pronouncing that the president possessed "no knowledge of diplomacy and no personal acquaintances or correspondents from abroad"; thus "he willingly entrusted foreign policy to his Secretary of State."[7]

Alternately, scholars turn for evidence of Lincoln's noninvolvement in foreign affairs to Secretary of State William Seward, who recalled that the recently inaugurated president confided that Seward would have to manage the international policies of the country "of which I know so little, and with which I reckon you are familiar."[8]

Richard Carwardine and Doris Kearns Goodwin both depart from the established narrative about Lincoln's foreign policy expertise. Accounting for Lincoln's habitual self-deprecation and his secretary of state's braggadocio, they note the ability that he displayed during the foreign relations crises with Great Britain during the last two months of 1861. Goodwin says that Lincoln deserves much credit for the "sophisticated prowess" with which he responded to that country's diplomatic protest.[9] Still, their reconsideration does not extend beyond the diplomatic crisis of late 1861 with Great Britain.

Historians of U.S. foreign policy and international relations place the president in a broader perspective. The path of Oren's research for American involvement in northern Africa during the Civil War guided me to his chief authority, Jay Monaghan's *Diplomat in Carpet Slippers: Abraham Lincoln Deals with Foreign Affairs*, first published in 1945. As a narrative of the Lincoln administration's foreign efforts, the book dealt more with events and less with their relationship to Lincoln's life and domestic affairs.

Howard Jones and Kevin Peraino both update and add scholarly depth to Monaghan's survey. Jones, who has written extensively about the Civil War and Lincoln, notes, "Lincoln realized early in his presidency that the slavery issue proved that domestic and foreign affairs were inseparable." Recently, Peraino analyzes more extensively the president's vital role in foreign affairs by unraveling his complex relationship with his secretary of state and showing the president's crucial role in the 1861 diplomatic crisis with Great Britain and the conflict with France during Napoleon III's 1862 Mexican incursion.[10]

This book revises Lincoln biographies and studies of his presidency. It demonstrates that a Lincoln portrait within a national frame eliminates from view crucial components of his thinking. When Lincoln became president, although he may have possessed slight knowledge of the formal conduct of foreign affairs, as he freely admitted, he had great experience thinking about the worldwide progress of republicanism. In his political career, he intended to perpetuate the republic of the United States and make it "more perfect" by ending the institution of human slavery within its boundaries.

After the bombardment of Fort Sumter in April 1861, it was predictable that, given the European and hemispheric events of his youth, he should insist on the global significance of the need to preserve the republic of the United States when, on July 4, he addressed the Congress, whose members had assembled for a special session. He wanted the voters in the United States to see the conflict between the states as he did – from a republican and global perspective:

It presents to the whole family of man, the question, whether a constitutional republic, or a democracy – a government of the people, by the same people – can, or cannot, maintain its territorial integrity, against its own domestic foes. It presents the question, whether discontented individuals...can...break up their Government, and thus practically put an end to free government upon the earth. It forces us to ask: "Is there, in all republics, this inherent, and fatal weakness?"[11]

The president's reference to the whole family of man and his interpretation of the Fort Sumter bombardment raised the question central to the existence of republics since Roman days. Was their demise foreordained? Moreover, in this quotation Lincoln reveals the core of his global view. Thinking globally in his terms meant understanding that political history since the Enlightenment had possessed one main theme, namely the rise of republican thought and government in the Americas and Europe. Concomitantly, republican government implied a government resting on the consent of free men, as the Declaration of Independence had said. Lincoln thought the United States in the 1850s and 1860s occupied an exceptional place in the history and, he assumed, the progress of republicanism.[12]

Republicans worldwide knew that they had lost the foremost champion of their causes when John Wilkes Booth, the famous actor turned infamous assassin, fired his fatal shot in April 1865. Accordingly, this book begins with the worldwide reaction to the death of President Abraham Lincoln. This global response inspires awe by running far beyond the sympathy letters from kings, queens, prime ministers, and presidents, who, with notable exceptions, followed established etiquette and diplomatic protocol. Everyday people around the globe poured out their sorrow and their high estimation for the U.S. president with telling words and material tributes.

The remaining chapters tell how Lincoln won that worldwide esteem. Chapters 2 through 4 explain how his global thinking developed during his pre-presidential years with specific reference to the issue of slavery, the Hungarian revolution, and political turmoil in the German states. Whereas as a young man he had taught himself the skills of speech, writing, and logic that gained him entry into the literate, genteel society of Victorian America, in the late 1840s, following his term in Congress and the visits of German and Hungarian patriots to the United States, his ambition developed to include an international dimension. He began to see that praise of U.S. history and political system had contemporary relevance. Political reformers in the German states, France, and Great Britain shared his republican political ideals. Absorbing their lessons, Lincoln began to shape his appearance and his message. He wanted to become an opponent of autocracy as was Lajos Kossuth in Hungary, and a champion of republicanism and free labor as was John Bright in England and the self-exiled Comte de Gasparin for France.[13]

The next three chapters trace how his thinking matured and received implementation with encouragement from sea captain and author James Riley and Member of Parliament John Bright, as well as German émigrés Francis Lieber, a political scientist, and John George Nicolay, his personal secretary.

A concluding chapter elevates *Our American Cousin*, some say the most popular comedy of the nineteenth-century stage, from its current status as a frivolous British comedy. (See Figure I.1.) More than laughs, the comedy presented serious political and cultural commentary by upholding the ideals of free men, free labor, and free land. When Booth, Confederate partisan and pro-slavery advocate, shot Abraham Lincoln, he disrupted a theatrical presentation situated in the midst of the nineteenth-century culture war between government by the people and government by inherited right. As Lincoln chuckled at the play, he received his last global lesson. By implication, the play affirmed the rightness of the Union victory and the preservation of the republic of the United States. Directly, it affirmed the conviction of liberals around the globe that ascendance of republican governments everywhere, especially in the Atlantic world, was inevitable.

For now, one example will illustrate the global context in which Lincoln lived. A second example will demonstrate how his global thinking affected his thinking by exposing the global dimension of the phrase in the Gettysburg Address: "all men are created equal."

Consider the nickname, "the Tycoon," by which Nicolay and John Hay, his private secretaries, affectionately referred to their boss, the president. Unraveling how the term came to be applied to Lincoln shows that politically active and informed people of the 1850s and 1860s were acutely aware of the U.S. commercial and diplomatic engagement with the world. Today, we call men such as Andrew Carnegie or J. Pierpont Morgan tycoons to evoke the great wealth and power that they often

FIGURE I.I. Playbill for Ford's Theatre, Friday evening, April 14, 1865. Courtesy of Library of Congress, Rare Book and Special Collections Division.

deployed for suspect ends. Abraham Lincoln does not seem to qualify for that usually pejorative term. In 1858, "tycoon" possessed an entirely opposite meaning. Internet-powered research through U.S. newspaper databases of the 1850s and 1860s revealed that the term surfaced in diplomatic correspondence and on the printed page in late 1858. In that year, Townsend Harris, whom President Franklin Pierce had appointed as the first consul general to Japan two years previously, negotiated with

FIGURE I.2. "Reception of the Japanese Embassadors at the White House, May 17, 1860," *Harper's Weekly: A Journal of Civilization*, May 26, 1860, 329. Courtesy of Archives and Special Collections, Franklin & Marshall College, Lancaster, PA.

that country the Treaty of Amity and Commerce, known as the Harris Treaty. At the consul general's insistence, provisions in the treaty had stipulated that ratified versions of it should be exchanged in the U.S. capital. Thus, Harris demanded from Japan and secured for his country the Asian nation's first-ever official diplomatic visit to a Western nation. Describing his mission to the emperor in a letter to Commodore Matthew C. Perry, who had opened Japan to merchants from the United States in 1854, Harris explained that the Japanese ruler was known as the Taikun, or Tycoon, meaning "great ruler."[14]

Two years after the original treaty negotiations, U.S. Navy ships delivered a sizeable delegation of three Japanese ambassadors, their retinue of almost six dozen aides and translators, and fifty tons of baggage to Washington. To pay for elaborate receptions in their honor, Congress had appropriated $50,000.[15]

The visit of the seventy-one Japanese diplomats to Washington during the spring of 1860, their reception at the Executive Mansion by President James Buchanan, and subsequent gala parades and festivities in east coast cities transformed the emperor's title into the sobriquet of the day. (See Figure I.2.) Within a few weeks, journalists were applying the word to public figures and even to their own employers. In early June 1860, reporters for the *New York Herald* called James Gordon Bennett, its editor and publisher, a tycoon. In following years, journalists so labeled General John Frémont, New York City Mayor Fernando Wood, and other powerful men in the public eye.[16]

In newspapers, linkage of Lincoln and the Japanese Tycoon initially occurred unintentionally and subsequently intentionally because of the heated rhetoric evoked by the presidential contest of 1860. After the Japanese mission to the United States had its audience at the Executive Mansion during the third week of May, it proceeded to receptions in Baltimore, Philadelphia, and New York City. During the same week in May, but in Chicago, the Republican Party nominated Lincoln as its candidate for president. Thus, the term "tycoon" referring to the Japanese emperor frequently appeared on the same newspaper page as did reports of the Republican Party convention. Many papers featured stories about the Japanese Tycoon and his emissaries to the United States on the front page or even in the same column with stories about the Chicago convention and its nominee. Eight months later, the coincidence of their mutual newsworthiness reoccurred when the president-elect departed Springfield for the national capital and his inauguration. When the *New York Herald* announced the start of his railroad trip to Washington, an adjacent column reported the hospitality extended by the Tycoon to the U.S. mission then arriving in Japan.[17]

Intentional linkage of the Republican nominee to the Japanese emperor's title occurred as the presidential campaign moved forward through the summer into the intensity of the fall presidential campaign. A Democratic commentator ridiculed Lincoln by predicting that he would "never *adorn* the White House." If he were to be elected, the writer suggested, at public receptions in the mansion "guests might be provided with cut-glass prisms, which might, by their distortions, bring Old Abe's features into something not altogether repulsive." Were these adjustments impossible, the president should "adopt the Japanese Tycoon style, and give audience *behind a screen*."[18]

Given John Hay's admiration for Lincoln, he probably had no such pejorative intention when he referred in his diary and private correspondence to his employer as "The Tycoon."[19] As was customary for the Taikun, Hay intended the Americanized version of the title to mean a great and good ruler. As an aspiring journalist and witty diarist, Lincoln's secretary simply was adapting the trendy language of his day.

Foreign affairs since the opening of Japan had made "tycoon" a familiar word in the lexicon of the United States. In the summer of 1860,

Laura Keene, the star and owner of the theatre company that presented *Our American Cousin* at Ford's Theatre in 1865, advertised her current production: *Tycoon: Or Young America in Japan.* A Republican Party songbook, published during the 1860 campaign, referred to the Japanese ruler as The Tycoon.[20] As cultural awareness of Japan developed in the United States, mentions of tycoon proliferated, John Hay took note, and the word entered his parlance as a shorthand means of referring to his new boss, the president.

Unraveling the origins of the Tycoon nickname for Lincoln had revealed that a more complete understanding of the president called for a vision that included the engagement of the United States with the nations of the world. By 1863, the Japanese government had contracted for the building of three warships in the United States, although subsequent political unrest in that country prevented their delivery. In addition, the Tycoon had sent several gifts, including a full suit of Samurai armor, to Lincoln, thus inspiring wags writing for Democratic newspapers to call the president "another iron-clad."[21]

Returning to consideration of the Gettysburg Address, besides Lincoln's dedication to Union victory, his words show that he had received, mentally digested, and absorbed into his being global lessons about republicanism. In that brief November speech, when the president pronounced that all men are created equal, his audience, both then and now, understood that he referred to African Americans and whites. Additionally, many among his listeners at the cemetery that day understood a meaning that twenty-first century readers of the speech do not grasp. Remembering the political controversies that had affected the years of 1854 through 1860, the audience at Gettysburg, especially recent German-American immigrants and the descendants of German-American immigrants, realized that the president intended an even broader meaning when he proclaimed "all men." Lincoln's words implied that both native-born citizens of the United States and immigrants who intended to become its citizens should receive equal treatment under the laws of the national government. Second, the president did not add the final phrase of the address – from the earth – as a final rhetorical flourish. When he included the defining phrases of republicanism – "a government of the people, by the people, for the people" – in his concluding clause, "that . . . shall not perish from the earth" – he did so because he meant it.

He had learned his global lessons in his lifelong classroom – the Atlantic world.

# I

# The Second Shot Heard 'Round the World

We will never know whether a British regular or a Massachusetts militia-man fired the first shot on the morning of April 19, 1775. It started a military skirmish that reverberated through lands on both sides of the Atlantic Ocean. The blast announced a new era in transatlantic world history that scholars now call the age of democratic revolutions. On July 4, 1776, representatives of the thirteen American colonies to the Second Continental Congress meeting in Philadelphia adopted the Declaration of Independence. Its words politically defined the new era with a bold statement of the bedrock beliefs of republicans around the world: all men are created equal, and governments depend on the consent of the governed.

The evening of April 14, 1865, five days short of four score and ten years after the confrontations at the village green in Lexington and the North Bridge in Concord, a single gunman fired another blast. Like the first shot, its report also resounded, first around the country and then around the world. Throughout the United States, people soon learned that John Wilkes Booth, the famous actor and sympathizer with the Confederate States of America, had pulled the trigger.

On the night of April 14, 1865, he purposefully had made his way from an alley behind Ford's Theatre in Washington, up to its Dress Circle, and into the presidential box, where Mary and Abraham Lincoln and their guests were enjoying the popular comedy. After drawing a derringer pistol from a concealed pocket stitched into the inside right leg of his tall leather boots, Booth waited for the hero of Laura Keene's *Our American Cousin* to draw guffaws from the audience with his line: "I guess I know enough to turn you inside out, old gal – you sockdologizing old man-trap." As the presidential couple and members of the audience roared at the absurdity

FIGURE 1.1. "The Assassination of President Lincoln at Ford's Theatre on the Night of April 14, 1865," *Harper's Weekly*, April 29, 1865, 260. Courtesy of Archives and Special Collections, Franklin & Marshall College, Lancaster, PA.

of these words, Booth squeezed the pistol's trigger and sent a lead ball into the skull of the President of the United States. Coming to rest just behind his right eye socket, the bullet ended his conscious life. (See Figure 1.1.)

Overcoming their shock and horror, doctors and soldiers carried the mortally wounded leader from the theater, across 10th Street, and to a second-floor bedroom in a three-story brick house. In the home of Anna and William Petersen a German-American couple, the unconscious Lincoln lay on a bed too short for his six-foot-four body while his blood and brain tissue oozed onto the pillow under his head. By 7:22 the next morning, his life had ended.[1]

Reports of the assassination took twelve days to cross the Atlantic Ocean by ship. From England, telegrams sped to the capitals of Europe and to U.S. ministers and consuls on the continent. A combination of boat and wire then carried the news to the southern countries of the Americas, to Africa, and to Asia. By late May, governments and people everywhere within reach of telegraphs, railroads, and sea lanes had learned of the assassination and the nearly simultaneous vicious attack on Secretary of State William H. Seward, who was currently bed-ridden with severe injuries suffered in a recent carriage accident. On the night of April 14, Booth had led a team of plotters in an attempt to decapitate the executive branch of the U.S. national government by assassinating its president, vice president, and secretary of state.

From around the globe, U.S. ministers and consuls conveyed to Washington the official public reaction to the president's death and the extraordinary efforts of people to explain what they thought he had represented. The condolence letters and expressions of grief composed in response to the assassination promptly became templates upon which mourners etched the meanings that they attached to Lincoln's life, his presidency, and the country that he had led. To the people of the world, he had stood for republicanism and its realization in the United States of America.

In four years, Abraham Lincoln had ascended to the status of global hero. The forty-nine months of Lincoln's presidency had brought him renown and reversed the initial impressions of him that foreigners had held in 1860. After his surprise nomination by the Republican Party, the British minister to the United States reported to the Foreign Office that he had never heard prominent Democrats or Republicans mention the candidate's name. Lincoln was, he reported, "a rough farmer who began life as a farm labourer and got on by a talent for stump speaking. Little more is known of him."[2]

By April 1865, Lincoln's name recognition had risen. The letters and memorials that people around the globe wrote in the months following his assassination to his widow Mary, the secretary of state, and/or U.S. ministers worldwide transport us to a singular moment in global history. At that moment, the world's people saw the United States and its slain president as the embodiments of republican government and republicanism. This moment in history wields so much power that it can neutralize present-day concerns about U.S. world dominance, past imperialistic ventures, cultural ascendance, and the worldwide sales reach of Hollywood films, Facebook, McDonald's, Google, Coca-Cola, Proctor and Gamble, and other American companies. The international community of 1865, especially its members with republican hopes, conceived of the United States politically as Lincoln had. To use the words of his 1862 annual message to Congress, the country was "the last best, hope of earth."

Throughout the world, the evidences of grief at the events of April 14 appeared in manifold forms. To mourn this towering national leader, officials followed established conventions. Monarchs sent their condolences, prime ministers delivered elegies, and parliaments and town councils passed commemorative resolutions. Diplomats wore mourning clothes, memorial services were held, naval fleets and honor guards boomed salutes, newspapers bordered their pages in black, businesses and government offices temporarily closed, and flags flew at half-staff. Beyond the ordinary official manifestations of mourning expressed in these conventional ways, monarchs and citizens also did the extraordinary.

This chapter describes several of the extraordinary ways in which people memorialized the assassinated president before it presents analysis of the extraordinary words found in the communications transmitted to the state department and Mary Lincoln during the spring and early summer of 1865. These words illustrate that people around the world had cast Lincoln and the United States in starring roles in the rise of republicanism.

Among the heads of European governments, Queen Victoria of Great Britain broke through diplomatic etiquette, which discouraged private communications, to compose a personal letter to Mary Lincoln. From Osborne, the royal residence on the Isle of Wight, where Prince Albert and she had often enjoyed the spring months, she handwrote a letter to "Mrs. President Lincoln" the day after learning of the assassination. She explained why she was making this exceptional gesture to Mrs. Lincoln, "a stranger," with whom she had neither met nor corresponded. The terrific horror of the crime had forced her to sympathize with the new widow because she too recently had lost "my own beloved Husband, who was the <u>Light</u> of my Life, –my Stay–<u>my All</u>." To the queen, "recently" meant slightly less than four years previously. Her husband, Prince Albert, had died in December 1861 at the age of forty-two. (See Figure 1.2.)

Lincoln and the prince had shared antislavery positions and a commitment to free labor. Like the deceased president, Albert had promoted emancipation, opposed establishment of the Confederate States of America (CSA), and supported preservation of the United States as one nation. In his last days and in declining health, he had edited the response of the British Crown to the seizure of Confederate emissaries on the British mail ship *Trent* as they made their way to Europe to represent the cause of the seceded states. From the draft of the message that the Foreign Office had prepared and would issue in the queen's name, he eliminated diplomatic insults and softened the language of protest. Through his revisions to this message, he had taken a key role in making more likely an apology from the United States, a prerequisite for a peaceful end to the crisis.[3] Although in her letter to Mary Lincoln, Queen Victoria described her sympathy as that of one widow to another, the bonds between the two

FIGURE 1.2. Prince Consort Albert and Queen Victoria. This carte de visite rested in the Lincoln Family Album, which the family assembled while living in the Executive Mansion. Date of photograph is probably 1860. ALPLM cat. in LR 209 #15 and by name. 4″ × 2.25.″ Courtesy of the Abraham Lincoln Presidential Library & Museum (ALPLM).

families ran deeper. The convictions that her husband and the president shared had forged an identity between the two men that their unfortunate deaths made complete. Her kind words veiled her deeper understanding of the two leaders' place in the history of the nineteenth century.

In the capital of Prussia, Minister President Otto von Bismarck, government ministers, and members of the diplomatic corps attended a memorial service in a Berlin church filled to capacity and surrounded by an overflow of mourners who had been denied entrance. The service had been scheduled for a modestly sized house of worship until the overwhelming public response forced its relocation into the Dorothea Church, which the minister from the United States described as the largest available church in the city.[4] A delegation from the lower house of the Prussian House of Deputies previously had presented the minister with a resolution commemorating Lincoln, which two-thirds of its members had signed.

The delegation that carried the resolution to the U.S. embassy included veterans of the revolutions of 1848 and 1849 as well as the fathers of sons who had ventured to the United States and enlisted in the Union army. The son of one delegation member recently had perished during the Union army siege of Petersburg, Virginia, the crucial battle before the fall of Richmond, Virginia, and the retreat of the Army of Northern Virginia, commanded by General Robert E. Lee, to Appomattox Court House where on April 9 he surrendered his army. The Germans who delivered the resolutions truly represented the Prussian people. As well as their own sons, the sons of approximately 187,000 other families from the German states had traveled to the United States and joined the military that preserved the republic of the United States.[5]

In South America and Europe, national and local governments memorialized the slain president by erecting monuments and renaming towns, streets, and squares. To honor the deceased leader, the province of Buenos Aires promised to call the next town founded within its boundaries after the deceased president, and it did so on July 19 of that year. Today, an Argentinean town, some 300 miles west of Buenos Aires, calls itself Lincoln.[6] In the north of the Italian peninsula, the Montanelli Association for Mutual Education and Assistance, of which Giuseppe Garibaldi, the fighter for Italian independence and unification, served as honorary president, raised funds to build a monument to memorialize the assassinated president in the city of Pisa. In Cano, Italy, a small town near Como north of Milan, the town council unanimously voted to dedicate a square off the national road to Lincoln, whom its members called "the champion of human freedom." In Chiavenna, a town in the Italian Alps, the Society of Operatives elected the president posthumously to join Garibaldi and Giuseppe Mazzini as honorary members.[7]

French workingmen, liberal statesmen, and politicians manufactured and presented the most elaborate tributes to Lincoln, including a solid-gold medallion measuring four inches in diameter and a silk U.S. flag hand-woven in one piece. To fund the silk flag, a mutual aid society of silk weavers from Lyon, France, accepted donations of up to ten centimes per person that they solicited through an announcement placed exclusively in the liberal papers of their city and other cities in France. At least 25,000 people donated. (See Figure 1.3.)

Upon presenting the flag, which the weavers called "un drapeau d'honneur" [flag of honor], to the U.S. consul in Lyon, the workingmen explained that they had "suffered much" when the Civil War had closed to them a market essential to their prosperity. Nevertheless, no

FIGURE 1.3. Image of the silk flag commissioned by the Weavers' Association of Lyons, France. More than 25,000 working people contributed to the memorial. The effort was said to represent "the sincere admiration and affection of the liberal working class" for President Lincoln, "the Martyr of Liberty." The Association saw the war having emancipated "the colored people" and hoped for the emancipation of "the workmen of France." Flag image following page 15 and quotations from pages 14 and 15 in *Tributes to the Memory of Abraham Lincoln: Reproduction in Facsimile of Eighty-seven Memorials Addressed by Foreign Municipalities and Societies to the Government of the United States, Prepared under the Direction of the Secretary of State, in Accordance with a Joint Resolution of Congress, Approved Feb. 23, 1881* (Washington, DC: GPO, 1885).

weaver "would have wished for a postponement of the great solution for which you [the United States] were fighting on the battle-fields of liberty." If your countrymen "have emancipated the colored people, we, by association, solidarity and mutuality, endeavor to emancipate the workmen of France."[8] On the banner were embroidered in gold the words "Souscription populaire. A la république des Etats Unis offert en mémoir d'Abraham Lincoln." [Popular subscription. To the Republic of the United States offered in memory of Abraham Lincoln.][9]

For another memorial, 50,000 self-identified French democrats reputedly contributed a maximum of ten centimes each so that a gold medal could be struck and presented to Mrs. Lincoln. About four inches in

FIGURE 1.4, 1.4A. "Abraham Lincoln French Mourning Medal, 1865," front and back views. (French Medal Committee to Mrs. Lincoln, October 13, 1866, Series 4, Abraham Lincoln Papers, Manuscript Division, Library of Congress.)

diameter and one-quarter-inch thick, the handsome tribute displays a portrait of her husband's head in profile on one side and a tomb on its reverse side. At one end of the tomb, a winged victory proffers a crown of olive leaves, and on the other stand an African-American man and boy, probably representing recently freed slaves. The boy gestures with a palm frond toward an eagle hovering above the tomb. It carries a shield bearing the motto of the United States, while the man also gestures and carries a rifle, a symbol of his freedom and manhood. The altar's face bears the words: *"Lincoln, L'Honnête Homme/abolit l'esclavagie rétablit l'union/Sauva la République/sans veiler la statue de la liberté/il fut assassiné le 14 Avril/1865* [Lincoln: an honest man; abolished slavery, restored the union, and saved the Republic without veiling the statue of liberty. He was assassinated April 14, 1865.].[10] (See Figures 1.4, 1.4a.)

Delivery of the medal to the United States and its presentation took longer than expected. Local French police had confiscated subscription lists, and because Napoleon III had not permitted the imperial mint to strike the medal, it had to be sent to Geneva, Switzerland, for casting. The committee organizing the gift included leading French intellectuals and liberals including Louis Blanc, Victor Hugo, and Eugène Pelletan, who opposed many of Napoleon III's policies. They wrote Mrs. Lincoln, "If France had the freedom enjoyed by republican America, not thousands, but millions among us would have been counted as admirers."[11] Finally, early in January 1867, Mrs. Lincoln received the medal and expressed how the gift had profoundly touched her. It had been "given," she wrote, "in honor of his services in the cause of liberty, by those who in another land work for the same great end."[12]

The reference on the medal to Lincoln's not veiling the statue of liberty puzzles us in the present day. Edouard Laboulaye, a noted liberal and professor of comparative law at the Collège de France, and artist Auguste Bartholdi had not yet dreamed of France's future gift to the United States of "Liberty Enlightening the World," a mammoth sculpture, commonly known as the Statue of Liberty. Laboulaye would raise funds for that project and Bartholdi would become its sculptor. Still, in 1865, liberal French and American readers understood.

Readers of political fiction on both sides of the Atlantic Ocean would have been familiar with the writings of Laboulaye, a popular author and university professor of American constitutional history. The wording of the text on the French medal probably referenced a phrase from his book *Paris en Amérique*, which rapidly had exhausted three editions in his home country and then had been translated in 1863 into English for the American market. In this political essay, the primary spokesperson, "Truth," disputes with an antagonist who always will subordinate liberty in the present to the goal of preserving liberty in the long run. Countering its compromising adversary, "Truth" reasons in absolutes: "as soon as a citizen is unjustly attacked, all are menaced."[13] Had French liberals recognized the suspension of the constitutionally guaranteed right to habeas corpus and freedom of the press in various war zones of the United States during certain periods of its war, they would have had to reword their tribute. Instead, they focused on the freeing of the slaves and Lincoln's arguments that he enjoyed constitutional sanction as commander in chief for the Emancipation Proclamation of January 1, 1863.

The French ruler must have interpreted the mourning and celebration of the murdered president as a protest against his own regime since his obstruction of the medal's production was no unique event. After news of the assassination arrived in the French capital on April 26, a disturbance had erupted near the U.S. embassy in Paris. John Bigelow, the resident minister, had prepared to receive grieving Parisians, including a large deputation of students from law and medical schools. Assembling for a march to the minister's residence, the students had gathered at a bridge over the River Seine. After a throng of 1,500 or more mourners had formed, the police arrived with swords unsheathed to disperse them. A few groups of twenty or so protestors and marchers evaded the roundup and arrived at the embassy some three miles away, where another force of police barricaded its entrance.

As the Paris correspondent to *The New York Times* explained to his readers with understatement, "after a tussle, however, a certain number succeeded in getting in." Reporting on the incident to his superiors in the United States, Minister Bigelow observed that he had held "no idea that Mr. Lincoln had such a hold upon the heart of the young gentlemen of France."[14] This confrontation caused the minister to worry that a large public ceremony to commemorate the late president might cause the French police to react with repressive measures, and so the people of France and Americans in France mourned exclusively at private events.

Opponents of Napoleon III's rule had similar difficulties in organizing to express their respect for the slain president. Workers used the occasion of paying tribute to Lincoln by including criticism of the Emperor's policies in their condolences. For example, working people in Tours explained that they lived "in a city where there is only one newspaper, where the press speaks only the official language of the prefecture, where liberty is limited by policemen and public functionaries, and where democracy's warmest partisans are among the common people." Thus, they apologized for their inability to collect more than 208 signatures on their letter of sympathy and remembrance.[15]

French politicians, labor leaders, and opinion makers, including Louis Blanc and Victor Hugo, drew upon Lincoln's assassination to assert that France and the United States had a place in the global history of republicanism. By celebrating Lincoln, they showed that despite Napoleon's repressive legislative acts of 1851, liberty survived in their country. As liberal Benjamin Gastineau explained the high import of the popular collection for the medal, "le jour n'est pas éloigné où réunissant l'Europe et l'Amérique sur le terrain de la liberté et du droit, *ces démocraties solidaires formeront les Etats-Unis des deux mondes!*" [The day is not far off, when Europe and America reuniting on the basis of liberty and right, these committed democracies shall form a United States of two worlds!] Presumably, Gastineau hoped for the unity of the republics of France and the United States in a figurative and not a literal sense.[16]

When people around the globe heard of the assassination, they dispatched letters and scrolls of condolence and sympathy to Mary Lincoln, the department of state, and/or U.S. ministers and consuls. An 1885 volume published by the department of state reports that 1,000 of those documents were then in its keeping.[17] This collection may represent the entirety of the written outpourings prompted by the assassination, although more probably it comprises a selection.

The American minister in France, for illustration, wrote to his superiors in Washington that he had transmitted in his diplomatic packet seventy-two letters from mourners, a "small proportion" of the correspondence that he had received.[18] Six months after Lincoln's death, he forwarded to the secretary of state another two volumes of translated commentary from newspapers that he deemed "of consequence." He observed to Seward that the late president's death had elicited from the people of France "latent respect for his character and for the cause to which his life was sacrificed which, till then," the French people had scarcely recognized publically.[19]

In London, a deluge of condolence notes flooded the U.S. ministry. Not anticipating the magnitude of the eventual response to the tragedy of April 14, Minister Charles Francis Adams initially wrote to Seward immediately after he learned of attacks on Lincoln and his secretary of state that his office was preparing to receive many letters. He expected that he could respond individually to those from prominent individuals and organizations but that he would need to prepare standard, formal replies for the remainder. A week later, he laid his initial plans aside and requested permission to send standardized responses to all letters and complained of the labor involved in producing handwritten ones.

A week after that modification of procedure, the volume of correspondence became so heavy that he apologized for the slight delays incurred in following the diplomatic instructions previously received from the United States. By June 2, the flow of condolences had swamped the ministry and caused Adams's griping to reach a new height: "Already the mere process of filing, cataloguing and acknowledging them has occupied one of my Secretaries the larger part of his time for some weeks."[20] Eventually the ministry received at least 460 condolence letters and resolutions from civic and government entities and an unrecorded number of private letters.

Most of the messages received by foreign legations were written in script on stationery of various sizes. Some are pieces as small as 4 × 6 inches, and others fit into boxes for legal papers (10.25 × 15.25 inches). Still others are large-sized documents that measure as much as 24 × 30 inches.[21]

The National Archives safeguards most of the larger documents, while the Abraham Lincoln Presidential Library and Museum in Springfield, Illinois, holds another twenty-nine examples, a few of which duplicate those in the National Archives.[22] Many of these pieces have experienced

a perilous history, despite their having the most visual appeal. The sentiments that they express appear on heavy paper stock or vellum in highly
formal and stylized calligraphy and script, sometimes with colorful illu-
mination and capital letters in gold leaf. Following the medieval or gothic
style text, formal signatures, occasionally accompanied by a seal pressed
into red or black wax, complete the documents. A few seals are affixed
to gilt or silver paper and have appended decorative ribbons. If the town
or corporate group sponsoring the condolence letter had one hundred or
so members, all its citizens or members often signed. Most often the lists
have exclusively male names, although occasionally they include signatures of women as do the resolutions sent by the inhabitants of Kettering,
in the county of Northampton, England.[23]

Unfortunately for historians and the public, merely a portion of
the larger original documents that reached the state department in the
nation's capital survive. In 1881, Congress authorized publication of
eighty-seven of them in facsimile in a commemorative volume. The selections for this volume were probably the most colorful and handsome of
the condolences received. Others of the actual larger documents, mostly
from Great Britain, moved from the state department to Memorial Hall
on the ground level of Lincoln's tomb in Oak Ridge Cemetery, Springfield, Illinois, sometime before 1905.[24] Eventually, to protect them from
weather changes and the touches of overly curious tourists, they were
transferred downtown to the Illinois State Historical Library, then in
2004 to the new Abraham Lincoln Presidential Library. Reputedly during World War I, the state department or National Archives transferred
several of the documents remaining in its possession for display in the
public library of the District of Columbia. That institution deaccessioned
them about 1947, of which process there is no known official record. We
have this story because a pedestrian chanced upon one of the documents
lying in a trash barrel and salvaged it.[25]

The surviving condolence letters, large and small, arrived from many
points of the globe and most levels of society. (See Figures 1.5, 1.6, 1.7.)
Almost every country in Europe, Latin America, the Caribbean, and South
America as well as a few rulers in Africa and Asia sent official expressions of grief. Local governments from the level of the province down
to the small town also prepared resolutions to honor President Lincoln
and to offer sympathy to his widow. Private associations and individual
citizens took occasion to write. Authors identified themselves specifically
as the "inhabitants of a borough" or "the members of a congregation."
Predictably, representatives of religious, antislavery, and emancipation

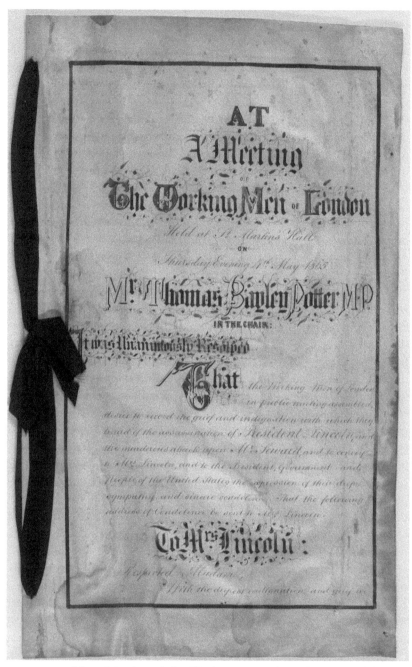

FIGURE 1.5. "At a Meeting of the Working Men of London...." Elaborate, uniquely composed, and calligraphed condolences to Mary Lincoln and the people of the United States came from hundreds of world towns and organizations. Some of the most remarkable came from the United Kingdom and were submitted to the U.S. ministry in London for forwarding to Washington. ALPLM cat. LB-4076p ca. 22″ × 13″. Courtesy of ALPLM.

FIGURE 1.6. "At a Public Meeting of the Inhabitants of the Borough of Leeds...." ALPLM cat. LB-4076h 21″ × 13.25″. Courtesy of the ALPLM.

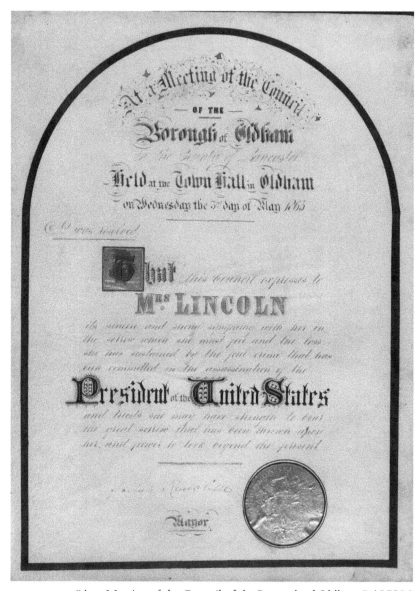

FIGURE 1.7. "At a Meeting of the Council of the Borough of Oldham." ALPLM cat. LB-4076r ca. 22″ × 15″. Courtesy of the ALPLM.

societies expressed their sorrow upon losing the leader who had done so much for their cause. Groups of the middle and upper classes including associations of financiers, merchants, and manufacturers told of their admiration for Lincoln and sympathy for his family and expressed their hopes for a revival of trade and commerce with the restoration of peace. Testaments from workingmen and women in England, Italy, Prussia, and various South American countries outnumbered the messages from associations with middle- and upper-class members. As the Allgemeiner Deutsche Arbeiter-Verein [General German Workers' Association] claimed, "while the aristocracy of the Old World took openly the part of the southern slaveholder, and while the middle class was divided in its opinions, the working-men in all countries of Europe have unanimously and firmly stood on the side of the Union."[26]

Like the French democrats and weavers who sent the silk flag and gold medal, workers seemed to assume a proud stance in preparing their memorials and to take care that they should be identified clearly as free laborers and as members of the working classes. The 270 townspeople who signed a letter in Selby, North Yorkshire, England, identified themselves by their profession or trade. The list included the leading citizens of the town – the curate, justice of the peace, banker, and merchant – plus its artisans and tradesmen, including teachers, stonemasons, farmers, hatters, shoemakers, butchers, shipwrights, a telegraph clerk, plumbers, and so on. In Hinton Martell, Dorset, England, its citizens assembled in the town schoolhouse and assured American minister Charles Francis Adams that no more "earnest and true sympathy" could be felt than that "by us, a few of the agricultural laborers of Dorset."[27]

People of color from Africa, Europe, the Caribbean, and the Pacific also expressed that the assassination had brought them a special loss. From Cape Coast in Africa (currently a city of Ghana, and in the 1860s a major trading city with a strong British and consular presence), the king of that city, the chief of Donasie, the king of Anamaboe, and the king of Winnebah described their appreciation for "the benefits that our race has derived from the results of events that have occurred during the administration of that great and good man."[28]

Free black workers in London, whose ancestors had been enslaved, claimed fellowship with "our brethren, the black laborers of the southern States."[29] In their memorial, the residents of Lahiana in the Sandwich Islands (now known as Hawaii) cited as the president's "mighty deeds, victory, peace, and the emancipation of those despised, like all of us of the colored races."[30] Joining the mourners of Lahiana were the Creoles of Guadeloupe, a French possession in the Caribbean since 1816. These people of color interpreted the war as one "for the freedom of an oppressed race."[31] As the Mauritian men who resided in London wrote, the war had occurred to bar "the lawless attempts of *a slave-holding* community to destroy the glorious, free, and united republic of George Washington."³²

The establishment of two categories promotes analysis of these letters and documents composed in response to Lincoln's death. The first category comprises basic condolence letters. They offered sympathy to the United States and Mrs. Lincoln for their loss and expressed hope that the country would resume its place in a peaceful world community. The second category includes letters from mourners who departed from the conventions of the basic condolence. They expressed horror at the crimes perpetrated on April 14 and frequently asserted the place of Lincoln and his country in the history of global republicanism.

Basic condolences arrived from rulers of countries without representative assemblies or with a more authoritarian nature, and consequently, these documents did not celebrate republicanism or note Lincoln's relationship to its preservation and development. Instead, they praised the admirable character of Lincoln and expressed hopes for future peace and prosperity. Through his foreign minister, Napoleon III conveyed his sympathy for the inestimable loss suffered by the United States. Without mention of any political position or military act of the deceased president, the French emperor lauded the president's moderation and his "exalted wisdom, as well as the examples of good sense, of courage, and of patriotism."³³ From St. Petersburg, the minister reported the grief shared by the high nobles who belonged to the Tsar's court. After the Tsar himself wrote Mary Lincoln, American Minister Cassius M. Clay commented, "There is but one sentiment of indignation and grief, at the death of our loved president throughout all Russia; shared alike by the Prince and the peasant."³⁴

The communication received from both the Tycoon of Japan and his majesty Shahinshah of Tehran, Persia, focused less on the person of the president and more on the nation. Both rulers conveyed through their representatives their sentiments of condolence. Additionally, the latter ruler sent both his best wishes for the continued prosperity and hopes for "perpetual amity between the two countries" to U.S. President Andrew Johnson, who had succeeded to the office from the vice presidency after the assassination.³⁵

For European rulers, whether leading an all-powerful government or heading a representative assembly, Booth's shot held larger implications about the maintenance of governmental authority. From Brutus's stabbing of Julius Caesar in the Roman Senate to attempts on the life of Napoleon III, assassins had stalked European leaders in the hopes of forcing governmental change. As the head of the conservative party in the Spanish Congress of Deputies noted, the "poison which corrodes the entrails of European societies has infiltrated itself beyond the Atlantic."[36] Assassins now targeted elected national authorities, hereditary rulers, and monarchs. Commentators realized that political murders imperiled constituted governing authorities. Whether their rulers claimed to possess mandates from divine powers or from the consent of the governed mattered little. Even if monarchies would disappear from the world, the political murders would persist. As the House of Peers in Portugal observed, Booth's crime constituted "essentially a regicide," which "a monarchical country cannot help but abhor and condemn."[37]

Most frequently, letters and remarks on Lincoln's death referred to his conciliatory plan for ending the four years of warfare in the United States. The press of many European countries had praised his conciliatory plan immediately after the words of his second inaugural address reached Europe in early April. Numerous remembrances, including missives from the House of Burgesses of Bremen (an independent city in what is now northern Germany), Napoleon III of France, the Swiss canton of St. Gall, and several British towns and boroughs such as Chippenham, Blackburn, Plymouth, Oldham, and Bath, to name a few, referred to the president's second inaugural address, which he had delivered a mere six weeks previously.[38] In that speech, Lincoln had invoked the one religious faith that united the then largely Christian United States and its seceded states. He had interpreted the war as retribution for 250 years of slavery and wondered if the God shared by Confederates and Unionists might demand that "every drop of blood drawn with the lash, shall be paid by another drawn with the sword" before the blood-soaked conflict ended.[39]

Unlike European revolutions and civil wars that had punished the vanquished with the guillotine and executioner's ax, the United States would demand no violent retribution after the war. Other letter writers worried that an odious crime such as the assassination of the victorious leader might inspire departures from Lincoln's announced policy of reconciliation, exacerbate the national temper, and encourage acts of personal and national vengeance. They asked the people and government of the United States to recall their slain leader's recently uttered merciful words.[40] In the second inaugural address, Lincoln had promised that the United States would hold "malice toward none" and offer "charity for all" to achieve "a lasting peace, among ourselves, and with all nations."[41]

The language used to condemn the crime and the criminal evoked the most negative and severe vocabulary. The "foul act" was an "atrocious murder" by a "ruthless assassin," who had committed "an odious wickedness," that was "the most detestable of crimes." Besides condemning the crime, the language also deprived its perpetrator of his humanness and his manhood. Not simply cowardly, Booth had been a "monster in human form," or a "fiend in human shape" to commit his "execrable crime."[42] Such castigating language contrasts sharply with the positive superlatives summoned to describe the crime's victim and the cause for which he stood. Thus, writers drew upon potent words to distance themselves from the criminal, to deny his humanity, and to identify themselves with his victim.

Working people, whether from Lyon, Turin, Berlin, Valparaiso, London, small British towns, or many other locales around the globe, claimed fellowship with the president. No matter to them that Lincoln never had worked as a factory laborer as did increasing numbers of the nineteenth-century working classes. Their letters and resolutions stand apart from the previously described basic condolences because they offered encomia that cast the president as the embodiment of the republican ideal. For instance, they proclaimed that he had risen "from the people, but he exalted the people among whom he arose." His life had instructed and encouraged the members of the Association of Anglo-Saxon Workingmen of Valparaiso, Chile, who apologized for "their want of proper language and flowing rhetoric" that compromised the full expression of their grief. Lincoln's example had taught workingmen such as them that no limit barred an "honest and hard-working man" from reaching to the highest "degrees of excellence and dignity." He had been, as a public meeting of the trading and working classes of Brighton, England, wrote, the first ruler elected from the ranks of those who worked with their hands "to the high position of ruler of one of the mightiest nations of the globe."[43]

Even the London-based central council of the International Working Men's Association, a communist organization of which Karl Marx was the German representative, had praise for the deceased president. Viewing human history as a progression from slavery, to free labor under capitalism, and to truly free labor under communism, the communists noted that the American people had chosen in the 1864 election "two men of labor," namely Lincoln and Vice President Andrew Johnson, who had started his working life as a tailor, "to initiate the new era of the emancipation of labor."[44] Workers in the United States, at least union members, did not enjoy that emancipation for almost sixty years. American Federation of Labor leader Samuel Gompers then called the Clayton Anti-Trust Act of 1914 "labor's Magna Carta." It permitted unions to spread through industries without threat of legal prosecution as combinations in restraint of trade under the antitrust laws.

Lincoln's personal transformation and rise from farm laborer and celebrated rail-splitter, to general store keeper, lawyer, politician, and president offered hope of upward mobility and the promise that representatives of working people could rule a country with high competence. As historian Daniel Walker Howe explains, Lincoln's own life embodied his commitment to human self-development as defined in terms of nineteenth-century aspirations of respectability and upward mobility.[45] These aspirations extended upward from members of the working classes and outward beyond the boundaries of the United States. "His memory," workingmen of London predicted, would be "endeared to, and enshrined in the hearts of the toiling millions of all countries, as one of the few uncrowned monarchs of the world." In short, various associations of workingmen in Europe and the Americas lamented their loss by saying, as did the people of Acireale, Sicily, "he was also ours."[46]

The expressions of condolence frequently described Lincoln as an exemplar of republicanism, both as a man and as a national leader. To the generosity that he had demonstrated in the second inaugural address by his recommendation of conciliation toward the enemies of the Union, mourners most often added the words "simple" and "honest." At this tragic time, they overlooked Lincoln and his wife's taste for the finer things, especially Mary's extravagances during the presidential years. His social and economic ascent as manifest in material goods may have seemed a tangible sign of an admirable transformation – from manual laborer in backwoods America to a prosperous, respectable member of its urban professional class.[47]

As Lincoln's career had advanced to make him a leading figure among Illinois lawyers and in his state's politics, the couple had furnished their home with purchases in the latest styles. Visitors to their front parlor saw on its mantel a three-piece suite of gilt girandoles or candelabra, probably manufactured in Philadelphia, and acquired in the late 1850s, while in the back parlor, the one that the family used, were bookcases, a stereo viewer, a writing table, and two globes – one of the earth and the other of the skies.[48]

Once in the Executive Mansion and before the death of their son Willie in February 1862, the Lincolns had hosted elaborate receptions.

The 500 guests who attended the most elaborate one feasted on beef, foie gras, quail, turkey, duck, partridge, and oysters followed by a dessert of spun-sugar confections and a cake shaped and frosted like Fort Sumter.[49] Additionally, as part of redecorating the Mansion, Mary purchased for state occasions a full dining set, breakfast set, and tea set of 666 pieces in royal purple color. Imported from France as blanks, or pieces without color and decoration, and then painted in the New York shop of E. O. Haughwout & Co. to avoid the higher tariffs levied on finished pieces, the porcelain pieces bore double gilt edging and a central decoration of the "Arms of the United States."[50]

None of these engagements with fashionable goods obtained in the commercial marketplace marred Lincoln's persona of republican simplicity. With selective vision, Lincoln enthusiasts could say that his tastes as a mature man as well as his humble origins added to the republican components of his character. The representatives of a Masonic Lodge in Choisy-le-Roi wrote that honor belonged to Lincoln "for the simplicity he brought from his home" to the Executive Mansion. He was "the most perfect model of a chief magistrate."[51] A retired merchant, representing the citizens of Caen, France, summed up the issue of republicanism: Lincoln demonstrated for the world "the manly virtues of the bright days of the Roman republic."[52]

Lincoln's admirers praised him for two interrelated achievements that promoted the republican character of the United States – he had preserved the Union and freed the slaves. The result was a republic of free men and free laborers. The significance of Lincoln as an exemplary republican linked directly to the significance of the United States as an exemplary republic. In the overblown language common in nineteenth-century expressions of sympathy, resolutions offered summary statements of the deceased president's accomplishments. He had broken "the shackles of four million of slaves," thus erasing "from the national escutcheon the reproachful stain of human thralldom," according to the letter sent by the association of Hellenic Greeks of Constantinople. The Bristol (England) Reform Union, which campaigned to obtain political rights, most importantly the right to vote, for the unenfranchised workers of England, wrote that Lincoln's death was a loss not only to his country but also "to the world at large." He had "endeared himself to all lovers of liberty by his devotion to the great cause of Negro Emancipation, and by his earnest desire to confer the blessings of equal rights and privileges on all, without distinction of party, creed, or color."[53]

Among adherents of republican political theory, those in France and Switzerland most frequently recalled the history instruction that past republics offered, especially as interpreted in the lessons of eighteenth-century French philosopher the Baron de Montesquieu. According to his discovery of supposed universal laws governing the fate of republican governments, earlier European history decreed that regional factions would tear them apart when they covered extensive territories. Applying Montesquieu's predictions, the survival of the United States with territory of 830,000 square miles in 1787 – approximately four times the area of France – was doubtful, while that of Switzerland, with less than 3 percent of that area, was more probable. Campaigning for ratification of the Constitution of 1787, James Madison had argued in *Federalist Number 10* that the division of the United States into states would exempt it from the French philosophe's dictum. Federalism would eliminate the dangers of disruption posed by a republican government ruling an extensive territory while permitting regional minorities within its borders to thrive. Until General Lee's surrender in 1865, the secession of eleven southern states in 1860 and 1861 and their formation into the Confederate States of America had seemed to prove Madison wrong and Montesquieu right, much to the dismay of European republicans.

With the defeat of Confederate armies in the spring of 1865, European advocates of free labor and governments dependent on the consent of the governed could rejoice. The resolutions from the workingmen of Wigan, a town in Lancashire, England, proclaimed that the war's outcome had brought "the complete falsification of the statements that American institutions were a failure." In Switzerland, an assembly of citizens of Bern applauded that "by their own inherent power the American people have themselves overcome the evil of which all the glorious republics of old have perished." They especially rejoiced that the Civil War had had this outcome because the Swiss had felt themselves to be too small a nation to influence neighboring states toward a future of representative government and universal manhood suffrage. After the triumph of the much larger United States, "Who would now deny that a republic can now maintain herself with great nations?"[54]

In extending condolences, the most passionate republicans predicted a role for the United States as an exemplar to nations around the globe. On behalf of the people of Switzerland, the President of the Council of State and his committee announced: "It is for you, strong and free people, to give an example to other people."[55] The United Workmen of Alessandria (a city in the Piedmont section of northern Italy) repeated the hope of the Swiss: that the American people and their federal government might "continue to serve as a model to free nations, and be a comfort and hope to those that mourn under the yoke of oppression."[56] From the Mechanic's Society and the Society of Progress of Forli, a town where the influence of Garibaldi was especially strong, came the hopes that the people of the United States would realize their inheritance of the principles of Lincoln and would extend their influence to Europe, and especially the Italian states, which they thought still enslaved under the rule of either the Pope or foreigners.[57]

Death has a way of muting criticism of the deceased and, in the case of a world-renowned figure such as Lincoln, of his nation – at least for a time. Missives expressing condolence and sympathy offered no balanced analyses of Lincoln's career or the conduct of the United States during the Civil War. Especially in the first thirty months of the war such criticism had been virulent from European cotton-manufacturing and shipping interests.

Now, as the people of Great Britain mourned, the direction of the commentary from even its cotton districts turned positive. For example, various groups in Liverpool, England, a port serving the cotton mills of Lancaster, where the criticism had been most severe and prevalent, regretted their castigation of the president during the first years of the war, when the cotton dearth had severely affected the British economy. During these years, the city's Chamber of Commerce had supported the Confederacy, and during the last years of the war a pro-southern organization in the city had taken up a collection for the aid of the "suffering poor" in the seceded states.[58] After Lincoln's death, the Financial Reform Association of Liverpool assured the people of the United States that affection for the deceased president and horror at the assassination would bury "in oblivion the remembrance of all such grievances, real or imaginary."[59] A newspaper reported that former secessionist sympathizers in the city "grieved as earnestly as the most fervent abolitionist of Massachusetts."[60] The workmen of Gateshead-on-Tyne, a town in northeastern England, even went so far as to offer regrets for the criticism "that persons of this nation have spoken and written in justification of the rebellion of the South."[61]

Despite the absence of explicit criticism, some reservations appeared. Whereas British emancipation societies were unanimous when expressing their condolences in praising the deceased president for his policies, they noted their previous unease with his gradual movement toward emancipation over the course of his four years and one month in office. Elected in November 1860, on the Republican Party platform that the federal government had the Constitutional right to control and prohibit slavery in its territories, "he gradually and cautiously developed an anti-slavery policy," they observed, "which resulted in the issue of the emancipation proclamation, by which every slave in the rebel States is now free; and he lived to see adopted by Congress an amendment to the Constitution abolishing slavery forever in the United States."[62]

The U.S. Senate had passed the Thirteenth Amendment by the required two-thirds vote of its members in April 1864. Then, encouraged by President Lincoln's lobbying and his reelection in November 1864, the House of Representatives had acted similarly in January 1865. Nine months later, regretfully recalling the slowness of the Union in moving toward emancipation at the war's beginning, self-identified "good liberals" of Andalusia, Spain, cautioned Andrew Johnson, Lincoln's successor, and urged him to promote ratification of the Thirteenth Amendment so that there would "be no more slaves for a single day."[63] By the end of December 1865, three-quarters of the states had approved the amendment, thereby making slavery and involuntary servitude unconstitutional throughout the United States.

When John Wilkes Booth shot his derringer pistol in Ford's Theatre in the spring of 1865, it was too late to save slavery or the Confederacy. The Emancipation Proclamation had taken effect, Lee's army had surrendered, and both houses of Congress had voted for the Thirteenth Amendment, which was on its way to ratification by the states. In the post–Civil War world, the enemies of free institutions no longer could taunt as hypocrites U.S. citizens who lived in the North or the South. Slavery existed nowhere in the United States. With the assassination of Lincoln, the leader who had done most to bring about these changes received global acclaim as the model republican. As the American minister to the Prussian state, Norman B. Judd, reported to Secretary of State Seward, "Mr. Lincoln is being canonized in Europe. A like unanimity of eulogy by sovereigns, parliaments, corporate bodies, by the people, and by all public journals was never before witnessed on this continent," and, as this chapter demonstrates, throughout the world.[64]

Assuredly, the people of each nation and of non-republican sympathies found different reasons for lauding the deceased president. Politically more conservative national leaders, groups, and citizens tended exclusively to emphasize his personal qualities and his generous and conciliatory policies that, they hoped, would continue and promote peace and prosperity in the United States and among nations. While adding to this elemental praise, his political sympathizers did not universally share the same reasons or points of emphasis. People of color and antislavery societies lauded Lincoln the emancipator. Swiss testimonials especially emphasized how the war had repudiated Montesquieu's theories, and French liberals and workingmen turned Lincoln, his loyalty to the Constitution, and emancipation into a foil for Napoleon III and his policies.

Despite these variations by nation, race, and class, the praise centered about the core propositions of the Declaration of Independence: that all men were created equal in their possession of life, liberty, and the pursuit of happiness and that governments should depend on the consent of the governed. As a dedicated Confederate, John Wilkes Booth had intended to promote the establishment of a government that did not depend on the consent of the governed. His shot that April night hit its immediate target and backfired in its long-term effects. People worldwide affirmed their commitment to republicanism based on free labor and free men who by the ballot consented to the rule of their governments.

Since the abrupt and tragic end to Lincoln's presidency, at most a half-dozen of his successors as president of the United States have won similar accolades from people around the world. Think of the cheering crowds that greeted Woodrow Wilson as he toured European capitals after World War I and of John F. Kennedy and Barack Obama addressing crowds in Berlin. To understand what Lincoln did to evoke such effusive mourning and garner praise as a great republican, this book analyzes selected events starting with his nomination as a candidate for the presidency. Simultaneously, it also looks backwards at his development as a politician and statesman to unearth the lessons from around the globe, and especially from Africa, Hungary, Great Britain, and the German states, that shaped his global understanding of the United States and its historical significance.

# 2

# African Lessons

At a tumultuous nominating convention in Chicago in May 1860, Republican Party delegates assembled in the recently built huge two-story meeting hall called the Wigwam. In the third round of balloting, a majority of the delegates cast their votes for Abraham Lincoln. From the cupola atop the Wigwam, a brass cannon then boomed to signal the choice of a candidate. The nominee's political friends quickly launched his bid for the presidency. Within a month, Lincoln's campaign biography was almost written.

Starting with Andrew Jackson's unsuccessful 1824 run for the office against John Quincy Adams, an authorized election-year biography had become a staple of presidential campaigns. These books touted the qualifications of the candidate to lead the American people. Benefiting from the printing and publishing innovations of the prewar decades, these cheap and mass-produced political works in English were intended to reach a national audience and sell inexpensively. Other editions were translated into the languages of immigrants to the United States and targeted their communities. From June 1860 through the election, thirteen campaign biographies in English, three in German, and two in Welsh publicized the Republican candidate's qualifications for the presidency.[1] Of these campaign pieces, Lincoln scholars consider the one written by John Locke Scripps, editor of the pro-Lincoln Chicago *Press and Tribune*, the most authoritative, the most widely circulated, and the most influential. For a few cents, the thirty-two-page booklet introduced the candidate to a broad public beyond the Republican Party faithful.

Readers learned of Lincoln's rise from his family's Kentucky log cabin, to splitting rails as a backwoodsman, to debating Democrat Stephen A.

Douglas as they campaigned for the U.S. Senate in 1858. As a skilled writer, Scripps made his points both explicitly and implicitly. Readers might learn of Lincoln's political positions, including those about slavery and its extension into the territories, through speeches taken from the 1858 Illinois Senate campaign. Scripps adopted less direct means when he established Lincoln as a pious, antislavery man – a candidate who appealed to evangelical voters dedicated to Christianity and social reform in the United States.[2]

To counter criticism of the Republican candidate's moral and intellectual qualifications for the nation's highest office in 1860, Scripps listed seven books as forming the heart of Lincoln's education: the Bible, Dilworth's Speller, Aesop's Fables, *Pilgrim's Progress*, the *Life of Franklin*, Mason Weems's Washington, and James Riley's *Narrative*.[3] Although Lincoln's actual choice of reading matter during his lifetime remains a topic that scholars dispute, the candidate had given Scripps an interview and did authorize, albeit implicitly, his biographer to include these seven titles in his biography.[4] Lincoln, the savvy politician, and certainly Scripps must have been aware of the message sent by including some books while excluding others. After the inauguration in March, Lincoln showed his gratitude to his biographer by appointing him to the lucrative and influential position of Chicago postmaster.[5]

Readers of Lincoln's biography would have recognized that his seven reading choices established him as a worthy national candidate, committed to God and country and opposed to the institution of human slavery. These titles implicitly refute many of the charges that the opposition press, foreign newspapers, and even members of his own party had leveled against the candidate during the campaign for the Republican nomination and that they would level against him during the presidential campaign of 1860. Impious, illiterate men did not teach themselves to read by studying Dilworth's Speller or the Bible. Aesop's fables certainly taught common sense and supplied a fund of wholesome, folksy stories. If a male reader took Benjamin Franklin's life lessons to heart, he would not want to remain a backwoodsman content with a life filled with material plenty while devoid of moral improvement. Instead, a morally and materially ambitious man would absorb Franklin's teachings and gain a place for himself and his family in the educated and professional middle class of the mid-nineteenth-century United States. George Washington's life taught lessons of moral probity and virtue, in the classical republican sense of putting one's self-interest aside while serving one's country. Finally, Riley's *Narrative* taught about the evils of slavery, in Africa and, by application, everywhere.

Among the seven books, the choice of Riley's *Narrative* stands forth both in the biography and in the minds of today's students of Lincoln. The book is unknown except in rarified scholarly circles. In 1860, its mention held inestimable importance, and heads would have nodded knowingly in response to its mention.[6] Of the seven books, it alone addressed a contemporary national issue that supplied the determining question of the 1860 election. What would be the future of slavery in the United States? As voters in the major slaveholding states desired, would slavery spread through the continental United States and even to territories that the nation might acquire in the Caribbean and Latin America? Or would the federal government prohibit the expansion of slavery into its current and future territories? In short, would the United States become, in the words of the Republican Party slogan of that year, a land of Free Soil, Free Labor, and Free Men?[7]

Besides a narrative of captivity and freedom, the *Narrative* teaches many lessons about Lincoln and his stand on slavery. From the narrative he learned how slavery existed as an institution in the flow of Western history and how it might be eliminated in the present moment from the United States. While it taught global lessons, it had local application.

The listing of Captain James Riley's *Narrative* in Scripps's campaign biography demonstrated that Lincoln had chosen to make a stand on slavery, one that he calculated would not alienate more voters than necessary. Readers in the know would grasp the candidate's position on the issue and the means that he supported for slavery's eradication. Riley's book had appeared in 1817 with the title: *An Authentic Narrative of the Loss of the American Brig Commerce, wrecked on the Western Coast of Africa, in the Month of August, 1815: With an Account of the Sufferings of her Surviving Officers and Crew, who Were Enslaved by the Wandering Arabs, on the Great African Desart, or Zahahrah; and Observations Historical, Geographical, &c. Made during the Travels of the Author, while a Slave to the Arabs, and in the Empire of Morocco.* Daunted by the extravagance of repeating this excessively long and very descriptive title, reviewers and cultural commentators in the early national and antebellum periods referred to it simply as Riley's *Narrative*.

Consider other books that Lincoln might have chosen to show his opposition to slavery and hopes for emancipation. As preparation for a speech in Springfield, Illinois, in which he intended to counter Senator Douglas's advocacy of popular sovereignty as a remedy for the question of whether slavery might extend into the territories of Kansas and Nebraska, he had studied for weeks in the state library in Springfield, according to the city's newspaper. Biographer Michael Burlingame explains that during Lincoln's preparation, he had consulted Leonard Bacon's *Slavery Discussed in Occasional Essays from 1833 to 1846*. A minister of the First Congregational Church in New Haven, Connecticut, Bacon had published these essays in the *Christian Spectator* and *New Englander*, the primary journals of his denomination.[8] Active in many antebellum reform causes, Bacon strongly opposed slavery, supported its gradual abolition, and promoted the settlement of the freed people in Liberia. Although his book generated little controversy among reviewers and would not have offended voters with any degree of antislavery feeling, its author enjoyed minimal name recognition beyond the northeastern and mid-Atlantic states.

If Lincoln had wanted to select a recently published book with name recognition across the United States, he could have mentioned Harriet Beecher Stowe's *Uncle Tom's Cabin, or Life among the Lowly*. First published in *The New Era*, a weekly abolitionist paper of the American and Foreign Anti-Slavery Society from June 1851 to April 1852, it was issued as a novel in 1852, quickly becoming "the world's first true blockbuster," according to book historian Michael Winship.[9]

Although the title of this novel in Lincoln's campaign biography might have encouraged abolitionists to vote for the Illinois Republican, it would have aroused controversy in every section of the United States. Even its mention would have alienated all but a smattering of voters residing south of the Mason-Dixon line and, more significantly for a presidential candidate, voters north of that line who were not thoroughly devoted to the antislavery cause. Shortly after the novel's publication, a scathing review in the *Southern Literary Messenger* denounced Stowe's work as "the most pernicious book that ever disgraced female authorship."[10]

Given this background, mention of Riley's *Narrative* in a campaign biography was a prudent and wise choice as the title had wide name recognition and demonstrated that Lincoln supported the crucial slogan of Republicanism: "Free Soil, Free Men, Free Labor." His selection of the *Narrative* showed his moral opposition to both slavery and its immediate abolition. Examination of the text and its juxtaposition to Lincoln's life shows that the book also had considerable educational value. It provided both global and historical lessons about slavery and, equally important, lessons about a possible process of emancipation.

Although no one can say exactly when the Republican presidential candidate read Riley's *Narrative*, its inclusion with the other six books implies that it may have been a highlight of his youthful reading, as his campaign biographer suggested, probably when his family lived in southern Indiana from 1816 to 1830, when Lincoln was seven to twenty-one years old. During this period, Riley traveled through Kentucky selling his book, and a Lexington printer published a new edition in 1823. In the same year, Henry Clay, the state's leading citizen whom its legislature elected to the Senate three times, hosted a reception for the author, really a sales event for the forthcoming edition of the *Narrative*. Seven years previously, Clay had served as the first president of the American Colonization Society (ACS). It promoted the emancipation of American slaves and the settlement of free blacks in Africa, or what its members considered to be repatriation to their homeland. Most of the several thousand African Americans freed by the ACS settled in Liberia, which the society had helped found in 1821–1822.

With transportation provided by traveling peddlers or settlers emigrating from Kentucky, the *Narrative* might have traveled in wagons or saddlebags some 120 miles northwest from Kentucky to the vicinity of the Lincoln family's home on Pigeon Creek in Perry County (now Spencer County), Indiana. There it could have landed in the home of one of the several families with more disposable income and more literate members who loaned reading material to the young Abraham. Since Riley's *Narrative* would have been a luxury purchase for the struggling Lincoln household during its Indiana years, it most likely did not buy its own copy. Alternately, if Lincoln's biographer Scripps is mistaken, his subject might have encountered the volume after his marriage to Mary Todd.[11]

Both Mary Todd, a native of Lexington, Kentucky, and Lincoln admired Clay, who had promoted sales of Riley's *Narrative*. The senator had touted the book, while the book endorsed his plan of colonization. In agreement as well with Clay's program to develop the economy of the United States through tariff policy and the building of federally funded canals, harbors, and other internal improvements, Lincoln served as an elector for Clay, the Whig Party candidate for president in 1844, by campaigning for him extensively through southern Illinois and into portions of Indiana and Kentucky. Meanwhile, his wife of two years and their one-year-old waited for his return in the family's recently purchased house in Springfield. Two years later in 1846, after the young Whig's own election to the House of Representatives, the Lincoln family, now doubled in size with the birth of a second son, visited Mary Todd's family in Lexington for a month in late 1847 while en route to Washington. While with the Todds, Lincoln took advantage of his father-in-law's extensive library and attended the launch of Clay's bid to be the presidential nominee of the Whig Party in 1848. At the event on November 13, for which Mary's father was vice chairman, Clay spoke for 150 minutes on the Mexican War and slavery.[12]

During that month in Lexington with Mary's family, Lincoln might have passed some of his free hours reading or rereading the *Narrative*. Most probably, Robert Todd, his father-in-law, owned a copy. He had been among the prominent guests at the 1823 fête for the author. Besides their high regard for Clay, the Lincolns most likely also shared delight in the adventures of Captain James Riley.[13]

If Lincoln did not spend time reading his father-in-law's copy while sojourning in Kentucky, we can speculate about when he did read it by following the findings of a recent analyst of the *Narrative*'s sales. On the one hand, few copies of the book sold outside the northeastern states, while, on the other hand, Riley's story appeared in redacted and reprinted versions in popular anthologies of pirates and African adventures.[14]

Consequently, if Lincoln did not read the book during his early years, he would have encountered it repeatedly in redacted forms and in references encountered in newspapers and journals throughout his pre-presidential life. After 1831, Riley's *Narrative* appeared, in much abbreviated form, in two children's editions. Given this information, we can imagine Papa Lincoln in the back parlor of his Springfield home reading the juvenile adventure book to young Robert or Willie at some time from the late 1840s through the 1850s.[15]

Probably because the Lincoln-Douglas senatorial debates throughout the fall of 1858 had underlined the differences between Democrats and the newly formed Republican Party, an enterprising New York City publisher issued a new edition of the *Narrative* in 1859.[16] As the presidential campaign of 1860 commenced, Riley's book remained a current topic in public discourse about slavery and reminded its readers of its current relevance to national issues.

From a practical viewpoint, many, if not most, of the readers of Scripps's 1860 biography would have recognized the reference to Riley, as they would not have recognized the reference to the minister Leonard Bacon, and the mention was not likely to provoke sectional controversy, as *Uncle Tom's Cabin* would have. By the 1840s, Captain Riley and Riley's *Narrative* had acquired name recognition among the reading public of the United States. In 1840, the *New Hampshire Sentinel* claimed that the story was "familiar to many of our readers." Farther south in Baltimore, Bayard Taylor, a popular mid-century author and lecturer, demonstrated that he could count on learned-society audiences to associate references to either the author's name or an abbreviated title to connote travel narratives, sea adventures, and Africa. Reviewers for *Godey's Lady's Book* and other publications made similar references with similar assurance that readers who opposed the antislavery movement would take no offense.[17] For example, when Riley's son published a sequel to his father's book in 1851, he included letters of praise for the original volume from readers in several states, including North Carolina and South Carolina. One reader mentioned that Riley's tale made him "willing to shoulder my gun, to go and seek redress of them Arabs," while another reader had an opposite reaction. He put the book down filled with "admiration" for the Arab trader who had made possible the captain's rescue.[18]

From what is known of the history of readers, Lincoln's involvement with this popular book surpassed involvement that we might describe as once-read-and-then-discarded. Instead, Lincoln enjoyed what reading scholars call an intensive involvement with Riley's *Narrative*, as well as his other six notable books. He drew lessons from them that took root deep in his self. In addition, his immersion in the journal literature of his era repeatedly would have recalled the book and its significance while providing assurance that his fellow Americans were participating in a similar experience.

Reading brought Lincoln into a public square of words that his countrymen, especially like-minded Whig and Republican voters, also occupied. We can enter this public square when we understand the content of Riley's book as well as the global and political context surrounding its publication.

Reviewing the meaning of "slavery" in the six other books in Lincoln's campaign biography reveals the many connotations of the word in the antebellum years. As a politically active Whig and then Republican politician who consumed newspapers from multiple locations, candidate Lincoln understood that mere mention of the Bible as an influential book did not signal his opposition to slavery. During his years of political activism in Illinois for the Whig Party and subsequently for the newly formed Republican Party, both pro-slavery and antislavery polemicists claimed that the Bible supported their positions. Widely published pro-slavery authors, such as Baptist minister and Virginia slaveholder Thornton Stringfellow, contended in *The Bible against Slavery* that Christians and Jews revered a God in the Old Testament that had recognized, sanctioned, and rewarded slaveholders. The Virginian provided scriptural evidence to reach his conclusion that "the conviction is forced upon the mind, that from Abraham's day, until the coming of Christ (a period of two thousand years) this institution found favor with God." When he addressed the New Testament, Stringfellow refuted contemporary anti-slavery partisans who said that its God excoriated slavery. Instead, he maintained that Jesus had condoned the holding of slaves and increased the obligation of servant to master by enjoining a servant "to render good will to his master."[19] First appearing in the Richmond, Virginia *Religious Herald* in 1841, Stringfellow's argument joined the 1860 Democratic Party campaign for the presidency when it was republished that year in an anthology of pro-slavery arguments called *Cotton is King*.[20]

Antislavery writers had two primary means of appropriating the authority of Scripture for their cause. The Reverend Theodore Dwight Weld, a leading abolitionist of the 1830s, had established the basic Bible-based antislavery argument against which later polemicists such as Stringfellow contended. Weld accused pro-slavery advocates of choosing and molding the words of the Bible to suit their own predilections by conflating the status of servants in ancient Israel with that of slaves in the antebellum United States. In the Bible, servants, he argued, were treated as humans, whereas in slaveholding states laws that had established and currently regulated slaves and slavery treated African Americans not as people but as things, property, or chattel. According to Weld, the Bible never referred to humans, whether servants or not, as property. Servants of Biblical times could earn their freedom, rarely remained slaves for life, and their children did not inherit their slave status. As Weld wrote: "servants became and continued such of their own accord." Accordingly, he inferred that they also did not "work without pay."[21]

Given the potency of pro-slavery writers' Biblical proof, the most popular and influential antislavery writers of the 1850s set aside the issue of slaves versus servants in the Old Testament and publicized the antislavery spirit that they perceived in the New Testament. In *Uncle Tom's Cabin*, Stowe showed the limitations of the Bible as an antislavery document. Major and minor characters draw on the words of the Old Testament to support both the pro and anti sides of the debate. While some Biblical verses vindicated possession of human property, other verses condemned the practice.

The impasse called forth a new tactic. Both Stowe and her famous preacher brother, Henry Ward Beecher, bypassed the verses of the Old Testament. To counter pro-slavery polemics, in their sermons and fiction, the Beechers relied on celebration of the humanitarian spirit that they inferred from the New Testament. As Henry preached on Thanksgiving Day, 1860, Christ "had come to open prison doors, to deliver captives, to loose those that are bound."[22] The import that Henry Ward and, by implication, his sister desired for the slaves of the United States, especially after Lincoln's election of November 6, could not have been clearer.

Despite Weld's research and logic and the Beechers' evocation of New Testament stories, pro-slavery writers such as Stringfellow made the more persuasive case in the court of public opinion. As noted scholar Mark A. Noll writes, their interpretations of the Bible "made the most sense to the broadest public." Belief in Biblical inerrancy made most evangelicals unwilling to ignore completely the words of the Old Testament. The arguments of the Beechers and other antislavery Biblical apologists led Christian believers to the top of a slippery slope that threatened to slide them toward rejection of the Bible as truth.[23] Had Lincoln wanted to demonstrate in his campaign biography by Scripps that he stood in moral opposition to slavery, reference to the Bible would not work. Its inclusion must have served other necessary purposes, such as reassuring the pious American that he was no unbeliever and shared their reverence for the Divine word and its authority.

Similar ambiguity on the slavery issue appeared in the listing of both Weems's biography of George Washington and *The Life of Franklin*. Famous for the anecdote of the young Virginian confessing to his father Augustine that he had hacked his prized English cherry tree with a new hatchet, the Weems biography of the general and patriot obfuscated when it discussed the issue of slavery. Weems never called the laborers slaves who worked in the fields of Mount Vernon, the Washingtons' plantation. He describes the president riding into his fields in early morning to observe "his overseers and servants." Their industrious labor applied to the well-manured fields produced bountiful harvests of wheat and Indian corn from which, Weems observed, the plantation owner's "servants fared plentifully. His cattle never had the hollow horn [a disease of cattle]."[24]

In fact, George Washington's father had owned slaves and had left the future president ten of them after his death in 1743. With the addition of slaves from the dowry of his wife, Martha, purchases of more slaves during the Washingtons' lifetimes, and the addition of the slaves' descendants to the plantation labor force, by the time the former president died in 1799, more than three hundred slaves lived at and labored on the Mount Vernon plantation. Nevertheless, in the hagiographic biography, Weems's word choice throws a cloak of invisibility over the enslaved people who labored at Mount Vernon.

In contrast, from the life of *Franklin*, Lincoln would have learned an overt lesson about slavery, although one that still muted its criticism of the institution in the United States. This biography describes how Franklin had assumed the presidency of a society to abolish the slave trade after returning from his diplomatic posting to France. While not giving the actual name of the society, Weems euphemistically refers to it in a list of Franklin's memberships as "a society for abolishing the slave trade; the relief of free negroes, unlawfully held in bondage; and for bettering the condition of free blacks."[25] In fact, Franklin assumed the presidency of the Society for the Promoting the Abolition of Slavery and the Relief of Negroes Unlawfully Held in Bondage. In Weems's reference to the antislavery organization, which Franklin led in his last years, the biographer bypasses use of the word "abolition" and terms the institution of slavery "unlawful bondage." By referring solely to the slave trade, illegally enslaved African Americans, and "free blacks," Weems blunts the implications of Franklin's antislavery activity by describing them in softer terms unlikely to undercut slaveholding.

Weems's reference to the demise of the slave trade should have generated no controversy. In the nation of the 1790s, the end of slave importation rested as a settled issue. A dozen years previously, the Constitutional Convention held in Franklin's hometown had debated the topic and had agreed that the new federal government would have the power to abolish the importation of slaves to the United States twenty years after the Constitution's ratification, or as early as 1808.

Significantly, Weems's biography excludes any reference to Franklin's activities in support of the Quaker abolition society with an actual name that would have offended pro-slavery readers. His prose omits possible offense to them even though well-informed readers would have known that Franklin's society did not touch slavery in states where laws made its existence legal. It opposed only the holding of previously freed slaves whose claims to freedom owners had not recognized or whom slave catchers had wrongfully captured.

Unlike Weems's Franklin, the real Franklin used strong words in his antislavery writings to condemn the institution. In 1789, to raise funds for the society, a circular appeared under his signature. In it, he dramatically termed slavery "such an atrocious abasement of human nature" that "the galling chains that bind his [and her] body do also fetter his [and her] intellectual faculties, and impair the social affections of the heart." To enjoy freedom in its full sense, freed slaves thus needed more than freedom; they also required preparation for "the exercise and enjoyment of civil liberty."[26]

Almost all the books that Lincoln's campaign biographer deemed notable include the noun "slave" or the adjective "slavish," while referring to human slavery neither as an institution nor in a global context. Noah Webster's dictionary of the early nineteenth century provides a guide to the use of the words "slave" and "slavish." It says that a person could be a slave in three different ways. First, a person might work incredibly hard, like a beast of burden. Second, a person might live in total dependency on another, or third, s/he might exist under the rule of a vice, passion, or tyrant. In Aesop's fable "The Farmer and the Stork," the stork complains that it slaves for his parents, and in "The Wolves and the Sheepdogs," the wolves lure the dogs by arguing that they slave for humans in return for sheep bones that their owners discard after stripping them of meat. In the second instance, Dilworth's speller taught the beginning reader from the verse: "And he that to this Vice [lying] becomes a Slave,/In Fire and Brimstone, shall his Portion have."[27] For the third meaning, *Pilgrim's Progress* told more advanced readers that no man could "be a living monument of grace, that is a slave to his own corruption."[28]

To illustrate the possibility of being a slave in a political sense, examples appear in Weems's *Life of Washington*. The biographer praised his subject as a patriot. He had defended his country "from slavery," or the absolute control that the colonists perceived Great Britain attempting to exercise over them through imposition of taxes such as those of the Stamp Act and Tea Acts.[29]

Of the seven books that Lincoln mentioned to Scripps, Riley's *Narrative* alone discusses the institution of slavery explicitly and illustrates the evils of holding humans as property. Its lessons about the treatment of slaves fascinated pre–Civil War readers because the captors of American and European sailors wrecked off the coasts of Africa or seized from European and American vessels demanded from their white captives trying physical labor while brutally punishing them. Because the captives found themselves wholly dependent on the will of another and had to work arduously with no reward besides a modicum of food and shelter, the transatlantic Christian public easily thought of the captives as slaves. Rather than learning cerebrally about the inhumanity of slavery from the pleas of British and American antislavery partisans, the narratives gave their white readers first-person access to the slaves' physical and mental experiences.[30] Barbary narratives transformed slavery from a concept of an institution that never affected whites because it exclusively controlled the labor and the morality of a population considered inferior in their capacity for self-governance. Readers now could empathetically enter into the torture of slavery by seeing how the institution affected people like themselves. They could visualize slavery in personal terms and understand the institution's inhumanity. By naming Riley's *Narrative*, Lincoln invited white readers to enter the imaginative world of slavery as presidential candidate Lincoln once had and as millions of African Americans in the United States lived it – every day of their lives. And if these readers declined this invitation, they might consider the contemporary campaign against slavery as a nationalistic endeavor similar to President Thomas Jefferson's and President Monroe's naval campaigns against the Barbary pirates.

Additionally, captivity narratives had what we might call feel-good endings. White slaves could tell their stories because they had made a successful escape. The freed whites accredited their survival and release largely to their physical and, more important, moral strength rooted in their Christian faith. Like the gospel story of Christ in the Judean desert and like the trials of Bunyan's pilgrim on the way to the Celestial City, the captives faced temptation from their non-Christian masters, while prevailing over them because of their religious fortitude.

Riley's *Narrative* became one of the most popular captivity narratives because of these internal and external factors. In the story, a variety of sensational delights neutralized the potential cloying effect of the character-strengthening story. The captain told of exotic places, sea adventure and shipwreck, desert treks, encounters with peoples that Christian Americans deemed savage and heathen, and instances of extreme human brutality. Even if readers encountered abbreviated versions of the *Narrative* in books such as Samuel Goodrich's *Lights and Shadows of African History* or *The Narratives of an Old Traveller*, they would still meet, as the subtitle of the second book promised, "*Perils and Hair-breadth Escapes from Shipwreck, Famine, Wild Beasts, Savages, etc.*"[31]

Captain Riley's *Narrative* begins with the story of a commercial voyage in 1815 that should have proceeded from the Connecticut River town of Middletown to New Orleans, to the Cape of Gibraltar, to the Cape Verde Islands, and then ended at Riley's home port in Connecticut. As captain of the merchant brig *Commerce*, he had planned this complex voyage, yet an ordinary one for New England merchants, to try to recoup his fortunes that had suffered seriously during the recently ended War of 1812 between his country and Great Britain. Because of the hostility between Britain and France during the Napoleonic Wars, whose later years overlapped with the War of 1812, Riley had lost a well-loaded ship when, in 1808, French consular officials confiscated it and its cargo. This calamity had sunk the captain into debt and caused his creditors to seize his Connecticut house and homestead of fifteen acres.

In February 1815, Senate ratification of the Treaty of Ghent officially ended the conflict with Britain, and the debt-plagued captain promptly raised funds for another sea venture. He planned to transport bricks and hay from Connecticut to New Orleans and to trade those goods for a more valuable cargo of flour and tobacco. In Gibraltar, he would swap them for brandy and wine, and with this even more valuable shipload sail to the Canary Islands, where he would exchange that cargo for salt for subsequent sale in Connecticut at a substantial profit.

Foul weather destroyed Riley's plan, wrecked the ship, cost the death of many crewmembers, and caused the enslavement of the survivors. After departing Gibraltar, the *Commerce* met catastrophe in August off the northwest African coast. As its captain navigated his vessel between the Canary Islands and the mainland, dark clouds and fierce winds prevented accurate navigation and the sighting of coastal landmarks. Without knowledge of his ship's position, Riley caused it to founder on a sandbar, on Cape Bogador.

Throughout the *Narrative* of his voyage and subsequent adventures, Riley provided Lincoln and his fellow readers with graphic descriptions of his incredible mental and physical perils while attributing his eventual rescue to intercessions by divine Providence. Describing the first African people encountered in sensational and frightening terms, he stressed their ferocity and near-animal natures while forcefully stating their propensity to cannibalism, in case his readers did not make the inference. The leader "had about him to cover his nakedness, a piece of coarse woollen [sic] cloth, that reached from below his breast nearly to his knees; his hair was long and bushy, resembling a *pitch mop*, sticking out every way six or eight inches from his head; his face resembled that of an ourang-outang [sic] more than a human being; his eyes were red and fiery; his mouth, which stretched nearly from ear to ear, was well lined with sound teeth; and a long curling beard, which descended from his upper lip and chin down upon his breast, gave him altogether a most horrid appearance, and I could not imagine that those well set teeth were sharpened for the purpose of eating human flesh!"[32]

After convincing his terrified crewmen that to remain among such people courted death, the captain had his sailors launch their ship's longboat into towering surf. With its waves pounding against the fragile and overloaded craft, which Riley describes as writhing "like an old basket," he asked his crew to doff their hats and pray to the "great Creator and preserver of the universe." Then, "as if by divine command," the wind stilled, the seas calmed, and the crew escaped the life-threatening brutes on shore. By the intercession of divine Providence, Riley felt that he and his men had been saved from a hostile people much as the book of Exodus relates that Moses and the Jews had been able to escape the Pharaoh's soldiers by passing through the Red Sea.[33]

After reaching calm waters, Riley's crew navigated southward in hopes of locating a friendly merchant ship or a beach suitable for a landing. After a few days of roasting in the tropical sun and with little potable liquid or food, the sailors' despair moved their captain to head the boat toward land regardless of hazards. Indeed, a reef and heavy surf soon mangled the longboat and forced its crew to struggle ashore. After a perilous climb over rocky cliffs bordering the beach and with little food to eat and their urine, which they captured in empty wine bottles, exclusively to drink, the sailors eventually reached the plain of the Sahara desert. Sighting Arab traders, they imagined imminent relief for their thirst and hunger. Sadly, they had not reached safety but simply exchanged the perils of the sea for those of the desert. The Arabs stripped the clothes from their captives and fought one another with scimitars and knives for possession of them.

As the rival groups divvied up the crewmembers, the sailors felt themselves transformed into commodities. As Riley described, the Arabs "examined every bone to see if all was right in its place, with the same cautious circumspection that a jockey would use, who was about buying a horse; while we, poor trembling wretches, strove with all possible care and anxiety to hide every fault and infirmity."[34] Beatings inflicted by their male and female owners inflicted less injury than did the hardship of the trek. With blistered, nude bodies and feet lacerated on the sharp stones of the desert surface, the men were forced to straddle bareback the rear of camels' humps. A master's wife and children rode in a basket atop the hump and the master himself guided the camel from a saddle mounted on the hump's foreside. (See Figures 2.1, 2.2.)

Instead of the desert cutting and burning the soles of the crew's feet, now "blood dripped from their heels" because camel hide and hair abraded their crotches and upper legs. Parched with thirst and weak from hunger, the naked men quenched their thirst with fetid water and camel milk, and sometimes with camel urine. If they were lucky, they found snails and enjoyed variety in their diet. In the midst of this intense suffering, Riley, now weighing less than half his former 240 pounds,

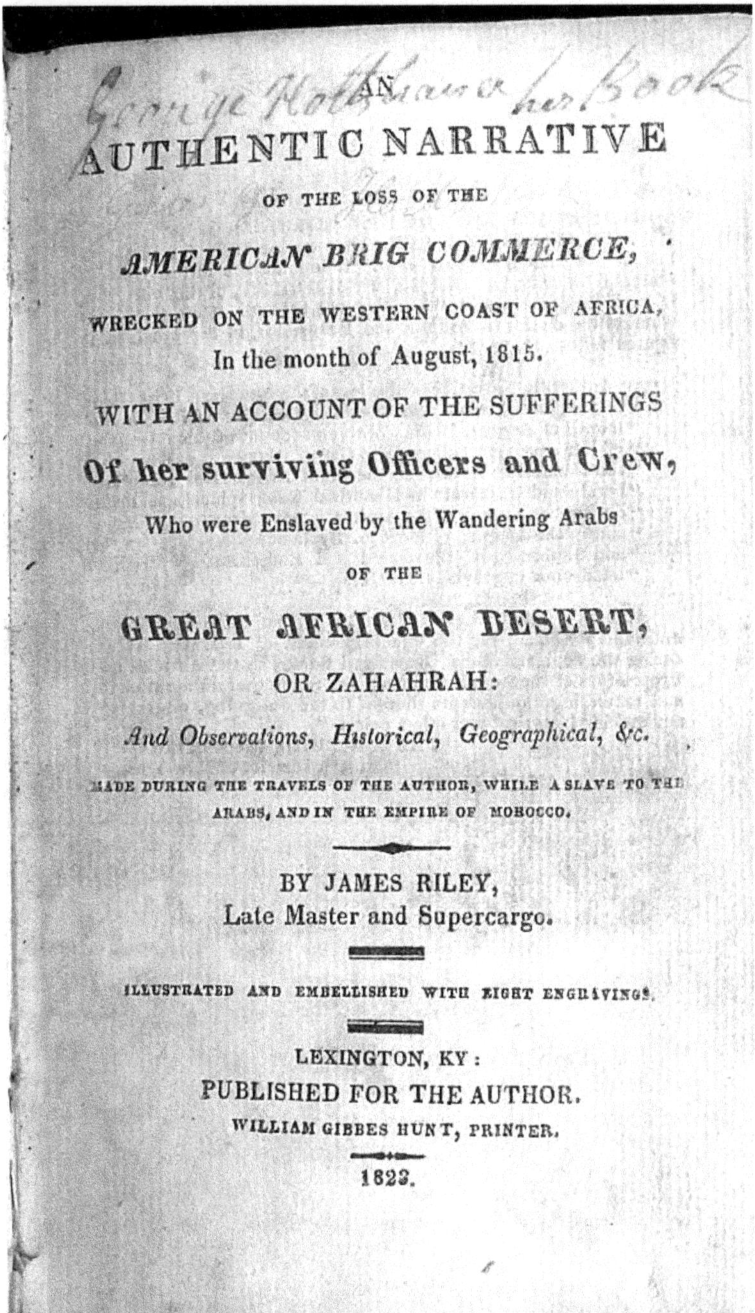

AN

# AUTHENTIC NARRATIVE

OF THE LOSS OF THE

## AMERICAN BRIG COMMERCE,

WRECKED ON THE WESTERN COAST OF AFRICA,

In the month of August, 1815.

WITH AN ACCOUNT OF THE SUFFERINGS

### Of her surviving Officers and Crew,

Who were Enslaved by the Wandering Arabs

OF THE

## GREAT AFRICAN DESERT,

OR ZAHAHRAH:

*And Observations, Historical, Geographical, &c.*

MADE DURING THE TRAVELS OF THE AUTHOR, WHILE A SLAVE TO THE
ARABS, AND IN THE EMPIRE OF MOROCCO.

———◆———

### BY JAMES RILEY,
Late Master and Supercargo.

▬▬▬▬▬

ILLUSTRATED AND EMBELLISHED WITH EIGHT ENGRAVINGS.

▬▬▬▬

LEXINGTON, KY:
PUBLISHED FOR THE AUTHOR.

WILLIAM GIBBES HUNT, PRINTER.

—◆—

1823.

FIGURE 2.1. Henry Clay hosted what we call a book party for James Riley when
the author visited Lexington to peddle the locally printed edition of his *Authentic
Narrative*. Lincoln's father-in-law attended the event. Image courtesy of Special
Collections Research Center, University of Kentucky, Lexington.

Capture of the Author and ten of his crew, by a tribe of wandering Arabs.

FIGURE 2.2. This illustration from the Lexington edition of Riley's *Narrative* shows the author and his crew being captured by Arabs. The traders stripped the captives of their clothes, assessed their health and physique, and divvied up their new slaves among them. If one examines the illustration closely, one can see how a captive might have sat on the rear of a camel's hump. Image courtesy of Special Collections Research Center, University of Kentucky, Lexington.

saved himself from suicide once again by summoning his faith "that 'the Judge of all the earth would do right'."[35]

The destiny of Riley and four members of the crew took a new turn when their owners met Sidi Hamet, another Arab trader. Luckily for the sailors, this man too had suffered from trading ventures that had cost him his fortune and family. Upon encountering Riley and his men, the Arab trader must have estimated that he could ransom the whites in Morocco to the north and recoup his losses. With wile and bravery, Riley played upon the Arab's entrepreneurial spirit, promising him that the European powers in Swearah or Mogadore (now known as Essaouira, Morocco) would pay handsomely for the white slaves. Sidi Hamet soon computed that he could buy them for several blankets and a bundle of ostrich feathers and resell them profitably.

In reality, Riley had duped the Arab. Knowing no one in that trading port, Riley had been hoping that some Europeans or Americans would empathize with the plight of their fellow Christians and would advance the ransom without any guarantee of repayment. If the captain had misjudged, the consequence would be fearful. Sidi Hamet had vowed that if he did not receive a ransom, he would slit the captain's throat and sell back into slavery his crewmen and the fifteen-year-old cabin boy.

After surviving the physically and mentally punishing 800-mile trek across the Sahara and evading bands of robbers, the captives and their new owner neared Mogadore. One last time they escaped from danger, in this case from Sidi Hamet's greedy father-in-law, who coveted the promised ransom. While the father-in-law kept the Americans, Hamet took a note from Riley to give to any white European whom he might find in the Moroccan port city. In the scribbled note, Riley begged its reader to consider "all the ties that bind man to man, by those of kindred blood, and everything you hold most dear." If the plight of the enslaved Americans moved the note's reader, he was to ransom the men with two double-barreled guns and a sum of 920 dollars. This payment would buy the freedom of three crewmembers, the cabin boy, and the captain. After a series of fortunate events, the note did reach William Willshire, the British consul-general in Mogadore. Moved by Riley's supplications, the diplomat ransomed the sailors, thus saving Riley's neck and rescuing his crew from another descent into slavery.

Although we have no comments by Lincoln on Riley's *Narrative*, reviews of the *Narrative* that appeared in central publications of literary elites suggest that readers enjoyed more than the tale's gag-inducing stories of drinking urine and suppurating flesh. They most likely found Riley's detailed descriptions of Africa conventional because they added little new information to preexisting notions of northern Africa and its inhabitants. Even so, the *Narrative* introduced new information into a cultural conversation that had taken place over three centuries.[36]

Since at least the sixteenth century, seafarers from northern Africa, the western edge of the Islamic world, then called al-Maghrib, had preyed on European shipping.[37] Corsairs, as they were then known, from Morocco "and the semi-autonomous Ottoman regencies of Tripoli, Tunis, and Algiers" captured and ransomed European merchant vessels and their crews. American and Europeans had learned of the people of northern Africa and their customs from narratives that their former captives published.[38] Along with the Indian captivity narrative of North America, by the late 1790s, the so-called Barbary narrative had become a major genre of the English-reading Atlantic world.

With protection from the dominant Royal Navy, ships from the American colonies mostly avoided peril from seafaring marauders in the southwestern Mediterranean Sea until 1776. Despite the wartime Treaty of Alliance (1778) with France, which promised mutual aid against common enemies, the United States in the next decade increasingly began to lose merchant ships to the corsairs. After Moroccans captured the American brigantine *Betsey* in 1784, emissaries Benjamin Franklin, John Adams, and Thomas Jefferson conducted negotiations in Paris and gained its release in return for a so-called gift of $20,000 to the Moroccan ruler. This sum was the first of many payments of either tribute or ransom to the North Africans, whom Americans and Europeans called the Barbary pirates. Over the next thirty years, they captured 35 U.S. ships and held for ransom more than 700 sailors.[39]

In the early 1790s, the United States had no navy able to protect its ocean commerce. Presidents had to choose among paying exorbitant sums of tribute money, ransoming cargos and crews, or deploying the new country's minuscule military might. With little to no protection for their ships, U.S. captains piloting their ships through the Mediterranean Sea relied on their own initiatives. To protect their vessels, they counterfeited passes that resembled those that tribute-paying nations routinely purchased from African rulers, or they might hire Dutch or Spanish gunboats to escort their ships past the Barbary coast after they sailed through the straights of Gibraltar.

After the Treaty of Paris in 1783 recognized that the American colonies had won their independence from one of the most powerful European countries, Americans found tribute payments to the Barbary States intensely insulting. Not until 1794, and then only after a lengthy debate, did Congress act on President Washington's call for the construction of a navy. Because its creation took a decade, U.S. shipping remained vulnerable to Barbary piracy during the 1790s. In 1796, its treasury paid one million dollars, or one-sixth of its annual budget, to the ruler of Algiers to ransom American sailors. In this sense, the United States still had not gained independence for its ships at sea.[40]

To end the payment of tribute and ransom, the new nation fought two wars during the administrations of presidents Jefferson (1801–1809) and James Madison (1809–1817). The first Barbary War, or Tripolitan War, of 1801–1805, ended when the ruler of Tripoli agreed to free the 300 American prisoners under his control in return for a $60,000 ransom and release of Tripolitan prisoners held by the United States.[41] In the treaty, Jefferson did not secure promises of the end of the practice of tribute and ransom. Their continuation caused a second Barbary War to begin in 1815.

Having to defend its merchant marine and coasts from the British navy from 1812 through the end of 1814, the United States could not protect merchant ships in the Mediterranean Sea, and they once again became easy prey for the Barbary corsairs. After Major General Andrew Jackson's victory over British forces at New Orleans, in January 1815, inspired patriotic fervor, demand arose for an end to the predations by the pirates. A Christian, independent nation, Americans thought, should be able to vanquish foes lesser in both physical and moral strength. Tribute payments and the theft of cargoes not only supported the economies of the Barbary States but also outfitted their pirates. Besides hard currency and consumer goods, their naval marauding secured gunpowder, guns of war, and even gunships such as the *Betsey*.

After Senate ratification of the Treaty of Ghent in February 1815, President Madison deliberated until early spring before asking Congress for a declaration of war against the Barbary States. By mid-May, a squadron of ten warships had departed New York City harbor for the Mediterranean Sea to fight the second Barbary War, or Algerine War. By July 1, the naval expedition, commanded by Commodore Stephen Decatur, had vanquished the *Mashuda*, a previously captured and renamed U.S. ship. By the end of the month, Decatur's fleet had defeated twenty-nine ships, forced negotiations with the rulers of Algiers, Tunis, and Tripoli, and won compensation for seized ships and the release of American captives.[42]

Following the successful conclusion of the Barbary wars, patriotic fervor intensified in the United States. Authors and the press now lauded their county's might as they had deplored it twenty years earlier, when playwright Susanna Rowson had lamented the nation's weakness in *Slaves in Algiers* (1794) and novelist Royall Tyler ended *The Algerine Captive* (1797) with a plea for national strength.[43] In the country's material culture, decorative motifs of stars and stripes, heroes, and triumphant eagles surged to popularity.[44] As Americans settled territories in the midwestern United States, they named towns, townships, counties, and streets after the heroes and diplomats of the Barbary Wars, most notably Stephen Decatur, naval hero of both the Revolution and the recent wars. Patriotic fervor had sufficient strength even to penetrate frontier settlements of Kentucky and Indiana, where the young Lincoln was born and then lived from boyhood to young adulthood.

The first edition of Riley's *Narrative* thus enjoyed the good fortune to be published in the midst of this enthusiasm and a burgeoning of U.S. trade with the lands bordering the Mediterranean Sea. American merchants provided the region with 12 million gallons of rum annually.[45] Riley's shipwreck, captivity, and release demonstrated the prestige that the nation had acquired on the international stage. In the *Narrative*, a British diplomat makes possible the ransom of Riley and four of the *Commerce*'s crew. The British consul-general's payment of ransom to Sidi Hamet shows that the two nations' wartime enmity had no permanence; the lasting condition was one of peace and cooperation. As a result, international respect joined with the centuries-old feeling of Christian unity to free Riley's crew from captivity.

That Lincoln might admire the captain as a hero should not be surprising given the heroes in his six other favored books. The moral fortitude demanded from Riley during his captivity would have resonated with readers who admired the future-orientation and political virtue that Weems had highlighted and inscribed into the lives of Washington and Franklin. Like Washington, the general who thought of the welfare of his troops, Riley had thought first of the good of his crewmen. Not content with Sidi Hamet's buying him and no other crewmember, Riley imperiled his own life by arguing with his future master that he should purchase the youngest and weakest sailors. Like Franklin, Riley had scientific skills – in the sea captain's case, skills of navigation. He also had displayed Franklin-like shrewdness when bargaining for the freedom of his crew and himself.

Bunyan's hero Christian also resembled Riley with his faithful perseverance. While Bunyan's pilgrim avoided the temptations of the Seven Deadly Sins to drag him from the path to the Celestial City, Riley avoided temptation during his sea adventure and desert trek. Like Bunyan's pilgrim, he received a great reward after reaching his destination. On the desert, the captain might have given up by committing suicide and ending the tortures of dehydration, sun roasting, and hunger. Or he might have renounced his Christian faith and settled among Sidi Hamet's people as a Muslim. Overcoming these temptations, Riley gained his freedom and the status of a hero.

Beyond lessons about bravery and demonstration, the *Narrative* recounts a religious story. Riley intended his book to demonstrate that Providence, or God's plan, operates in human life. The seas had parted for the shipwrecked men's longboat, and the captain and the crew were the first white captives that the Moors knew to have survived crossing the Sahara desert. We know that Riley's book transmitted this message since redacted versions make the Providential narrative even more obvious. Peter Parley, author of many didactic children's books, concludes Riley's story with the observation that the captain had made a particular "Friend, who amid all his trials, never forsook him; nor could the surges of the ocean or the whirlwinds of the desert throw them apart. This Friend was the Christian's God."[46]

Finally, and of most importance for the election of 1860, the *Narrative* teaches about slavery in a way that the other six books did not. Unlike the Bible's contradictory positions on the institution of slavery, Riley opposes the institution openly. He gives personal testimony to its effects on human beings held in complete dependence and who suffer almost unbearable physical pain. Unlike Weems, Riley presents slavery as it was, with no cloak of synonyms or artfully chosen words from the politically correct lexicon of the early American republic.

Perhaps because prominent New York politician and opponent of slavery De Witt Clinton encouraged him to publish the *Narrative*, Riley included in the 1817 edition and subsequent editions a condemnation of not just slavery, but slavery as it was practiced in the United States. As he explained,

I have drank [sic] deep of the bitter cup of suffering and wo [sic]; have been dragged down to the lowest depths of human degradation and wretchedness; my naked frame exposed without shelter to the scorching skies and chilling night winds of the desart [sic], enduring the most excruciating torments, and groaning, a *wretched slave*, under the stripes inflicted by the hands of barbarous monsters, bearing indeed the human form, but unfeeling, merciless, and malignant as demons.[47]

Such experience let him see the evils of slavery in his own country and "pledge to exert all my remaining faculties in endeavours to redeem the enslaved, and to shiver in pieces the rod of oppression."[48] Despite his harsh words against slavery, Riley recommended future action identified with mild antislavery policies. He absolved slaveholders from moral guilt by observing that they might have inherited their slaves rather than having acquired them intentionally. Wishing that slaveholders should incur no financial harm, he endorsed gradual emancipation with compensation. Riley hoped that the federal government might devise a plan to fit the freedmen and women for "the necessary occupations of civilized life" so that they would never threaten "domestic peace or political tranquility." This plan would conform to "the eternal principles of justice and humanity" to "wither and extirpate the accursed tree of slavery, that has been suffered to take such deep root in our otherwise highly-favoured soil."[49]

Not only did Riley's *Narrative* reach a reading public whose patriotism had been energized by victory in the War of 1812; it also reached a public primed to think about United States slavery and its possible end, especially through the process recommended by the ACS. Despite opposition to colonization from white and black abolitionists who called for an immediate end to slavery in the United States, the *Narrative* became one of the forces in the antebellum United States that taught the young Lincoln, and later the office-seeking Lincoln, that colonization of former slaves might help end slavery and the discrimination affecting African Americans under the existing state and local laws of the United States.

During his congressional term and then his presidency, he publicly advocated plans for colonization whether in Africa, in the Caribbean, or in Central America. In March 1863, he gave final approval to a previously conceived scheme of New York financiers who intended to transport willing African Americans to Île-à-Vache, an island near Haiti, to cultivate Sea Island cotton, a premium crop.[50]

Riley's *Narrative* also taught readers about the historical location of slavery. The northwestern African states and the Barbary States, which extended as far east as Tripoli, did not prosper in the first decades of the nineteenth century. Riley commented that plagues of locusts and the current Moroccan ruler's prohibitions of trade with Christians negatively affected the economy. The regulations created a food scarcity and forced everyone except the wealthy to forgo wheat and to exist on a less plentiful and less nourishing diet of barley. Now, "superstition, fanaticism, and tyranny" reigned and had "swept away, with their pernicious breath, the whole wealth of its once industrious and highly favoured inhabitants."[51]

When Americans of Lincoln's day read the *Narrative*, they drew on prevailing views of history and global progress. Its placement of slavery in the Barbary States confirmed their preexisting notions about the past and implied what the people of the United States would have to do to get in step with progress toward a Providential future. They deemed the civilizations of northern Africa static and savage lands when compared with European nations and their own country. If the United States were to be a modern, prosperous country, why would it retain vestiges of a world now bypassed by innovation, commerce, and prosperity? As the Irish Anglican Bishop George Berkeley had written in 1726, "Europe breeds in her decay/... Westward the course of empire takes its way."[52] Surely Britain's defeat in the last two wars on the North American continent, and then victory over Napoleonic France, proved by the principle of transitivity that the United States was mightier than the mightiest of European countries and would soon be, if it was not already, a powerful empire.

Still, the *Narrative* promised that this area of Africa might regain its former prosperity and coexist with Christian nations. Riley told of being heartened when he met some of Morocco's inhabitants – so different from the frightening people whom he had met on the beach after the initial shipwreck. Before reaching Mogadore, Riley and his men had dealt with an emissary from Willshire, Rais bel Cossim. This Moor impressed the captain with his ability to speak a smattering of English and Spanish as well as with his diplomacy and resourcefulness. Through flattery and pretense, he succeeded in freeing the Americans.

The Moor also saved Riley spiritually. The emaciated and sun-roasted captain had descended into despondency so deep that he had wanted to escape the pain of living. Hearing Riley's plaints, the Moor lectured him on the religious fellowship shared by Muslims and Christians. He chastised the Christian for daring "to distrust the power of that God who has preserved you so long by miracles?"[53] The Moor's words stunned Riley, when he continued, "We are all children of the same heavenly Father." No matter whether we are pagans or what our religion might be, "we must perform his will." At this point, the fellowship of all believers embraced both the Moor and Riley and forced the Christian to question the lessons of United States culture that Moors were "the worst of barbarians."[54] Despite Riley and the Moor's omission of Jews in evocation of religious brotherhood, Riley's *Narrative* supported a hopeful vision for a new nation with expanding foreign trade. Under leaders such as the Moor surely northern Africa could progress and join the peaceful, and profitable, Atlantic world of commerce. The ransoming of Christians need no longer sustain its economy.

Finally, the most important lesson that Lincoln might have taken from Riley concerned the method of emancipation. Slaveholders, even those of the desert whom Americans and Europeans thought the most uncivilized, frequently parted with their slaves for profit. Riley's readers learned that the ransoming of captives was embedded in the economic systems of the Barbary States. Ransoms supported both the so-called pirates and the rulers of these states. The possibility and feasibility of liberating slaves in the United States through a process that included compensation might have suggested itself to many of Riley's readers, including Lincoln, who wondered how slaveholders in the United States could be parted from their property. They must have hoped it would not be through bloody, horrific conflicts like the Haitian Revolution of the 1790s or the conquests of Simon Bolivar in Venezuela and Central America of the 1820s.

The emancipation lessons from the narrative correlated with historical experience during Lincoln's lifetime. Every instance of emancipation in the major slave societies of the Americas in the nineteenth century had incorporated compensation for slave owners. They received either cash or bonds from a central government, or labor time from the enslaved people. Further, the U.S. Constitution implied that slaveholders had a right to compensation. Its Fifth Amendment specifies that the federal government can take no property from its owners without due process of law. Because in the pre–Civil War United States, many state constitutions still provided that slaves were property, the federal government could not end slaveholding in peacetime without compensation to the slaveholders.

Additionally, no emancipation plan in the Atlantic world had compensated enslaved people for their time served in slavery.[55] Riley's discussion of emancipation confirmed and conformed to the historical understanding of Lincoln's lifetime: compensation to slave owners without recompense to the enslaved people had been and could still be a way to end slavery. This process promised both a constitutional and peaceful way of eliminating this impediment to the westward progress of a U.S. empire of free labor.

Historians recount that in the territories of North America that would become the United States, "untold thousands of enslaved African Americans were liberated by payments to their masters" between 1607 and 1860. Despite the most ardent antislavery activists' opposition to compensation to slaveholders, payment to them afforded the usual route to freedom. Although abolitionists declaimed that morality forbade slaveholders receiving payment for human lives and labor, humanity often dictated that payment was prudent. Freedom could be lawfully guaranteed or families reunited when freed slaves and their humanitarian supporters paid slaveholders. Antislavery activists including Henry Ward Beecher, Quakers, and even African Americans who had liberated themselves by fleeing from the slaveholding states to the northern states or Canada campaigned against buying people out of enslavement. Still, abolitionists' vocal opposition did not bar everyone, including abolitionists, from emancipating a lucky few of the millions of people who lived in slavery by compensating slaveholders for the wrong of holding human property.[56]

Lincoln, as well as other readers, learned multiple lessons from Riley's *Narrative*. As many previous scholars have observed, it did demonstrate graphically the evils of slavery, while this closer reading and contextualization of the book reveals that it performed much greater political and cultural work. Through the book's and Riley's association with both colonization and Henry Clay, the volume demonstrated by its inclusion in Lincoln's presidential campaign biography that the Republican candidate belonged to a global antislavery tradition, although one disparaged by extreme abolitionists on the one hand and by pro-slavery advocates on the other.

More important for Lincoln's understanding of the place of slavery in world history, the volume taught that slavery existed as an atavism in Christian, republican countries. The United States could stagnate like the Barbary States or it could prosper with free labor. Finally, the *Narrative* showed that American free laborers could liberate themselves from the degradation of competition with an unfree labor force through government-sponsored programs of compensated emancipation. Since the federal government of President Monroe eventually had reimbursed Riley for the cost of his crewmen's and his ransom, why should it not pay for the ransom of other slaves, albeit African Americans in the United States?

Such an understanding of compensated emancipation underlay Lincoln's proposals for emancipation in the national capital while he was a representative to the Illinois legislature and member of the thirtieth Congress from March 1847 to March 1849. His effort while a member of Congress continued the attempts that he had first made as a representative in the Illinois state legislature in 1837. Then, he had proposed that Congress possessed the power to abolish slavery in the District of Columbia with the concurrence of the city's white voters. With a fellow representative, he presented to the state assembly a protest of its condemnation of anti-slavery associations and their pamphlets that described slaveholders as "cruel brutes."[57]

Twelve years later as a Whig member of Congress from Illinois, Lincoln proposed a plan of compensated emancipation for the enslaved people of Washington. In other words, he implemented the lessons of Riley's *Narrative*. In the District of Columbia and in the lands of the United States that were not yet states, antislavery adherents believed that the federal government possessed the power to emancipate. Within their own borders, states had the exclusive power to emancipate slaves, as most states above the Missouri Compromise line had done prior to its passage in 1820.

Between that year and Lincoln's sole congressional term, the issue of slavery and the slave trade in the capital bubbled to the surface of political debate. In the early 1830s, antislavery members of Congress had presented to that body numerous petitions from constituents seeking to have the national government abolish slavery in the capital district. In response, starting in 1836, pro-slavery congressmen, led by John Calhoun of South Carolina, had approved resolutions that sent antislavery petitions directly to committee without debate. This procedure avoided violation of the Constitutional right of citizens "to petition their Government for a redress of grievances" as it caused petitions to bypass debate on the floor of the House of Representatives by stipulating that no debate occur before the petitions were tabled. Calhoun's resolution, commonly known as the gag rule, remained in force until 1844, when Representative John Quincy Adams assembled a coalition of Whigs and Democrats to vote it down.

Adams had been roused to oppose the gag rule because of House members censure of Ohio Representative Joshua Giddings, a passionate abolitionist, for violating it. By introducing nine resolutions for debate in the House, Giddings had reacted to slaveholders' attempt to regain their slaves, or compensation for them after 15 slaves had revolted in 1841 on the ship *Creole* during their transfer from Hampton Roads, Virginia, to the New Orleans slave market. Giddings's resolutions proposed in essence that the *Creole's* rebels were not mutineers and that their revolt on the high seas had won them permanent status as free people.

After the slaves aboard the *Creole* as human cargo had won control of the vessel, they sailed to the British-owned Caribbean island of Nassau, where an act of Parliament had ended slavery in 1834. On the island, an Admiralty court ruled that the *Creole's* cargo of African Americans no longer were property. To reach its decision, the court relied on the precedent of the 1772 Somerset Case. Lord Mansfield, the judge in that case, had ruled that a slave transported to Britain from the colony of Massachusetts could not be compelled by his master to return to his slave status in a British colony. Developing the antislavery implications of Lord Mansfield's decision, legal authorities on both sides of the Atlantic Ocean had reached agreement by the end of the American Revolution that slavery did not exist in a locality unless positive law in that locality had established it.[58]

When the founding fathers of the United States composed their country's constitution in 1789, they recognized the Somerset precedent by inclusion of a provision for the return of fugitive slaves. The principle that positive law alone could establish slavery and that slavery did not exist in a territory without the existence of positive law made necessary in the Constitution article 4, section 2, clause 3, the so-called fugitive slave clause. Without its presence, the Somerset precedent would have applied in the United States. Enslaved people could have freed themselves by escaping their owners and claiming refuge in a place where no state or local law had established that humans could be property. Because of the Constitution's fugitive slave clause, enslaved people could not exit their slave status by escaping to free states or territories. The Constitution nullified the Somerset precedent in the United States.

When slaveholders in the United States protested the Nassau Admiralty Court's ruling in the *Creole* case, they were attempting to overturn application of the Somerset precedent. Giddings saw the issue differently. He objected to the slaveowners' efforts to establish the slaves on the *Creole* as mutineers. He introduced into Congress resolutions that affirmed the implications of the Somerset precedent for both the transatlantic slave trade and the coastal slave trade in the Americas. Because slavery could exist exclusively by positive law, it could not exist where there was no positive law and where natural law prevailed, such as on the high seas. Rebellion on the ocean, to which local laws did not extend, and then arrival in a port where no law recognized the enslavement of people meant that slaves who revolted successfully on the high seas had not acted as mutineers and now were permanently free people. The implications of Giddings's resolutions so aroused the southern members of Congress and northern congressmen wishing to preserve institutional comity that he earned their censure and resigned his seat in protest. In the special election to replace him, his Ohio constituents vindicated his stand on the *Creole* issue by reelecting him by a huge majority.[59]

In August 1846, about sixteen months before Lincoln's congressional term, discussion of slavery heated up once again when Pennsylvania Congressman David Wilmot introduced his resolution or proviso stipulating that slavery or involuntary servitude should not exist in the territories that might be gained from the Mexican War. Backed by antislavery Democrats and Whigs, including the representative from Illinois once he assumed his seat in Congress, the proviso failed to overcome opposition from proslavery Democrats and Whigs who blocked its passage in the Senate. When the war officially ended with the signing of the Treaty of Guadalupe Hidalgo on February 2, 1848, Congress still had to decide whether the lands Mexico had ceded to the United States would become slave states or free states. The resolution of this question would determine whether proslavery or antislavery Senators remained about evenly split and whether or not the federal government would pursue policies friendly to the institution of slavery and its extension throughout the present territories of the United States and any lands that it might acquire in future years.

After Lincoln was sworn into his seat in the House of Representatives in December 1847, the novice federal legislator and his family moved into the boardinghouse in which his predecessor in Congress from the Seventh Illinois district previously had taken rooms. In practice, the boardinghouse was a school for antislavery thought and politics. Mrs. Ann Sprigg's establishment had a reputation for the Whiggish if not the antislavery proclivities of its residents, the most extreme of which were held by Joshua Giddings.

When Massachusetts representative John Quincy Adams collapsed on the House floor about three months after Lincoln had assumed his seat in the House, Giddings inherited his friend and political ally's former role as the most prominent antislavery proponent among his House colleagues. Lincoln found himself in frequent company with the abolitionist when they ate at a common dining table in the Sprigg lodging house. There, residents might discuss current doings in Congress, and Giddings might share his knowledge of antislavery arguments, including the Somerset precedent. Residence at the boardinghouse also gave newcomers, like Lincoln, opportunity to absorb the ways of Washington.[60]

Those ways included the direct experience of slavery. On January 14, six weeks after the Lincoln family had settled into its rooms, three slave hunters broke into Mrs. Sprigg's residence during the evening meal and seized Henry Wilson, an African-American waiter whose owner had hired him out to Mrs. Sprigg. After clamping Wilson in irons, the intruders transferred him to a slave trader who intended to ship the unfortunate man to the markets of New Orleans. For some time before his abduction, Wilson and his wife, a free African American, had been devoting their wages from employment at the Sprigg house to buy his freedom. Merely a small percentage of the $300 total price remained unpaid to his owner when she reneged on her agreement and sold him to the slave trader. Subsequently, because of the efforts of antislavery activists in the capital city, the slave trader accepted a monetary settlement and Wilson returned to his family and work at the Sprigg boardinghouse.[61]

In April, three months after Wilson's abduction, the attempted escape of seventy-seven slaves engulfed the national capital in violent controversy. Two white abolitionists had assembled seventy-seven slaves from the Washington area and secretly embarked with them on the ship *Pearl*, which would have transported them northward to freedom in a free state. Subsequently, their capture, the imprisonment of the abolitionists who had arranged the escape, and protests from people on both sides of the slavery issue incited mob violence, contentious debates in both houses of Congress, and President James K. Polk's calling of a cabinet meeting to ensure that its members did not join the rioters.[62]

As these incidents unfolded, Lincoln, Giddings, and their fellow House members were debating the issues of the slave trade and slavery in Washington, the exclusion of slavery from the new territories of California and New Mexico, and whether slaveholders deserved compensation for their slaves freed during the Seminole War. Except for two instances, Lincoln and the radical abolitionist voted the same way on slavery-related issues.[63] (See Table 2.1.)

When the second session of Lincoln's congressional term began in December 1848, he took a stand in Congress on the issue of the slave trade in the capital and the abolition of the institution of slavery.[64] That month, the Senate started intensive discussion on the future of the territories gained from the Mexican War. Concomitantly, the House debated whether to abolish slavery and/or the slave trade in Washington. The new congressman first opposed his messmate's resolution to ban the slave trade in the District of Columbia because it did not seek the consent of white citizens in the district and, he believed, it overreached in its condemnation of slavery. Lincoln estimated that Giddings's proposal was extreme and would not win sufficient votes because of its aforementioned provisions, and additionally because it would have allowed slaves and free blacks to vote on whether the slave trade should be banned from the national capital. Subsequently, he also voted against a bill committing a House committee to produce a bill banning the slave trade. Although these votes seemingly show Lincoln supporting pro-slavery legislatives, he actually was promoting his own antislavery measures. His "no" votes left the way open for congressional action on a bill that he was readying. In addition to banning the slave trade in the district, his bill went further and would have ended slavery in the district.[65]

From his year of congressional experience and from conversations with his messmates at the Sprigg house, Lincoln had learned where a compromise might lie. It would satisfy, he hoped, both conservative Whigs, who demanded that the white citizens of the district approve congressional action with regard to their property, and slaveholders, who wanted a stronger fugitive slave law to facilitate the return of escaped slaves. By the novice representative's calculations, his bill seemed more likely to win votes than did Giddings's bill because it could attract the support of

TABLE 2.1. *Abraham Lincoln's Congressional Career*

| | | |
|---|---|---|
| 1846 | August 3 | Elected to the U.S. House of Representatives from the Seventh Congressional District of Illinois. |
| 1847 | November | En route to Washington, Mary, Abraham, and their children stay with the Todd family in Lexington, Kentucky. |
| | December 3 | Takes his seat in the Thirtieth Congress. |
| | December 21 | Votes against tabling a memorial from citizens of the District of Columbia requesting the repeal of all laws authorizing or sanctioning the slave trade in the District. |
| | December 28 | Votes against tabling a petition from Indiana citizens praying for abolition of the slave trade and slavery in the District. |
| | December 30 | Votes against tabling a petition from Philadelphia citizens praying for passage of a law to appropriate monies from public land sales for the extinction of slavery in the United States. |
| 1848 | January 14 | Seizure of Henry Wilson, an African-American waiter, from Mrs. Sprigg's boardinghouse. |
| | January 17 | Votes against tabling a resolution to investigate the slave trade in the District and to consider transferring the U.S. capital to a free state. Infuriated by the seizure of Henry Wilson, Joshua Giddings had introduced the resolution, which eventually passed. |
| | January 31 | Votes against tabling Giddings's resolution asking for appointment of a committee to inquire under what authority the slave trade exists in the District. |
| | February 23 | Former president and representative John Quincy Adams dies after suffering a stroke in the House of Representatives two days prior. |
| | February 26 | Serves on the Committee on Arrangements for Adams's funeral and burial. |
| | April 10 | Votes to support the Senate resolution congratulating the people of France on their republican revolution. |
| | August 2 | Votes against an amendment to an Oregon territory bill that would have permitted slavery in the territory. Votes for admission of the Oregon territory with slavery prohibited. |
| | December 18 | Votes against reconsideration of a bill excluding slavery from New Mexico and California. Votes for tabling Giddings's bill calling for a referendum on slavery by black and white male residents of the District. |

TABLE 2.1 (*continued*)

|  |  |  |
|---|---|---|
| | December 21 | Votes against a bill directing the Committee on the District of Columbia to report a bill abolishing slavery in the District. |
| | December 29 | Votes to table a bill granting compensation for a slave transported west in 1835. |
| 1849 | January 6 | Votes against a committee report to grant compensation for a slave transported west. |
| | January 10 | Proposes his amendment to a bill abolishing slavery in the district. See, "A bill for an act to abolish slavery in the District of Columbia, by the consent of the free white people of said District, and with compensation to owners" (Basler, CW 2:20–22). |
| | January 13 | Proposes that he will introduce his bill to abolish slavery in the District. |
| | January 19 | Votes against reconsideration of a bill to give compensation for a slave transported west. |
| | January 31 | Votes against a motion to table a bill reported by the Committee on the District to abolish slavery in the District. The motion passes. |
| | February 28 | Presents a petition from the citizens of Morgan County, IL, praying that Congress abolish the slave trade in the District. |
| | March 4 | Completes his congressional term. |

Whigs who opposed Giddings's plan. After Lincoln won approval for his proposed bill from both the antislavery Giddings and pro-slavery William Seaton, the mayor of Washington, he presented a draft to the House of Representatives in early January 1849.

The bill's various provisions had the effect of abolishing the slave trade in the national capital. To satisfy slaveholders, it proposed that municipal authorities in Washington be "empowered and required" to return slaves who had fled into the district to their owners, thus deactivating the Somerset precedent. As Riley had proposed years earlier, emancipation, in Lincoln's plan, would be gradual, so that the freed people could acquire skills with which to support themselves. The bill mandated that the children born to slaves in the District after January 1, 1850 would labor as "apprentices" for their mothers' owners until they reached adulthood (determination of the exact age of adulthood lay in the future). The apprenticed children would compensate their former owners through years of unfree labor. Plus, his emancipation plan would take effect only with the approval of a majority of qualified voters, white male citizens, in the District. Despite inclusion of these provisions intended to address slaveholders' interests, the plan incurred strident opposition from influential southern legislators. They launched a lobbying campaign to turn prominent Washington municipal officials against Lincoln's emancipation proposal. With the defeat of the bill made certain by this pro-slavery campaign, the novice legislator never pushed it to a vote on the floor of the House.[66]

The issue of the slave trade in Washington remained a hot topic through 1849 to the end of the thirtieth Congress in early March. During the last week of Lincoln's term, he introduced a petition from citizens in Morgan County, Illinois. They begged Congress to ban the slave trade and slavery from the national capital.[67]

Soon after the ex-congressman returned to Illinois, the issue of slavery in the capital city resurfaced as a component of the Compromise of 1850, which dealt with the unresolved territorial questions arising from the Mexican War. When proposed by Senator Henry Clay, the Compromise banned slave trading in Washington, thereby winning the votes of antislavery legislators who also had to accept the pro-slavery provisions of the legislation, including strengthening enforcement of federal fugitive slave laws.

For Lincoln, the model of the emancipation process in Riley's *Narrative*, his residence at Mrs. Sprigg's boardinghouse, and the debates of the thirtieth Congress over his antislavery proposal endured into his presidential years. The *Narrative*'s influence dimmed when the military and political exigencies of 1862 and 1863 demanded a new approach to abolishing slavery during wartime in the United States. Eric Foner has shown, in his prize-winning investigation of Lincoln's role in the end of slavery, that Representative Lincoln's plan of 1849 to emancipate slaves in the national capital, gradually and with compensation, remained his preferred policy until, as commander in chief, he signed the final Emancipation Proclamation on January 1, 1863.[68]

# 3

## European Lessons

One month after winning reelection in 1864, President Lincoln gave an interview to Benson Lossing, a prominent historian of the American Revolution then preparing an illustrated history of the ongoing war. During their early December meeting in the Executive Mansion, Lossing did not raise questions about the crucial military and constitutional events of that year.[1] Instead, the historian sought to clarify stories surrounding the surreptitious arrival of the president-elect into the nation's capital in February 1861. Four years later, these stories did not seem sideshows to the main events of the president's first term. Lincoln's attempt to refute them tells much about how he was trying to shape his legacy for a republican audience, in the United States and around the globe.

Plots to assassinate Lincoln bracket his presidency. Threats to Lincoln and his family started to arrive during the heated last months of the presidential campaign and became increasingly virulent after his election – even before South Carolina seceded on December 20, 1860. Such letters continued to appear until he departed Springfield for Washington on February 11.

These missives contained scathing words and illustrations that threatened the president-elect or informed him of plots against his life. In early January, he showed his friend Henry Clay Whitney, a fellow Illinois lawyer, an image of himself from *Harper's Weekly* that a critic had altered by inserting a gallows, a noose, and a black executioner's cap. From Louisiana, a critic damned him at least thirty times in a short letter of three paragraphs. The letter began: "God damn your god damned old Hellfired god damned soul to hell."[2] Besides damning Lincoln, another correspondent composed an epistolary tantrum. He called Lincoln a "sundde of a bith" and a "goddam Black nigger," swearing at him to kiss his "Ass, suck my prick and call my Bolics [testicles] your uncle Dick." Carried away by his language, the correspondent signed the letter and then told Lincoln as an afterthought what might happen if he did not resign: six more states would secede.[3]

Cautioned by letters such as these and the threats that appeared in the pro-secession media, Lincoln and his confidants planned his railroad trip from Springfield, Illinois, to Washington for the inauguration on March 4. As the president-elect wrote Major David Hunter when he invited his presence on the train, the journey would "have to be a circuitous and rather tedious one."[4] The itinerary was designed to maximize his exposure to northern supporters and to minimize travel in states that had voted for opposition candidates John Bell, John Breckinridge, and Stephen Douglas.

Besides skirting danger, the trip planners wanted to introduce the president-elect to the American people. Besides politically active ex-Whigs and Republicans in the Midwest and Northeast, few Americans had seen or heard the Illinoisan. Voters knew him mostly through his campaign biography, speeches, and broadsides. So the route planners also wanted to let his supporters connect with him personally during the railway trip. A direct route by train took about half of the 1,900 miles of his planned, presumably safe, route. Along the way, he delivered at least 101 speeches for which records exist. On three days of the eleven-day trip, he spoke as many as twelve times and on two days, thirteen times. During the journey, he addressed state legislatures and visited mayors, raised flags, received bouquets, shook hands, and, of course, kissed young girls. Estimates of the number of people who saw him reach 750,000.[5]

Departing Springfield the day before his fifty-second birthday on February 12, the presidential train included two cars for passengers. The Lincoln family had use of the saloon, a luxurious railway car in 1860 talk. In the smoking car rode two bodyguards, Lincoln's secretaries, and the family's two personal servants – Ellen, whose last name and race are unknown, and William Johnson, an African American – as well as members of a Committee of Escort, Lincoln friends, and reporters. The train stopped frequently, either to refuel or to switch engines, as it rolled from the tracks owned by one railway company to those owned by another, altogether eighteen changes. Cheering crowds greeted the Lincoln special at his overnight stops, including Indianapolis, Indiana; Cincinnati, Cleveland, and Columbus, Ohio; Pittsburgh and Philadelphia, Pennsylvania; and Buffalo, Albany, and New York City, New York. More than

50 percent of the electorate had cast ballots for the president-elect in each of these four states.

Despite the friendly crowds, the stop on February 16 in Buffalo, then the nation's tenth-largest city and a thriving transportation link between the ports of the East Coast and Great Lakes, revealed how a friendly, energized crowd could transform into a threatening mob. As the *Commercial Advertiser* reported, the city had caught "Lincoln fever." As Lincoln exited the train to greet ex-President Millard Fillmore and the city's mayor, enthusiastic Buffalonians pressed themselves against the dignitaries. Protected from the mob by a circle of supporters and soldiers, the president-elect's party pushed its way through the cheering bodies thronging the depot to carriages parked on the street. One of Lincoln's escorts from Illinois, Major David Hunter, a Republican Lincoln supporter, had his shoulder broken or dislocated in the melee and was one of many victims of the "Lincoln fever."[6]

Departing from Buffalo on February 17, the train rolled across the nearly 300 miles to Albany, where it turned south to follow the Hudson River to New York City. Finally, the train and its exhausted passengers reached Philadelphia at 4 PM on February 21. Forcing their way once more through well-wishers, the travelers completed a four-mile carriage ride through streets lined with crowds of up to 100,000 people waiting to see the president-elect and his party as they proceeded to their rooms in the Continental Hotel. The night was not to be a restful one for Mr. Lincoln, and not simply because of crowds swarming in and about the hotel.

At 10 PM, detective Allan Pinkerton, Philadelphia, Wilmington and Baltimore Railroad (PW&BR) President Samuel Morse Felton, and Norman B. Judd, a fellow Republican from Illinois and the man who had placed Lincoln's name in nomination at the 1860 Chicago convention, informed Lincoln that his pre-inaugural trip was about to turn dangerous. If he proceeded according to the published timetable, peril awaited him in Baltimore, thirty-six hours later. Secessionist supporters formed an active minority in Maryland. In that state, Lincoln's presidential ticket had received fewer than 2,300 votes of the 90,000 votes cast in 1860. In its major city and railroad crossroads, Republicans had braved scorn and harassment when casting their ballots. Since the election, reports had circulated of militias in training to reverse the outcome of the election. Newspapers urged protests during the passage of the presidential party through the city.

Pinkerton and the president-elect knew one another by name if not by sight. They were fellow Illinoisans who frequently had railroads, especially the Illinois Central, as clients. The detective probably voted for the Republican candidate in the 1860 campaign as the best of a bad lot. While the other presidential contenders supported slavery and the right of new states to establish it as an institution, only the Republican had opposed the extension of slavery to U.S. territories. Pinkerton held more extreme antislavery positions. He had taken an activist position on the slavery issue when he worked for the underground railroad in the 1850s, purportedly as a station conductor.

While Pinkerton's accounts of the impending danger in Baltimore affected Lincoln's planning, they did not deter his determination to hold to the published schedule. On February 22, George Washington's birthday, he intended to visit Philadelphia's Independence Hall, where he was scheduled to raise the Stars and Stripes. He wanted to celebrate the birthplace of the American republic on the birthday of its first president. Lincoln gave a simple reason: the words of the Declaration, which had been signed there, held a central place in his political philosophy. He also worried about appearances. Like so many new presidents, especially those confronting the possibility of war, the president-elect wanted to present himself as a strong leader. He fretted that his fellow citizens might perceive as cowardly a president who slipped into the national capital under the cloak of darkness to assume his leadership position.

Late in the evening before his Independence Hall appearance, about 11 PM, Lincoln received word of threats that had been forwarded from his future secretary of state in Washington. William Seward's son, Frederick, had traveled from the capital to deliver his father's message into the president-elect's hand. This new evidence confirmed the existence of a plot. Conspirators planned to attack the presidential party in a Baltimore railroad station or as its members left the city on the Baltimore and Ohio Railroad to the national capital.

Seward's father had learned of the impending danger earlier that day from Winfield Scott, commanding general of the United States Army. Earlier on the same day, Scott had listened to operatives sent by the superintendent of police in New York City. In the first weeks of January, one of his chiefs had received troubling information about the president-elect's safety. Subsequently, the superintendent had launched an investigation of a supposed plan to attack Lincoln as he traversed Baltimore. In January, their agents had traveled to that city, where they posed as secessionists. They joined a pro-Confederate secret militia and participated in its drills and field exercises until discovery. This intelligence from Seward confirmed the warnings that Pinkerton previously had delivered. Seward's and Pinkerton's sources had investigated and reached their conclusions independently, thus making their warnings persuasive to Lincoln, the lawyer who appreciated the power of facts.

Pinkerton had become indirectly involved in investigating threats against the president-elect. In late January, Felton had hired the detective after rumors suggested that pro-secessionists might sabotage the tracks of the PW&BR. After Pinkerton's operatives had infiltrated secessionist ranks, they discovered that the conspirators aimed to destroy more than the railroad. They intended to have the president-elect murdered before his train departed Baltimore on its way southward to the nation's capital. If the assassination attempt failed, they would sever railroad access to Washington from every direction but the south and take over the nation's government in the name of the Confederate States of America, which had adopted a provisional constitution on February 8.[7]

About 6:30, the morning after learning of the Baltimore plots, Lincoln traveled to Independence Hall in a barouche drawn by white horses adorned with white plumes. Once there, he was to make a few remarks at a sunrise ceremony in which he would raise the national banner over the historic site. This moment would be the first time that a flag of thirty-four stars, representing thirty-four states, flew at the landmark. The most recently added star represented Kansas, which had entered the Union on January 29 as a free state after having been ravaged by violent, bloody confrontations between its pro-slavery and antislavery settlers during the previous five years.

Theodore Cuyler, president of the select council (later the city council) of Philadelphia, welcomed the president-elect with prepared remarks upon his entry to Independence Hall. The political import of his words disturbed Lincoln and impelled him to respond. The council president had expressed hopes that the seven states already seceded from the Union would rejoin the United States, that military action would be unnecessary to make them do so, and that concessions would succeed in motivating their return. In the political debates of early 1861, the word *concessions* carried a coded meaning implying that the Republican Party should renounce its intention to prohibit the extension of slavery into the nation's territories.

In his unprepared and impromptu response, Lincoln held true to the promise of the Republican platform and restated his bedrock beliefs. The crowd cheered his avowal that he had never "had a feeling politically that did not spring from the sentiments embodied in the Declaration of Independence." Visiting Independence Hall held great meaning for him.

He had "often pondered over the dangers which were incurred by the men who assembled here and adopted that Declaration of Independence." Then, he remembered "the toils that were endured by the officers and soldiers of the army, who achieved that Independence." Such thoughts inspired rumination about "what great principle or idea it was that had kept this Confederacy [of the United States] so long together. It was...something in that Declaration giving liberty, not alone to the people of this country, but hope to the world for all future time." After waiting for the applause to subside, he continued with a pronouncement that showed his determination to grant no concessions: the Declaration of the signers "gave promise that in due time the weights should be lifted from the shoulders of all men, and that all should have an equal chance. (Cheers.)... " Then, recalling the warnings from Pinkerton and others of the night before, the modest speaker concluded with an apology for his immodest words: he proclaimed the promise of the Declaration for all the people of the thirteen colonies and the globe.

Because Lincoln had not anticipated that the occasion would call for substantial remarks, he admitted to having spoken extemporaneously. He had supposed the occasion "was merely to do something toward raising the flag. I may, therefore, have said something indiscreet." After his audience voiced cries of "no, no," Lincoln concluded with the prophetic words, "I have said nothing but what I am willing to live by and, if it be the pleasure of Almighty God, die by."[8]

As the last line of quoted words suggests, the danger of assuming the presidency pressed on his thinking with such force that he released his worries in verbal expression. With no foreknowledge of April 14, 1865, he had in mind solely the recent cautions from Pinkerton and Seward when he committed himself to emulating the bravery of the signers of the Declaration. If their cause had failed, their signatures would have provided evidence for conviction of treason and a death sentence.

Lincoln's words on Washington's birthday showed that he rejected the advice that he had just received from Theodore Cuyler. The president-elect always read the first two paragraphs of the Declaration as a promise of what eventually would come to be in the United States rather than as a description of what was in the American colonies of 1776. Accordingly, it was a self-evident truth that all men should be equal. Politically astute listeners of that day recognized that the emphasis on the word *all* in Lincoln's remarks underlined that in his personal beliefs he did not exclude any man from the Declaration's promise that "all men were created equal." This promise, he believed, had given the signers of the

FIGURE 3.1. In this photograph taken by F. DeBourg Richards of Abraham and Tad Lincoln on February 22, 1861, the father and son stand in a crowd on the platform outside of Independence Hall, Philadelphia, as they prepare to raise the U.S. flag showing a new star for Kansas, admitted to statehood on January 29. Known as photo O-48 in Lincoln iconography. ALPLM cat. LPh1272m, a print from Meserve collection, at 2 1/8 in × 3 1/4 inches. Courtesy of the ALPLM.

Declaration and the soldiers of the Revolution resolve to resist tyranny. Its promises eventually would apply "to the world." Racial or national peculiarities would not make the Declaration's words exclusive, with application to some men of one color and national origin. If the Declaration's words applied to all men, they applied to all men, in all nations, for all time.

As the sun appeared about 7 AM, Lincoln, his son Tad, and other dignitaries emerged from Independence Hall onto a grandstand. (See Figure 3.1.) Father and son took their places around the flagstaff. Instead of listening to his father, Tad leaned on the balcony edge and inspected the aligned ranks of Scott's legion, veterans from the Mexican War, who stood at attention resplendent in dress uniforms. After welcoming the expansion of the nation to include "five hundred millions of a free and happy people" and a prayer from the presiding clergyman, Lincoln pulled on the flagstaff halyard to raise the new banner over the historic building. The crowd's cheering fed into a band's playing of the "Star Spangl'd Banner." As its last notes resounded, cannon boomed to end the ceremony.

Two hours later, Lincoln departed for Harrisburg, capital of a state with electoral votes that had been crucial to his November victory. The stop there was his way of thanking Governor Andrew Curtin and his fellow Pennsylvania Republicans. To guarantee the train's safe passage, flagmen stood at one-mile intervals along the railway. Sixty miles west of Philadelphia and forty miles east of Harrisburg lay Lancaster, hometown of the current U.S. president, Democrat James Buchanan. While the Democrat drew support from the state's agricultural areas, especially those around his hometown, Pennsylvania congressmen such as Republican Thaddeus Stevens, who represented Lancaster city, drew support from artisans, merchants, and manufacturers tied to an emerging economy based on industry.

At the train station in the center of Lancaster, an immense crowd awaited the president-elect's arrival. Many of them had stood in bracing cold for two hours to gain a vantage point. While a local reporter claimed the locals "lustily cheered" Lincoln, his secretary John Hay commented that its members seemed less than enthusiastic, perhaps no more than curious. In spite of the lackluster reception, the exhausted and hoarse president-elect appeared before them and spoke briefly. Not surprisingly, he repeated the substance of his Philadelphia remarks. Again the speaker promised to remain true to the Constitution "and Union of all the states, and to the perpetual liberty of all the people."[9]

Later that day in Harrisburg, after the governor's welcome, Lincoln attended a reception at the state capitol, made more brief remarks, and dutifully shook even more hands during a packed event at his hotel.[10] That evening during a small dinner in his honor, the newly elected chief executive made an unannounced and hasty departure. Most of the guests remained unaware of the Baltimore threat and the president-elect's new plans. He exited their company to board a private train for Philadelphia, where he changed to a regularly scheduled train to Washington. Soon after Lincoln's departure from Harrisburg, Pinkerton had the telegraph wires that connected the city to Baltimore severed so that no news about the whereabouts of their intended victim could reach the plotters. Service would be restored at 8 AM on the twenty-third. By that hour, the president-elect should have safely reached the nation's capital.

Before leaving for the Harrisburg depot, Lincoln left his easily recognized top hat and luggage with his wife in their hotel rooms. Having donned traveling clothes and an old overcoat, he folded a soft felt hat into his pocket. Reputedly, he had received the hat as a gift from friends during his stop in New York City a few days previously. They had given him a new beaver top hat but inserted the soft, wide-brimmed hat in the box as an extra.[11] To face the chill of the February evening, he might have worn the coat like a cloak, buttoned at the neck and over his shoulders, and carried a shawl for additional warmth during the journey in the poorly heated railway car. Departing the hotel, he took a carriage with Governor Curtin. Before driving to the depot, they misled the onlookers by heading for the governor's mansion. After that feint, they hastened to the Harrisburg terminal.

During the four-hour ride to Philadelphia, Lincoln, his well-armed bodyguard, Ward Hill Lamon, and several railroad officials sat in darkness. In the saloon, lamps remained unlit. Bystanders along the tracks might be curious about the passengers on the unscheduled train and recognize Lincoln's well-known profile. Upon arrival in Philadelphia, Lincoln and his party took a carriage from the east-west train station to the depot serving the north-south route. Lincoln now had left the safety of the special train for passage on a regularly scheduled train filled with passengers who might have voted either for or against him in the election. Together the citizens and their future president journeyed to Baltimore and their eventual destinations. If the trip went as planned, the passengers on the regular 11 PM train from Philadelphia to Washington would never realize their proximity to presidential history.

Lincoln and his bodyguard took berths on a sleeper car, where Pinkerton and his agent Kate Warne joined them. The female detective previously had bought their tickets and arranged for sleeping car berths. Before the arrival of the Washington-bound passengers, she had posed for the conductor as the sister of an ailing man who needed to recline and to remain in his berth during the southbound trip. Pocketing her bribe, the conductor helped her reserve berths in the rear of the sleeping car, where it would be easiest to defend Lincoln from intruders.

Guided by his sister and leaning on her arm, the supposedly sickly brother shuffled his way through the station to the sleeping car. Slowly the sister directed her stooped sibling, who wore an overcoat, shawl, and soft-crowned hat, to his reserved space. Once at his berth, Lincoln lay down, probably uncomfortably, since his height exceeded the length of the compartment. A flimsy curtain along the length of the bunk separated him from the aisle and potential kidnappers or assassins. To guard their invaluable passenger, Warne, Lamon, and Pinkerton took berths nearby. Occasionally moving from his bunk to the platform behind the sleeping car, the private detective watched for all-clear signs from agents whom he had posted with signaling lanterns at vulnerable points along the route, such as bridges and ferry crossings. Rumors had suggested that an attempt might be made to derail the cars at these locations.

Later that night, the train with its ordinary passengers and one very consequential occupant journeyed uneventfully across Baltimore while the city's population, largely hostile to the Republican Party cause, slept. When the train arrived at the city's President Street Station, crews detached the engine from the passenger and sleeping cars. Once harnessed to the cars, horses pulled them for about one mile to the city's southern depot. Coupled once again to an engine, the train continued to its depot in Washington.

Lincoln's nighttime, unannounced trip allowed him to travel across the city between 3 and 4 AM. In daylight, Baltimoreans who overwhelmingly had voted for a Democrat in November might have recognized the president-elect, causing passions, fanned by articles and editorials in the leading newspaper, to erupt in violence.[12]

The next morning in Harrisburg, upon discovering that Lincoln had departed the previous evening, journalists who had traveled with the Lincoln party howled. They discounted the fears that had motivated Pinkerton and Lincoln's closest supporters to make their secret, nighttime departure. Newspapers criticized the president-elect for an exit from the Pennsylvania capital that they called undignified and unbefitting a chief magistrate. He had acted "like a fugitive hotly pursued by the ministers of justice."[13] The Baltimore papers printed the most extreme criticism. They denied existence of a plot or danger from residents of their city, and their stories made Lincoln seem ridiculous. They already had found Lincoln's actions deficient and embarrassing; now they described his "stealthy and ignoble adventure" that "will inevitably draw down upon us the derision of all civilized nations."[14]

When the *New York Times* published its correspondent's account of the president-elect's secret journey, the damage to the president's image and reputation intensified. Joseph Howard, Jr., the paper's reporter, had accompanied the presidential party on its journey as far as Harrisburg. Although Howard supported Lincoln and believed a plot existed to harm him, he fabricated the details of his account when he described Lincoln's abrupt departure from the Pennsylvania capital on the evening of the twenty-second. On the morning of the twenty-third, he had learned about the president-elect's unexpected exit at the same time as everyone else in the Harrisburg hotel. Obviously miffed at his exclusion from the select few who had accompanied Lincoln to Philadelphia, Howard invented fiction in his telegraphed dispatch to New York City. It clothed Lincoln in a disguise of a "Scotch plaid cap and a very long military cloak," thus

THE MacLINCOLN HARRISBURG HIGHLAND FLING.

FIGURE 3.2. "The MacLincoln Harrisburg Highland Fling." This cartoon appeared in the New York comic weekly *Vanity Fair* on March 9, 1861, p. 113, at 4.5″ × 3.25″; no artist named. Courtesy of the ALPLM.

providing fodder for more critical journalists and cartoonists.[15] He may have chosen these words to chide Pinkerton for leaving him behind. The private detective was a native of Scotland and a former cop. Hence, the allusion to a Scotch cop via mention of a Scottish cap.[16]

To ridicule Lincoln, cartoonists seized upon Howard's colorful and highly inaccurate report. In cartoons and illustrations, they set a Scottish cap on Lincoln's head and transformed his overcoat into a heavy shawl or long cape that wrapped him from neck to toes. From Lincoln's 1861 arrival in the capital city and through the reelection campaign of 1864, the president's critics deployed this image to refute his Republican Party sobriquet as a muscled, manly, industrious Rail Splitter. Lincoln detractors denied that any plot to harm the president or to impede his progress through Maryland ever existed. Their imagery of a skulking Lincoln in a Scottish hat evoked associations that challenged Lincoln's masculinity and his fitness for leadership.

On March 9, *Vanity Fair* published an image of "The MacLincoln" dancing the Highland fling in full Scottish regalia of tam-o-shanter, kilt, sporran, and ghillie brogues. (See Figure 3.2.) In 1861, this was neither the attire nor the behavior of a real man ready to lead his country into war. Because famous events of British history were common knowledge among literate Americans in the mid-nineteenth century, these cartoons would have recalled the flight of Bonnie Prince Charlie, who had disguised himself first in a maid's clothing and then in Highland attire while seeking to escape to France after the bloody battle of Culloden on April 16, 1746. The reference impugned the Republican president-elect by associating him with royalty and, even worse, a rebel seeking to fracture the unity of Great Britain.[17]

During the campaign of 1864, anti-Lincoln cartoonists once again lampooned the president by evoking memories of the Baltimore incident by inserting a Scottish hat into their images. In one cartoon, the commander-in-chief stands in the middle of the Antietam battlefield holding a tartan cap. (See Figure 3.3.) Two years previously on that battlefield, 12,400 Union soldiers had died, received wounds, become captives, or gone missing. In this 1864 image, the president asks Lamon, his friend, frequent bodyguard, and now U.S. marshal in Washington, to sing him an amusing song from a blackface minstrel show. Meanwhile, Lincoln's campaign opponent, George McClellan, tends to a wounded soldier whom he had commanded in the battle. Thus the cartoon encouraged voters to view Lincoln, who pledged to continue the war, as demeaning the soldiers' sacrifice by indulging in racial humor, while they might think of McClellan, who wanted to end the war's carnage, as caring for the soldiers and their welfare.

Another cartoon represents a sleeping President Lincoln in the midst of a nightmare predicting his loss in the 1864 campaign. (See Figure 3.4.) In the dream, the goddess Liberty expels the president from the White House with a kick and the threat of her heaving at him a head severed from a black soldier. In undignified fashion, Lincoln flees the mansion while holding a Scottish cap on his head. In contrast, a dignified McClellan strides into the mansion with his suitcase in hand ready to assume the presidency. Bedeviled by images such as these in the months prior to his election victory, Lincoln obviously wanted to end the Baltimore stigma. It had affected his entrance into the presidency and now it promised to persist into his second term.

He gained the opportunity to correct the Scottish cap story when Benson Lossing arrived at the Executive Mansion in December 1864. In the ensuing interview with the noted historian, Lincoln chose to recall his controversial entry into Washington in February four years ago. When remembering his journey through Baltimore while president-elect, Lincoln insisted that he had not worn a Scottish cap but the soft-brimmed hat

FIGURE 3.3. "The Commander-in-Chief conciliating the Soldier's Votes on the Battle Field." This anti-Lincoln cartoon was based on newspaper stories running in the *New York World* from April 1864 through the November election. The articles accused the president of gross disregard for soldiers when he visited the Antietam battlefield. As the election approached, the *World* copublished this image as a lithograph on wove paper; 29.4 × 41.8 cm. Courtesy of the Library of Congress. For discussion of the *World*'s accusations and the print, see Harold Holzer, *Lincoln and the Power of the Press*, 502–504.

that he had received in New York City. It was known as a Kossuth hat. Such a hat carried associations opposite from that of the cartoons that had called into question his bravery and capacity for leadership.

In April 1848, Louis Kossuth, or Kossuth Lajos in his homeland, a Hungarian liberal, came to the attention of newspaper readers in the United States, including Lincoln, who represented the Illinois 7th district in the House of Representatives. In Illinois, Kossuth supporters convened meetings across the state to draft messages of support. Inspired by the French revolution of the previous February, Kossuth, a gifted orator, called in April for a new constitutional government in Austria and a separate

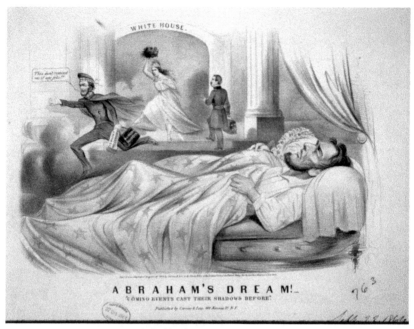

FIGURE 3.4. "Abraham's Dream!–'Coming Events Cast their Shadows Before'."
The artist of this Currier and Ives lithograph portrays Lincoln, who believed that
dreams might foretell the future, envisioning his expulsion from the Executive
Mansion after McClellan's probable election victory, an outcome that the pres-
ident and numerous others thought likely in August and early September 1864.
Courtesy of the Library of Congress Prints and Photographs Division.

parliamentary government for Hungary. In response, the Austrian government, in such turmoil that its Chancellor had to resign, conceded to
some of the Hungarian revolutionary's demands.

In response to the Austrian concessions, Kossuth guided the Hungarian parliament to enact reforms, such as an end to Austrian taxation of
the Hungarian nobility. Nevertheless, all the Hungarian people did not
support his initiatives. Strong resistance arose both to his opposition to
Austrian rule and to his reforms. Enmity between Romanians and Croats
and the Magyars, Kossuth's ethnic group, flared into war. Now, the peoples of Hungary fought among themselves. Kossuth's followers struggled
for independence from Austria against ethnic groups who supported rule
by Austria and an end to Magyar dominance of the Hungarian parliament. When Kossuth's forces verged on triumph, Austria intervened. For
a time in the spring of 1849, Kossuth's Magyar-led forces gained the
military advantage.

Facing potential defeat, the Austrian emperor appealed to the Russian tsar, who dispatched his armies. Overwhelmed by the intervention of Russian power, the Hungarian republicans confronted defeat, trial, and lengthy imprisonment or execution. To escape the Austrian crackdown on the political and military leaders of the revolution, Kossuth and a small number of supporters fled their homeland. Eventually, they found refuge in the Ottoman Empire, whose ruler defied diplomatic pressure from Russia and Austria that he return the Hungarians, and instead extended them asylum.

In the United States, President Zachary Taylor, who had come to national prominence as a victorious general in the Mexican-American War, interested himself in the Hungarian revolution and described his support in his annual message delivered to Congress on the state of the Union in December 1849. Because he had found the American people deeply sympathetic to the Hungarian declaration of independence from Austria the preceding spring, he had dispatched an emissary to Europe. Taylor had charged him to prepare "to be the first to welcome independent Hungary into the family of nations" if the revolutionaries succeeded in establishing a permanent government.[18] The intervention of the powerful Russian army on the side of Austria during the summer of 1849 soon extinguished any hope of Hungary's becoming an independent republic.

Evidently word of the surrender of the Hungarian army in August did not reach Springfield, Illinois, in sufficient time to discourage sympathetic citizens from acting on its behalf. On the evening of September 6, ex-Congressman Lincoln and other public-spirited citizens, including many ladies, according to newspaper reports, met to express support for the Hungarian cause. The resolution that Lincoln and others drafted called on the national government to recognize the new republican government at the earliest moment, greeted the "freemen" of Hungary as brothers, and claimed to violate no country's rights.[19]

During Kossuth's two years of exile, U.S. politicians campaigned to do something for the Hungarians. On January 9, 1850, Senator William Seward from New York presented a resolution to investigate whether public lands could be made available to the expatriates if they chose to settle permanently in the United States. Congressional records show that several state legislatures joined this cause and offered land to the Hungarians. Finally on March 3, 1851, Congress approved a resolution to help the exiles by giving them transportation to the United States and the opportunity to settle there permanently. About a dozen states had promised land to the Hungarians if they would become permanent

FIGURE 3.5. "Grand reception of Kossuth: 'The champion of Hungarian Independence' at the City Hall, New York, December 6, 1851." A German translation of the lithograph's title appears beside the English version, thus showing the multiple markets in the United States to which the publisher, N. Currier of New York, intended to sell. Courtesy of Library of Congress Prints and Photographs Division.

settlers. So, the resolution promised the future immigrants "a safe and permanent asylum within the limits of this republic" and requested that the president make available for their transportation a naval vessel currently in the Mediterranean Sea.[20] After the resolution's approval by President Fillmore, the United States extended an invitation to Kossuth to visit, the first one by the government of the United States to a foreigner since 1824, when President James Monroe had invited the Marquis de Lafayette to join the celebration of the fiftieth anniversary of 1776.

Kossuth and his party reached the United States on December 5, 1851. (See Figure 3.5.) Before he departed from New York City in mid-July 1852, he had traveled to the major East Coast cities, the South, and the Midwest – home to many German and Hungarian exiles from the failed revolutions of 1848. Supporters learned as the tour through the United States proceeded that Kossuth had no intention of settling in their country's western states or territories. He attempted instead to raise money and support for intervention in Hungary and expulsion of the occupying Austrians.

Even before Kossuth's arrival in the United States, he had generated tremendous excitement. His role in the Hungarian revolution had previously made him a hero to many Americans, especially in the southern states. In New Orleans, hatmakers named a broad-brimmed, soft-crowned hat after him. One horse lover and breeder even named a stallion trotter for the patriot. Composers of dances hoped to sell sheet music for the new Kossuth polka. In the weeks before the Kossuth entourage reached the United States, a New York City orchestra performed a "Kossuth March," and the National Theater of the same city presented *The Hungarians and Their Struggle for Independence*. The satirical work *Kossuth's Kum* or "Kossuth Come" ran at Brougham's Theater in New York and then in other cities that the hero visited during his American tour.[21]

After his arrival in New York City on December 6, his fame reached even larger audiences and generated even more enthusiasm. Books appeared, mementoes multiplied, and the Kossuth hat and beard became all the rage. John Genin, a hatmaker with a store located along the parade route in New York City, gave away soft-brimmed hats to the Hungarian refugees accompanying Kossuth as they marched up Broadway to City Hall. Immediately, the demand for the hat increased to the extent that hat manufacturers subsequently honored Genin's entrepreneurial initiative with a silver coffee or tea service worth $1,200. A munificent gift, but one worth much less than $500,000 the hat reputedly generated in revenue.[22] (See Figure 3.6.) Besides the hat, "Magyar-mania," as New York City diarist George Templeton Strong called the phenomenon, reached sufficient proportions by mid-1852 to support production of at least four books – two on Hungarian history and two on Kossuth himself; fairs given to support his independence movement; more articles of clothing such as pants, cravats, and overcoats; sheet music for Kossuth galops (lively dances) and waltzes; and numerous collectibles bearing his portrait, including glass flasks for liquor and jewelry brooches.[23]

Contemporary media consultants have much to learn from Kossuth's ascendancy in American popularity and subsequent fall from the spotlight. Adept with languages – he spoke French, Italian, and German– he had taught himself English while reading the plays of Shakespeare during imprisonment for purported sedition against Austrian rule of Hungary. Thus, he could speak directly to dignitaries, journalists, and crowds of supporters when he visited England and the United States after his liberation from the Ottoman Empire.

FIGURE 3.6. "Liberty our aim! Washington our example!" Edwin H. Brigham designed this wood engraving (38 × 39.4 cm.) for a kerchief most likely to commemorate Kossuth's New England tour of 1852. It shows the political context in which Americans saw the Hungarian. The design features central portraits of George Washington, Kossuth, and Giuseppe Mazzini. A border of shields with the names of historical figures references patriots who opposed tyranny or fought for their countries' independence, such as the Roman Brutus, the Irishman Thomas Francis Meagher, and the Venezuelan Simon Bolivar. Courtesy of Library of Congress Prints and Photographs Division.

Kossuth also knew to adjust his message to his audience. During a stop in England while en route to the United States, he delivered several public addresses. He pointedly praised that country's system of government, which depended on local, municipal institutions. He predicted that England would not suffer, and did not need to suffer, revolutions such as those that other European countries had experienced in the 1840s. Its constitutional monarchy excluded no class, according to him, from the benefit of free institutions. With such institutions it would forever be, in his words, "great glorious, and free."[24]

Similarly, he prepared audiences in the United States to cheer at his arrival by flattering them with praise for their history and heroes. Members of Kossuth's retinue researched U.S. history to furnish him with timely, laudatory references for documents and speeches that he would present during and even before his visit. After President Taylor had prepared to recognize an independent Hungary and after Kossuth escaped to Turkey, the exile addressed a letter to the people of the United States, which newspapers across the country published. He thanked the president for his efforts while claiming a common heritage for his country and the United States. During his tour through the United States, he inserted historical local color wherever he visited. In Boston, he spoke of how the small company of refugees who had landed at Plymouth Rock after their voyage on the *Mayflower* had brought with them the seeds that had "developed into a tree of freedom...a glorious evidence of mankind's sovereign capacity for self-government."[25]

He also seasoned his remarks with names that Americans revered, most especially that of George Washington. Words such as these won the allegiance of a vast audience of Americans: "May God bless your country forever! May it have the glorious destiny to share with other nations the blessings of that liberty which constitutes its own happiness and fame! May your great example, noble Americans, be to other nations the source of social virtue; your power be the terror of all tyrants – the protector of the distressed; and your free country ever continue to be the asylum for the oppressed of all nations."[26]

Finally, Kossuth intuitively understood the power of the press as a vehicle for popularizing his cause. As a journalist noted before his arrival in New York City, "the populace had had their feelings so worked up by the stories of his splendid fight for liberty in Hungary that they turned out in a vast mob when word was passed about the city that the ship bearing him and his party was coming up the bay."[27] The noise of the crowd's enthusiasm drowned out his speech at Castle Garden in Battery Park at the foot of Manhattan Island. Kossuth did not seek to be heard above the cheers; he simply stopped his oral performance and proceeded to the carriage that carried him as a visiting hero up Broadway to the park in front of New York City Hall.

In spite of the interruption, the next day his words praising Americans and their history of republicanism reached an audience many times larger than the one that had jammed the venue at Castle Garden. Newspapers ran the story for a national audience from the copy that Kossuth had distributed after the disruption. Articles, editorials, and advertisements in the press magnified the Hungarian's appeal. No wonder that on the day of his arrival in New York City, a major daily newspaper titled him "The greatest living man at this moment."[28]

Having arrived in the United States in December 1851, Kossuth benefited from a moment when its people were receptive to the Hungarian's message. Nine years previously the country had settled boundary disputes with Great Britain on its northeastern border and, in the previous five years, on its northwestern border. Following annexation of Texas in 1845, the U.S. Army had disputed its southern boundary with Mexico. Then, it launched successful military campaigns against that country and forced it to cede lands greater in extent than those of Thomas Jefferson's Louisiana Purchase of 1803. The United States now stretched from the Atlantic Ocean to the Pacific Ocean. Further, the discovery of gold in recently acquired California brought the promise of immense wealth such as that which enriched the Spanish Empire after its conquest of the Aztecs and Incas.[29]

This moment of national expansion and optimism encouraged many Americans to believe that their country had ascended to global power. Comparing the development of a nation to human development, they imagined that the United States had reached a stage in its life when the narrow confines of its childhood no longer restrained development. Ready to leave its so-called crib, or the North American continent, the Young America movement claimed, their country might now stride onto a larger playing field to assume its destined world role. Newly elected Michigan Congressman Alexander Buel told his honored colleagues in 1848 that the country could be an "emissary of American freedom amongst the nations of the earth."[30] Other Democratic politicians such as Stephen Douglas of Illinois and Lewis Cass of Michigan took up the cry along with journalists such as John L. O'Sullivan and James Gordon Bennett. O'Sullivan justified American expansion with the invented term "manifest destiny," while Bennett began to publish his pro-expansionist editorials in Europe in order to inform its would-be revolutionaries of America's "lofty and sublime principles of republicanism."[31]

The enthusiasm of Young Americans extended beyond the borders of the Democratic Party. Young Whigs also heard the call. In Connecticut, Noah Porter, a young minister who in 1871 became president of Yale College, dreamed of French scholars in dim garrets inciting the revolutions of the 1830s through their powerful words.[32] In the momentous year of 1848, revolutions in France, the German states, and Kossuth's Hungary produced the thinking that the world had entered a republican moment. Many Americans cheered the ascendance of republican-led revolutions in Europe and believed that the end of monarchy on that continent had arrived. The example of the United States shone like a North Star to guide republicans on both sides of the Atlantic Ocean.

In the U.S. Senate, Whigs and Democrats voted unanimously in praise of the efforts of the French people to establish a republic. And, in the House of Representatives on April 10 of that revolutionary year, Representative Lincoln voted "yea" along with 174 of his colleagues on the resolution that "the efforts of France to establish civil liberties on the basis of a republican form of government command the admiration and receive the warmest sympathies of the American people." Only two representatives cast "nay" votes.[33]

Despite the initial blast of enthusiasm for Kossuth upon his arrival in New York City in December 1851, criticism gained force during the next six months of his tour through the country. The press could have a negative as well as a positive impact. Word of his flattery of British institutions while in that country angered Irish Americans in the United States. Kossuth's British speeches evoked condemnation from American Irish Catholic leaders such as Archbishop John Hughes of New York City, who deplored British suppression of the Young Irelander Rebellion of 1848.

During the Hungarian patriot's visit to various U.S. cities through mid-July 1852, interest groups and politicians tried to persuade him to declare his position on the divisive issues that the passage of the Compromise of 1850 and its Fugitive Slave Law recently had evoked. Antislavery northerners, states rights southerners, and other political groups debated whether Kossuth advocated or opposed their political stances.

Initially, southerners had lauded Kossuth because he seemed to stand for the right of a state to defy the centralizing tendency of a powerful government. His appeal stemmed from an analogy comparing Austria to the United States. The oppressive Hapsburg rulers seemed to resemble federal authorities, while the Hungarian rebels seemed like Southerners with their pro–states rights stance. Unfortunately for Kossuth, as his American tour progressed, Southerners became fearful of him as his cause attracted support from antislavery New Englanders. These northerners found similarity between fugitive slaves and the Hungarian exiles. Both fled persecution and sought refuge in the free American states. Critics of slavery further noted that in Hungary Kossuth had abolished serfdom, while in the United States abolitionists sought an end to another system of unfree labor.

Despite the supplications of antislavery leaders, Kossuth resisted speaking against slavery, and sympathetic public figures questioned his silence. Especially in the antislavery newspapers of New England and New York, writers condemned his rejection of the request from an African-American committee to declare himself in opposition to slavery. Within weeks, leaders of the abolitionist movement, including William Lloyd Garrison, Lucretia Mott, and Wendell Phillips, had condemned the Hungarian's campaign for his country's freedom as hypocritical since he refused even to declare for freedom for slaves in their country. According to the abolitionist, "The freedom of twelve millions [slaves] had purchased the silence of Kossuth for a year."[34] Kossuth suffered the fate of many moderates as he tried to negotiate a position that offended neither extreme – neither proslavery nor antislavery Americans. Attacks from both sides diminished his popularity.

To add to his difficulties, Kossuth profoundly misinterpreted the vociferous cheering that had greeted him at every public appearance during his first weeks in the United States. Enthusiasm for the bravery and achievements of the patriot did not imply monetary or military support for the cause of an independent Hungary. When applauding Kossuth, recent immigrants to the United States from Austria, Hungary, and the German states lauded their own political sympathies and commitments. Native-born Americans transformed celebration of the Magyar hero into a proxy for celebration of their own history.

Through feting a Hungarian revolutionary, American citizens, including Representative Lincoln, might feel that they were commemorating their own revolution of 1776. They hoped that revolutions against colonialism and monarchy meant that republican governments were spreading worldwide and making the ideals of the Declaration of Independence into a reality. During the initial New York City parade, banners flew proclaiming "Welcome to Kossuth, Freedom's Champion, Freedom's Exile." Along with portraits of Kossuth and the Sultan of Turkey, who had harbored him during his exile, there hung portraits of American Revolutionary patriots Washington and Lafayette. A volume of prize essays, which Philadelphia schoolchildren had composed to honor Kossuth, contained thirty-eight essays of which nineteen compared the Hungarian to Washington. The essays noted that hatred of tyranny resided in the hearts of Americans and caused them to welcome "him who would fain have proved himself a Washington to Hungary."[35]

Heartened by the cheers and enthusiastic newspaper reviews, Kossuth went public on December 11 before a New York audience with his hopes that the U.S. government would depart from the nation's established policy of not intervening in European domestic affairs. The Hungarian interpreted Washington's advice in his Farewell Address much as members of Young America currently did. The cautions of the first president, he reasoned, had applied to the United States solely in its infancy. Now that his country had grown in power sufficient to combat Great Britain in the War of 1812 and the Tripolitan powers in 1815, it had adequate strength to extend its protection to South American republics threatened by European recolonization.

Thus, Kossuth reasoned, the United States now might apply the essence of the Monroe Doctrine to Europe. When the president issued his doctrine in 1823, no steam-powered ocean ships had connected Europe and North America. Over the next twenty-seven years, faster transport and communication, he argued, had rendered obsolete the limitations on American foreign policy that the Monroe Doctrine had established. They had no more current relevance than did the limitations that Washington had recommended in his Farewell Address of 1796.[36]

Kossuth's reasoning impressed some legislators at the state level, but quelled the enthusiasm of many statesmen, especially those in the national capital. They could laud the foreign visitor as the George Washington of Hungary while denying foreign aid to a Kossuth-led revolution. The Pennsylvania legislature voted a resolution in support of Kossuth's doctrine, while the legislature of Maryland disavowed it. National leaders stopped cheering the Hungarian and condemned his attempt to incite a warlike spirit in U.S. foreign policy. In the national capital, leaders pondered diplomatic procedure during Kossuth's impending visit. Welcomes extended to the Hungarian probably would insult Austria and its ally, Russia.[37]

Despite these misgivings in Washington, during the last days of Kossuth's stay in the city, citizens sympathetic to his cause in Springfield, Illinois, including Whig ex-Congressman Lincoln, his law partner William Herndon, Democratic Judge Lyman Trumbull, and other leading citizens called a meeting to compose a resolution endorsing Kossuth and his campaign. Their representatives and senators in Washington would learn of their support for Hungary when the resolution was delivered.

Even though the committee agreed that Kossuth was "the most worthy and distinguished representative of the cause of civil and religious liberty on the continent of Europe," its members had no unanimity on the question of whether the United States should intervene in his country's affairs. Much as Lincoln had favored a resolution supporting the French revolution of 1848 while a congressman, now he argued for expressing support for the cause of the Hungarian patriots. Still, he opposed military or diplomatic intervention in their country's domestic affairs. This temperate position must have represented the opinion of Lincoln and the minority, as the majority of the Springfield committee voted for a resolution ratifying Kossuth's position. The Illinois committee deplored the intervention by the Russians in Hungarian affairs, approved the principle of the "mutuality of non-intervention," and proposed that it should become "a sacred principle of the international law."

With these words, the committee majority expressed its desire to end the United States' heritage of nonintervention in European affairs. It supported intervention in that continent's domestic conflicts and recommended that the U.S. policy of nonintervention become universally applicable. Just as the United States ought never to intervene in a European country's domestic affairs, "so no other government may interfere" in the affairs of another country. In other words, Russian intervention in Hungarian affairs violated this novel interpretation of the Monroe Doctrine. After this assertive statement, the Springfield committee added to its resolutions a Pontius Pilate–like step back from actual commitment. The majority decided that whether the United States "will, in fact, interfere in such case, is purely a question of policy, to be decided when the exigency arrives."[38] In effect, Lincoln's position prevailed when the committee adopted Kossuth's position merely in principle and not in practice.

While the Springfield committee debated the principle of nonintervention, Kossuth continued to meet with prominent statesmen in the national capital. In the final days of his visit, members of Young America arranged an audience with former Kentucky Senator Henry Clay, who was in declining health and would die in six months. Kossuth had sought to approach Clay because of his hope that he would speak for the Hungarian cause. In Kossuth's orations to American audiences, he had recalled Clay's speeches in support of the Greek Revolution and, when he had served as secretary of state in the late 1820s, for Latin American independence.[39]

Kossuth's visit to the ailing ex-senator did not produce the desired outcome. Worried by the success of Louis Napoleon's recent coup d'état of December 1851, which had overturned the Second French Republic, the elderly statesman told his foreign visitor that his country would not intervene militarily against European despots. Kossuth's cause received a powerful reversal in public esteem when newspapers published Clay's remarks that "[f]ar better is it for ourselves, for Hungary, and for the cause of liberty, that, adhering to our (the United States') wise, pacific system, and avoiding the distant wars of Europe, we should keep our lamp burning brightly on this Western shore, as a light to all nations, than to hazard its utter extinction amid the ruins of fallen and falling republics in Europe."[40]

Shortly after news of the Clay-Kossuth meeting reached a national audience, citizens in Springfield, Illinois, extended an invitation to the patriot to visit their city in March while he and his entourage traveled from speaking engagements in Indianapolis, Indiana, to those in St. Louis, Missouri. Judging by attendance at organizational meetings for the Kossuth visit, interest in Springfield soon dissipated. Either the Kossuth entourage did not respond to the invitation, or the behavior of Kossuth and his followers caused the committee to reconsider its offer. The Hungarian was pressing his American hosts too hard for donations. On a tour of western Pennsylvania, Kossuth had turned more of his attention to fundraising. He went public with his dismay that a substantial portion of the funds that pro-Kossuth committees had raised had been devoted to gala receptions and entertainments and that little money remained to fund Austrian overthrow. As the patriot demanded more focus on raising money for the Hungarian cause, organizing committees in American cities became wary.[41]

Kossuth reached New England in late spring after a disappointing trip through the southern United States. By April 1852, southerners had forgotten Kossuth, the revolutionary hero of 1848 after whom they had named hats and trotting stallions. Instead, they focused on his noncommittal stance on slavery and its extension. Further, anti-Kossuth articles placed in pro-Austrian newspapers had roused Catholic sentiments in Louisiana against the foreign visitor. Senator Daniel Webster's pro-Hungarian remarks during Kossuth's Washington stay had offended the Austrian ambassador, who sensed that his country had suffered an insult. Consequently, it suspended diplomatic relations with the United States, although it resumed them twelve months later. Finally, newspapers in Louisville, Kentucky, had spread more venom. They accused Kossuth of insulting Henry Clay, their home state's favorite statesman, during their meeting in Washington at which the aging senator had refused to support Kossuth's plea for intervention. By the time the Hungarian left the southern states, accolades from crowds and politicians had receded from the high tide of popular support that had washed over him in New York City.[42]

The New England visit from late April through the third week of May reversed the negative publicity of the last few weeks. Besides visiting the region's major cities and many of its towns, Kossuth toured sites in Massachusetts of significance during the American Revolution, notably

Lexington, Concord, and Charleston. In Boston, he spoke at Faneuil Hall. The political and literary notables of the region, including Ralph Waldo Emerson and Henry Wadsworth Longfellow, greeted him at tour stops and headlined rallies and receptions. Such notice once again earned the exile a prominent place in the national news and further educated Kossuth supporters, including Lincoln, about the international influence of their country, its history, and its patriots. In the thirty-four days of Kossuth's New England tour, the *New York Times*, a recently founded paper, published approximately thirty articles reporting the patriot's progress through the region. In newspapers throughout the northeastern and midwestern states, excluding New York and Massachusetts, at least sixty articles appeared.

In New Haven, Connecticut, and then in the twenty-four speeches and informal replies that Kossuth delivered during the New England tour, he emphasized the ties between the free people of the United States and those of Europe. "Such a nation will be connected," he declared, "by a thousand ties with the struggles which are about to be made by those who will fight with all the resolution of men loving freedom." Not only did Americans empathize with the efforts of European liberals; their nation also provided a model, Kossuth believed, for the nations of the world: "We claim a great influence from your country, an influence which no other power on earth can exert."[43] Readers of praise such as this had their preconceptions about the United States' unique world role confirmed. These sentiments belonged to a worldwide audience.

Knowledge of the so-called Magyar mania that affected Americans, including Lincoln, leads to a new understanding of his republicanism: it had both visual and verbal dimensions. The president denied the charges of detractors and journalists that he had worn Scottish attire when he entered Washington in February of 1861 because their aspersions contradicted the image that he was seeking to create of himself. His remarks to Benson Lossing in December 1864 carry greater significance than does a mere effort to correct an inaccuracy perpetrated by a hostile press.

From the start of his campaign for the presidency, Lincoln made certain that he appeared as a respectable, professional man. For example, he attired himself in a new suit when he had his portrait composed by photographer Mathew Brady before the Cooper Union address of February 1860. For that occasion, he had fashioned himself for an audience of Republican Party leaders of New York City. In February 1861, he was no less careful when he dressed for his trip to Washington and when he described his attire for posterity to a historian.

During his presidency, he tried to create an image of himself that appealed to an audience of liberals much larger than that of Republicans in the United States. Readers of the twenty-first century do not recognize that Lincoln had adopted the uniform of a European republican because they have overemphasized the influence of Grace Bedell, the eleven-year-old from Westfield, New York, whose letter to the Republican candidate suggested that he grow his whiskers. They would not if they had been attuned to Lincoln's appropriation of the image and message of Kossuth.

Prior to the Hungarian Revolution in 1848 and Kossuth's subsequent mission to the United States, Lincoln never mentioned Russia in his letters and speeches. The first mention of that country appears in the resolution that Lincoln composed in January 1852 with other residents of Springfield who supported the Hungarian revolution and Kossuth's cause.[44] Following that instance, Lincoln frequently mentioned Russia in his personal correspondence and public speeches. Usually he referred to the country as technologically backwards and as a repressive tyranny where individuals had no rights. Writing in 1855 to his friend Joshua Speed to explain his opposition to Know-Nothings who denied equal rights to foreigners and Catholics, Lincoln explained that he "should prefer emigrating to some country where they make no pretence of loving liberty–to Russia, for instance, where despotism can be taken pure, and without the base alloy of hypocracy."[45]

Next, consider the concluding words of Lincoln's address dedicating the national cemetery at Gettysburg on November 19, 1863. For its memorable conclusion, Lincoln owes some credit to Kossuth. The series of prepositional phrases: "of the people, by the people, and for the people" echo throughout history and have become some of Lincoln's most repeated words. In his pre-presidential career, the president frequently had written and spoken these phrases in combinations of two, although the phrases usually did not follow one another directly. For example, in the fourth debate with Senator Douglas, when discussing the Kansas question, Lincoln declaimed, "there was no provision for submitting the Constitution about to be made *for the people* of Kansas, to a vote *of the people* (my emphasis)." He carried these locutions into his presidency. While addressing Congress on July 4, 1861, he said, "a government of the people, by the same people."[46]

Lincoln wrote and heard these phrases at least daily during the years while he was a Whig member of the Illinois General Assembly, from 1834 to 1842. They appear as single units in the text of much of the legislation that he considered. Almost every bill introduced to the assembly, including those proposed by Lincoln, contained these words: "Be it enacted *by the people* of the State of Illinois represented in the General Assembly – That" such and such should happen. Review of Lincoln's speeches and legislation for the phrases "for the people" and "of the people" provides similar results. He frequently invoked the rights, justice, or liberties "of the people."

Much as he had adapted Leonard Bacon's words about the wrong of slavery to write Albert Hodges, in April 1864 that "if slavery is not wrong, nothing is wrong," he drew from his legislative experience when composing the Gettysburg Address. Lincoln's rhetorical genius took ordinary prepositional phrases that pervaded legislation and transformed them into a rhetorical masterpiece. He was not the first. In a powerful oration to the Ohio state legislature on February 8, 1852, Kossuth had declared, "The spirit of our age is democracy – all for the people and all by the people. Nothing about the people without the people."[47]

Kossuth's influence on Lincoln did not stop with ideas and words. It extended to Lincoln's personal appearance. People who greeted his train as it rolled from Harrisburg, through perilous Baltimore, and to Washington might not have easily recognized the president-elect. In the weeks between the fall campaign and his entrance to Washington the following February his appearance had changed. Posters and banners of 1860 had made American voters familiar with the clean-shaven image of candidate Lincoln. (See Figure 3.7.) By February 1861, a full beard enhanced the profile of president-elect Lincoln. (See Figure 3.8.)

The story explaining why he did so has been told and retold. In late October 1860, Grace Bedell, an eleven-year-old girl with four brothers, had written the candidate that he should grow a beard for both aesthetic and political reasons. A beard would fill out his thin face, she predicted, and if he did grow his whiskers, she would persuade her brothers to cast their ballots for him. Although Lincoln worried that people might think it "a piece of silly affection," he soon began to show more facial hair. We will never know if Grace fulfilled her side of the bargain by persuading her brothers to vote Republican, although candidate Lincoln did win New York state by the slim margin of less than 1 percent, or about 50,000 of the ballots cast.[48]

Almost four months later, in February 1861, as the train carrying the president-elect chugged along the shores of Lake Erie from Cleveland, Ohio, toward Buffalo, it briefly stopped at Westfield, New York. There Lincoln met the influential Grace Bedell. After his supporters ran to fetch her, he descended from the train platform to give "her several hearty

FIGURE 3.7. William Marsh, an English immigrant, took the photograph on which this carte-devisite was based on May 20, 1860, in Springfield, Illinois, two days after Lincoln won the Republican Party nomination at the Chicago convention. Photo known as O-22. ALPLM cat. LPh819. 7 × 5 inches. Courtesy of the ALPLM.

FIGURE 3.8. "Abraham Lincoln, bust portrait." Samuel G. Altschuler's photographic portrait of the president-elect on November 25, 1860, is reputedly the first first to show his beard. Courtesy of Library of Congress Prints and Photographs Division Washington.

kisses," according to a newspaper. Lincoln told the applauding crowd that she had written him several months ago "a very pretty letter." Consequently, he had started to let his beard grow – to improve "my personal appearance; acting *partly* upon her suggestion [my emphasis]."[49]

Lincoln scholars never have accounted for that word *partly*. Given the impact of Kossuth on Lincoln's rhetoric, choice of clothing, and references to Russia, Kossuth probably played a role in Lincoln's qualification of Grace's influence. In the transatlantic world, facial hair on the chin had suggested eccentricity and won little acceptance in respectable circles. Before the Hungarian patriot's visit to the United States in 1851–1852, beards had little popularity among respectable middle-class men. In his novels of the late forties and early fifties, Herman Melville referred to a "whiskerando" as a non-white ruffian. In *Redburn*, he is "dark-skinned," and "a half-clad reeling whiskerando," while he grasps for the virtuous heroine in *Pierre*.[50]

Beginning in the 1840s, beards began to be associated with republican or liberal sympathies. Journalists suggested that they connoted the revolutions of the day. During and after Kossuth's visit, journalists noted a fashion shift in the United States. As the mania for the Hungarian republican affected the minds of the males in his U.S. audiences, symptoms appeared on their cheeks. Suddenly trimmed beards became fashionable and no longer suggested piratical brigands.

We might think of images from the 1850s of journalist-poet Walt Whitman. In his younger days, the poet sported Kossuth-like facial hair and sometimes posed for photographs holding or wearing a soft-brimmed hat, also known as a Kossuth hat. An Indiana journalist commented in 1852 that since the Hungarian's tour of the United States began, "we do not recollect having seen so many whiskerandos in Indianapolis as during the past week."[51] Obviously, Kossuth and the revolutions of 1848 had effected a change; few dark-skinned pirates inhabited the Midwest. By the middle of the decade, fashionable men could follow European fashion by applying a new product "La Salle's Original Whiskerando" to their beards. Advertisements promised the buyers that the formula, imported from Paris, would cause beards to grow "luxuriantly."[52]

In Springfield, fashionable young men loyal to the Republican Party wore well-trimmed beards, and the president-elect had to witness this fashion trend in his daily life. Both his assistant John George Nicolay, a German émigré, and Elmer Ellsworth, who had stumped for him in the Springfield area while studying law in the Lincoln-Herndon law office, sported well-trimmed facial hair. (See Figures 3.9 and 3.10.)

FIGURE 3.9. John Nicolay, Carte de Visite, taken by Mathew B. Brady, after Nicolay's arrival in Washington in March 1861. Showing stylish facial hair, the German American had worked for the Republican presidential candidate in Springfield and now served as his private secretary. ALPLM cat. in Meserve collection F3, #263 printed at 2 1/8 in × 3 1/4 inches. Courtesy of the ALPLM.

Eight years after the Kossuth visit, Grace Bedell's suggestion to Lincoln fell on a mind primed to condemn Russian predations and to capitalize on the positive connotations of facial hair. He not only would look more handsome, he also would look more republican – to an audience of liberals in the United States and beyond.

Wearing a Kossuth hat and a beard upon his entry to Washington as president-elect, Lincoln intended to communicate by appearance what he had often communicated in words. He showed that he wanted to be seen as a manly leader who, like Kossuth, would remain true to his republican principles. In Lincoln's case, slavery would not extend while he labored for the reunification of his country. Kossuth's visit had taught Lincoln that the fate of republicanism in the United States mattered to the world, and especially to those republicans whose countries had suffered defeats in the crucial year of 1848. Smears from detractors who dressed him in Scottish attire defaced the republican image that Lincoln cultivated.[53]

COL. ELMER E. ELLSWORTH.

Entered according to Act of Congress in the year 1861, by M
B. Brady, in the Clerks' office of the District Court of the United States for the Southern District of New York.

FIGURE 3.10. Carte-de-visite of Elmer E. Ellsworth by Mathew Brady. During the fall of 1860, Ellsworth studied law in the Lincoln & Herndon law office, campaigned for the Republican candidate in central Illinois, and became a favorite of the entire Lincoln family. This portrait shows the early growth of facial hair on his chin. He had risen to fame after he led a Zouave drill unit on a twenty-city tour. Before fascinated audiences, the unit of young men demonstrated complex rifle drills and movements inspired by the French foreign legion during the Crimean War. Ellsworth had written in 1859 a *Manual of Arms for Light Infantry . . . arranged for the U.S. Zouave Cadets, Governor's Guard of Illinois.* After the surrender of Fort Sumter, Ellsworth recruited New York City firefighters into a new Zouave unit. On May 24, 1861, while leading his command into Alexandria, Virginia, he became the first commissioned officer to be killed. A pro-Confederate hotel owner shot him after he removed a CSA flag from display. Ellsworth's death evoked tears from Lincoln and propelled his young friend to even greater fame. Within days, publishers were profiting by issuing his image on cdv's, sheet music, illustrated stationery, etc. ALPLM cat. Taper Collection / TLCDV 003. overall: 4 in × 2 5/16 inches. Courtesy of the ALPLM.

Thus, when historian Benson Lossing interviewed him in December 1864, Lincoln discussed events with personal significance. Although a modest man, the president knew the power of visual imagery. From the beginning of his one Congressional term in 1847 through his presidency, he appeared in more than 100 photographs and sat as well for numerous sculptors, sketch artists, and painters.[54] With this awareness of his image, a man such as he would have attempted to shape the story that historian Lossing told. Confronted repeatedly throughout his first term with demeaning cartoons of himself in Scottish garb, Lincoln told his version of the Baltimore incident in his interview with Lossing purposefully, but ingenuously. He was attempting to restore the republican image that he had so carefully fashioned for his entrance into the nation's capital.

In Lossing's illustrated book on the Civil War and then in many editions of his histories for families and schools, the author portrayed the president as he wished: in republican garb. From the historian's portrait in words, readers took an impression of the president-elect as a brave man ready to preserve republican government once he had sworn, "to the best of my Ability, preserve, protect and defend the Constitution of the United States." Prepared to command the struggle for national reunification, here was a leader who deserved to rank with the great republicans of Europe. These men wore Kossuth hats, labeled Russia a despotism, and had beards.

# 4

# German Lessons

The winter following the outbreak of the German and Hungarian revolutions, Lincoln and about a dozen of his Springfield friends, including Amos W. French, his dentist, and William Herndon, his law partner, started to meet semiweekly in the lawyers' office for German language lessons. The teacher, an émigré who had moved recently to the Illinois capital from Philadelphia, knew insufficient English to explain why a German word that sounded like an English word had a quite different meaning or connotation in each language. For example, in English, the word *gift* means a present; in German, *Gift* means a poison. To explain these so-called false friends, Lincoln stepped into the breach. He might tell his fellow students, "the Germans have no word for thimble; they call it a finger hat (*Fingerhut*)." Thus, he illustrated the nuances of meaning with stories that generated "much merriment." Because of the ensuing laughter, "none of us mastered the language," the dentist recalled.[1]

Lincoln reputedly did learn a few elementary words, at least enough to tell German-American friends and acquaintances some years later that their surnames of Kaufmann and Schneider meant merchant and tailor. Along with an introduction to the language, participation in the classes may have inspired discussion of current European events, especially the activities of the Forty-Eighters and Louis Kossuth. Lincoln and Herndon's hosting the classes indicates that he must have anticipated some benefits. During the years following his term in Congress, when he supposedly had stepped away from political activity, the German lessons helped ready him for reentry. He was learning how to enlarge his political base to a new constituency in Illinois. Concomitantly, he was revising his thinking about the meaning of the Declaration of Independence to include a new and broader understanding of "all men are created equal."[2]

During the 1840s, approximately 400,000 Germans arrived in the United States. By 1860, approximately 1.3 million people in the United States claimed Prussia or other German states as their birthplaces. Merely 5 percent of these people resided in states that would secede in 1860–1861. In some states, especially those of the Midwest, German-born residents outnumbered Irish-born residents, the most numerous immigrant group in the entire country from the 1830s through the 1840s. In 1847, the U.S. consul at Bremen reported that 33,632 Germans emigrated. As the revolutions started in the German states, 92,947 departed in 1848. The number of emigrants remained above the 1847 level until an economic downturn affected the United States in 1857, when merely 23,095 Germans took ships for new homes.[3] In Illinois, foreign-born residents numbered 18.9 percent of the population in 1860, with the Irish-born numbering 5 percent of the entire population and German-born 7.6 percent. In the states of the north and current Midwest (Ohio, Illinois, Indiana, Michigan, Wisconsin, and Iowa), the Germans and other immigrant groups, concentrated in the cities. In Chicago, foreigners constituted 49.9 percent of the population, and in St. Louis 59.6 percent.[4]

German immigrants ventured across the Atlantic Ocean for ideological, political, and economic reasons. The impact of the industrial revolution, especially the mechanization of textile production, brought on economic distress in previously thriving communities of craftspeople. In the countryside, large landholders monopolized available resources. Agricultural laborers rarely could improve their lot by acquiring land. For these dependent workers, the low population density and territorial expanse of the United States offered opportunity to purchase farms and consequently to acquire both political autonomy and economic independence. Prussia drafted its male residents into compulsory military service at twenty years old, and in most German states, including Prussia, only landholders could vote. If a German disagreed with the causes for which his homeland fought, he could not vote against its policies unless he owned land. Thus, German men often had to fight for causes that they found unacceptable. Instead of soldiering in wars to which they had not voted consent, emigration often seemed preferable, usually to the United States and less frequently to Canada, Australia, or South America.

Europeans also thought of the United States during these decades as having a future that they could help shape. With lands in the country open for settling, if one overlooks the presence of Native Americans, as most Europeans did, settlers could mold the culture of the new lands into conformity with their own political or religious ideals. After all, in the first decades of the young republic, German Pietists pursuing the freedom to practice their religion had started settlements based on communal principles in Ebenezer, New York, and Economy, Pennsylvania. In ensuing decades, Scottish reformers such as Robert Owen and Frances Wright founded model communities in Indiana and Tennessee.

Most of the emigrating Germans left their homelands primarily for economic and religious reasons. In the United States, the availability of land offered economic opportunity, and the Constitution promised freedom to practice the religion of one's own choice. About one-third of the immigrants worshiped in the Catholic Church and gravitated toward settlement in rural areas, while the majority of the immigrants were practicing Protestants, mainly belonging to the Lutheran or German Reformed denominations.

In politics, the Democratic Party attracted the German immigrants. They became its loyal members when they acquired citizenship after waiting for the five-year period required by U.S. naturalization laws. The Democratic Party's celebration of the common man, acceptance of Catholics, promise of universal suffrage for white men, and criticism of an active, strong central government appealed to people who had fled the rule of invasive governments. Further, the Democratic Party did not promote Sabbatarian practices. The Whig Party, the Democrats' major adversary from the presidency of Andrew Jackson into the 1850s, alienated immigrants with its advocacy, at the national level, of a strong central government to promote national economic development, and on the local level of temperance legislation and Sunday closings, especially of saloons and beer gardens.[5]

A far smaller yet more influential number of Germans emigrated for political reasons. The republican principles of the North American nation had drawn them across the Atlantic. They admired the claims of the Declaration of Independence that all men were created equal and that governments should depend on the consent of the governed. They believed that the U.S. Constitution embodied these principles and frequently declared that the country's founding documents approached being perfect expressions of republicanism.[6]

Previous to their emigration from the German states, this politically liberal subgroup had been activists. They participated as soldiers or opinion-makers in the revolutions and political turmoil first unleashed by the Napoleonic Wars, subsequently manifest in 1830 in France, and later in the revolutions of 1848–1849, which affected France, the German states, Hungary, northern Ireland, and states in the Italian peninsula.

Among the many Germans emigrating for both economic and political motives was the family of John George Nicolay, who served Lincoln as his private secretary during his presidency. While in their homeland, Nicolay's family disdained aristocratic pretensions. Before emigrating in 1837, his father had supported his wife and four children by farming a small plot of land in Essingen, a town in a south-central German state, and by making barrels for local wineries. Nicolay family lore tells that the father decided to take his family to the United States after the province's ruling family decreed that its subjects had to stand at attention when one of their members passed them by. Male subjects of the rulers had to doff their hats in respect, even in foul weather. After Nicolay's father stood in the rain with a bared head, he departed with his family for a country where the government depended on the consent of the governed and did not order its citizens to show their subservience.[7]

Sometime after the Nicolay family arrived in the port of New Orleans, it settled in Cincinnati, Ohio, among a community of fellow Germans. The family lived there for several years until the death of Mrs. Nicolay. Then the father moved his sons and daughter from settlement to settlement until he reached rural Pike County, Illinois, where he transferred his barrel-making skills to renovating and running a gristmill with assistance from his older sons.

After his father's death at the age of forty-four, John George, the youngest son, had to become self-supporting at age fourteen. First working as a store clerk, he next landed a position in a printing office, which published a four-page weekly newspaper and supported the Whig party. By age twenty-two, he had advanced himself from news office handyman to editor and proprietor of the newspaper. His interest in antislavery politics and reputation as "an honest printer" brought him and his future employer, Abraham Lincoln, into contact in 1856.[8]

Unlike the motivation for emigration of the Nicolay family, politics alone pushed Francis Lieber from Germany. During his teen years, he had fought in the Napoleonic Wars. While defending his homeland against French forces, he received a life-threatening wound. After his recovery, he journeyed, like many young men of the early 1820s, to Greece to join its people's revolt against Ottoman rule. Returning to Berlin and finding in 1825 that his republican political ideas would cause his imprisonment, he fled to London. Two years later he found sanctuary, employment, and a new life in the United States. His oldest son returned to Germany from 1847 through 1849 to study at schools and universities in Berlin, Gottingen, and Freiburg, where he experienced firsthand the political protests of those years.[9]

The elder Lieber eventually won a professorship at South Carolina College, where he taught until sectional controversies made life in the southern state intolerable and career advancement impossible. He moved his family to New York City, where Columbia College soon offered him a chair. As its professor of history and political science, he became the expert on international law who helped the Lincoln administration formulate standards of military conduct for the Army.

Other German-American political émigrés resembled Lieber and the Nicolays in several ways. Many tended to settle in towns and small cities and to belong to Lutheran or German Reformed churches. Seeking the broadest intellectual and political freedom, some of these immigrants even took anticlerical stances opposed to religious establishments, whether Protestant or Catholic. Despite the immigrants' radical politics and opposition to slavery, their anticlericalism alienated them from the evangelically inspired and often church-based extreme antislavery positions of the American Antislavery Society led by Bostonian William Lloyd Garrison.

While the Garrisonians advocated for immediate abolition, the German Americans hoped for the eventual end of slavery. Like most Americans with antislavery sentiments, they saw slavery not as a national institution, but as one sectional and state-based. The Constitution had implied recognition of the institution, for example in the fugitive slave clause, rather than mandating permission for its extension to territories of the United States. Accordingly, state laws and not the federal Constitution had established slavery and transformed humans into property. These German Americans expected that over time slavery would end peacefully on account of its confinement to the slave states that existed in 1850, namely the slave states east of the Mississippi River and also the lands that lay west of the Mississippi, excepting Missouri, and south of the Missouri Compromise line. For them, the confinement of slavery would cause its eventual extinction while guaranteeing the availability of land in territories for settlement by free people.[10]

Like Lieber and Nicolay, many of the political refugees became educators and opinion-makers. They found employment in institutions of American secondary and higher education, or as writers and editors of newspapers and journals. In the German-American migration, about

FIGURE 4.1. Francis Lieber, Class of 1862, Class Photograph. Courtesy of the University Archives, Columbia University in the City of New York.

10 percent of the total had participated in the failed revolution of 1848–1849. This subgroup attained an influence in the intellectual, political, and cultural affairs of their new country that far exceeded their numbers. They found employment in or established German-language newspapers, and became political activists after acquiring citizenship. By the 1860s, German-language daily or weekly papers with European and American news existed in almost every northern and Midwestern city with a substantial number of German-born residents, and large cities sometimes had several. Chicago, for instance, had three daily German-language papers. Of these, the *Illinois Staats-Zeitung* had the second-largest circulation in the city of any paper, regardless of the language.[11]

Lincoln's knowledge of his hometown and his travels as a lawyer on the eighth judicial circuit of Illinois would have made him aware of the increasing numbers of German Americans in his state. While serving in the state legislature in Vandalia, the Illinois capital until 1839, Lincoln might have noticed the substantial German community that had begun arriving in the 1820s. In 1839, he most likely handled his first law suit in which his client had a German surname, namely Moses Hoffman in *Hoffman v. Wernwag*.

In 1840, when campaigning for Whig presidential candidate William Henry Harrison in the so-called Log Cabin and Hard Cider Campaign, Lincoln joined a group of party orators who traveled to southwest Illinois to hold a political rally in the sizeable German-American community of Belleville.[12] In that Democratic Party stronghold, the young politician delivered a lackluster speech. Critical of the present Democratic administration, he tried to win his audience with a humorous quip. It backfired. The anti–Bank of the United States policies of presidents Andrew Jackson and Martin Van Buren, he jested, had so depressed the economy that a horse had sold in Belleville for the paltry sum of twenty-seven dollars at a just-completed auction. Unfortunately for Lincoln, the town constable, the horse's owner, interrupted his remarks to say that the horse in question had sold for a fair price, considering that he had one blind eye.[13]

The impact of the European revolutions reached Illinois more directly in the fall of 1851. The Prussian poet and revolutionary Gottfried Kinkel arrived in the city in September, three months before Kossuth's triumphal entrance into New York City. Kinkel solicited fellow German émigrés and committed American republicans on behalf of a loan to support the revolutionary ambitions of his countrymen then in exile in London. Traveling down the East Coast to the national capital, he met with President Millard Fillmore and Senator Stephen Douglas of Illinois.[14] In addition to visiting major German-American population centers such as Buffalo, St. Louis, and Chicago, he also visited Belleville where various fund-raising events raised six hundred dollars for his cause.[15] These visits revealed the major institutions of organizational life that the German immigrant community had formed, including Young Men's Associations, Masons, Odd Fellows, singing groups, and instrumental groups, and women's clubs. Additionally, they testified to the importance to the revolutionaries of Gustav Körner, a resident of Belleville. By 1852, he had served a term in the Illinois legislature – the first German-born American to do so – been appointed by the governor to the State Supreme Court, and started a campaign for the lieutenant-governorship, which he won in the November balloting.[16]

After Lincoln's term ended in the House of Representatives in March 1849, he returned to his Springfield law practice. There he began his German lessons and offered his support to the cause of European republicans and liberals. The visits of both Kinkel and then Kossuth to the

United States received extensive coverage in both the English-language and German-language press. The observant Lincoln, prepared by his language classes, must have noticed the enthusiastic publicity. He attended and then led the meetings in Springfield in 1852 that crafted the resolutions supporting Kossuth and the Hungarian revolution, even though the former Congressman had supposedly removed himself from politics.

In early January, the ex-Whig Congressman along with Lyman Trumbull, a Democrat currently serving on the Illinois State Supreme Court, called a meeting of Democrats and Whigs to discuss inviting Kossuth to Springfield during his tour of Midwestern cities. They debated whether the United States should reverse the promise announced in the Monroe Doctrine that the North American country would not intervene in the internal affairs of European countries. At their meeting, Lincoln and other attendees discussed whether their country should involve itself in Hungarian affairs. Besides the rebellion in Kossuth's country, they noted, movements to establish independence or representative governments existed in Ireland, France, and the German states. Possibly, the resolutions of the Springfield meeting should acknowledge support for them as well as for Kossuth's efforts with regard to Hungary.

The Illinois committee approved a resolution on January 9 that urged: "That the sympathies of this country, and the benefits of its position, should be exerted in favor of the people of every nation struggling to be free; and whilst we meet to do honor to Kossuth and Hungary, we should not fail to pour out the tribute of our praise and approbation to the patriotic efforts of the Irish, the *Germans* [emphasis added] and the French, who have unsuccessfully fought to establish in their several governments the supremacy of the people."[17] The enthusiasm for Kossuth and the various European reformers shows that Lincoln and other Americans, many of them immigrants, viewed their own republican causes in transnational terms. As a Whig, Lincoln united in sympathy with German Americans and freedom-loving Democrats, while remaining separated from them by party allegiance.

Lincoln again expressed his understanding of the United States' membership in a transnational Atlantic community when he delivered on July 6, 1852, a passionate eulogy for the recently deceased Henry Clay, who had met with Kossuth in January. As a leading member of the Whig party, Clay's service to Kentucky and the nation included terms in the Senate and House of Representatives, plus terms as Speaker of the House and Secretary of State (1825–1829). The statesman's death deeply saddened both Abraham and Mary as the couple supported his politics with regard to national development and the future of slavery. Further, Clay had enjoyed a close relationship with Mary's family in Lexington, Kentucky, and she had known him since childhood.

The day after the death of Clay, Lincoln, as the Whig party leader in Springfield, began to organize a public tribute for the national party's former leader. On July 6, while offices and stores suspended business, the local Episcopal church held a memorial service followed by a ceremony in the state house.

As Lincoln eulogized the late Kentucky senator in the Illinois state house, he noted that the years of the European revolutions, the 1820s through 1840s, were a "remarkable era in human affairs." In Clay's life, Lincoln found a pattern. The deceased statesman had both sympathized with the independence movements in Greece and South America and praised his own country for being the home of free men. Lincoln discerned no contradiction in the statesman's support for republican causes and his possession of black slaves. In Lincoln's thinking, Clay merited exoneration from the charge of hypocrisy on the issue of slavery. He had opposed its extension in the United States, attempted to establish a program of gradual emancipation in Kentucky, and cofounded the American Colonization Society. As was typical of most Americans in the 1850s, Lincoln, and in his lifetime Clay, simultaneously lauded the freedom promised by the Declaration of Independence and available to white citizens while not advocating abolition of slavery at the national level and elimination of laws at the state level that established racial discrimination. Both men expected that slavery would perish and that freedom for all men eventually would prevail. They based their faith on the knowledge that the United States had at the heart of its republican creed the statement that "all men are created free and equal."

Therefore, Lincoln adopted Clay as a model, both for his moderate political position between Garrisonian abolitionists and Southern pro-slavery apologists and also his statesmanship that taught global lessons of republicanism. Not only did the senator love his country as "a free country," and burn with "zeal for its advancement, prosperity and glory"; he also recognized in its development "the advancement, prosperity and glory, of human liberty, human right and human nature. He desired the prosperity of his countrymen partly because they were his countrymen, but chiefly to show to the world that freemen could be prosperous."[18]

As yet, Lincoln's life had offered few opportunities to apply his global thinking in his political efforts. For the two years after Kossuth's visit, the party line dividing Whigs from German Americans remained fixed even as the numbers of immigrants from the German states increased. By 1854, German Americans had become sufficiently numerous in Springfield that the main body of Lutheran worshipers split into English-speaking and German-speaking congregations. The German-speakers built a new church merely three blocks from Lincoln and Herndon's law office. In Cook County, home to Chicago, where Lincoln traveled frequently on legal and political matters, the foreign-born population expanded to nearly 72,000 by 1860, and Lutherans worshiped in twenty-one churches.[19]

In 1854, party lines began to dissolve and re-form because of the political maneuvering of the Chairman of the Senate Committee on Territories, Democrat Stephen A. Douglas of Illinois. Although he had no intention of doing so, he catalyzed party realignment by introducing a bill intended to organize the lands north of Texas and Indian Territory and west of Missouri and Illinois into territories. If passed by Congress and signed by the president, his bill would open the territories of Kansas and Nebraska to new settlers, provide a railroad route from Midwestern cities to the Pacific Ocean, and win Douglas supporters, he hoped, among northern and southern Democrats. He expected to set the stage for successful reelection to the Senate in 1858 and an eventual run for the presidency. He had miscalculated.

One provision of the bill lost the ambitious senator support among party members who thought the Missouri Compromise of 1820 had settled the question of where slavery could spread in the former lands of the Louisiana Purchase. The Compromise had prohibited slavery above the line of 36° 30′, which ran along the southern border of Missouri and then slightly north of the southern border of Kansas territory. Douglas's bill would permit settlers in the Kansas-Nebraska territory to vote whether their state should permit slavery or should prohibit it. This practice followed the precedent of the Compromise of 1850, which had established that if settlers so voted, slavery might be established in Utah and New Mexico territories, which the United States had acquired in 1848 from the Mexican Republic by the Treaty of Guadalupe Hidalgo. Douglas touted popular sovereignty, as the practice was termed, as the rule of democracy. The voters of a future state would decide on the question of slavery in their state. Many Whigs and members of Douglas's own party disagreed with the senator. They maintained that the Missouri Compromise had established a precedent that honorable men should never revoke for reasons of political expediency as, they charged, Douglas now was proposing. When he presented his bill to Congress, it stirred opposition from many German Americans who had emigrated in the past thirty years.

On March 2, Senator John Clayton of Delaware further embittered that immigrant constituency. To court anti-immigrant voters in his home state, Clayton had introduced an amendment to Douglas's bill that would have repealed the section in it that permitted male residents who had declared their intention to become citizens to vote in the new territories on territorial matters. Advocating their disenfranchisement, Clayton reasoned that national policy should not encourage foreigners to settle the Midwest, to vote in its territorial governments, or to participate in the writing of new state constitutions. His proposal had precedent. Congress previously had barred foreigners from voting in several southern territories, including Louisiana, Arkansas, and Mississippi, to name a few, before they had become states. In the 1820s, that stipulation had met little opposition.

By 1854, the situation had changed. German-American politicians and newspaper reporters, led by the Forty-Eighters, erupted in protest. Within the month, crowds gathered in at least five states to hear anti-Douglas and anti-Nebraska bill speeches and to rally around a burning effigy of the senator.[20] In Chicago, alderman Francis A. Hofmann asked: "What is the object of this amendment! To advance slavery, to prevent foreigners from settling in that country, and casting their vote in favor of free labor, and in opposition to that terrible system of making capital out of the blood of their fellow men."[21] Hofmann spoke for his fellow Germans who saw Douglas's bill and Clayton's amendment as discouraging foreigners, who opposed slavery, and encouraging settlers dependent on slave labor. Elsewhere in Illinois, Nicolay's Pittsfield *Free Press* published articles and editorials supporting the opponents of the bill. In South Carolina, although Francis Lieber could say nothing publicly without jeopardizing his position as a college professor, in private he called the bill "nefarious" and legislation "begotten in wickedness," and expressed his determination to decamp for residence in a free state.[22]

The German Americans' revulsion to the Clayton amendment and to the Nebraska Bill reveals their commitment to free labor and free land. The extension of slavery to Midwestern lands would erase their reasons for emigrating and reduce their attraction to a republican United States. Forty-Eighters, who had come to the United States in the very late 1840s or early 1850s, would be eligible to apply for citizenship and to vote in 1854 or at least by the 1856 presidential election. No prior allegiance tied them to the Democratic Party. Even when the Kansas-Nebraska bill passed without the Clayton amendment, the Nebraska issue lived in the public mind and continued as a central issue in the fall 1854 elections. Douglas's introduction of his Nebraska Bill unsettled party allegiances and rendered uncertain whether German Americans would maintain their loyalty to his party.

This revival of the so-called slavery question also motivated Lincoln to resume partisan activism. In his 1860 campaign biography, he recalled that Douglas's bill, or as he called it "the repeal of the Missouri Compromise," jolted him into action "as he had never been before."[23] As the fall political campaigns started in late August 1854, he joined the debate at a Whig meeting in Scott County, Illinois, where he spoke for Richard Yates, a long-time friend, lawyer, and Whig member of Congress running for reelection on an anti-Nebraska platform. Lincoln's support mattered because if elected, Yates would represent some areas previously represented by Lincoln in Congress. A sympathetic reporter wrote that the former representative's speech addressed the topic, now "uppermost in the minds of the people," demonstrating "the great wrong and injustice of the repeal of the Missouri Compromise, and the extension of slavery into free territory."[24]

In the elections of 1854, pro-Nebraska Democrats lost congressional races across the northern states, especially in those states with large German-American populations such as New York, Ohio, Pennsylvania, and Illinois. In Illinois, pro-Douglas Democrats had their influence reduced considerably. Whereas they had held a majority of the nine Illinois congressional seats, now they held four seats. Despite the anti-Nebraska sweep across the country, Yates lost to the pro-Nebraska candidate, a Douglas ally. The campaign had been dirty. In a pro-Yates speech, Lincoln insinuated that Yates's opponent secretly supported Know-Nothings and their anti-immigrant organization. Meanwhile, Democrats leveled the same aspersion against Yates. The candidate attributed his loss to the rumor, reputedly false, that he had courted anti-immigrant support when he entered a Know-Nothing lodge.[25]

Unlike Yates, Lincoln won his contest to represent Sangamon County in the Illinois legislature. Encouraged by the enthusiastic reception of his anti-Nebraska speeches early in that campaign season, he had entered the political fray to run for a seat in the state legislature. Yates's election defeat and his own election win let Lincoln see the potential strength of the German-American vote, its commitment to free soil, and its antipathy to nativism.

During the fall campaign of 1854, speaking against the pro-Nebraska candidates in Illinois cities, Lincoln had developed his arguments from reviewing U.S. history to expression of a moral commitment to free territory. For example, when addressing a German-American audience in Bloomington on September 12, he showed why since the Louisiana Purchase in 1803, certain states had entered the union as free states and some as slave states. His words persuaded a reporter in attendance that he was devoted to freedom for all men. At some point during the rally, an array of German Americans, most likely members of a political and athletic club known as a *Turnverein*, escorted Lincoln to the podium. In Prussia, Lieber's participation in a *Turnverein*, an athletic association that provided cover for illegal political meetings, had caused the authorities in Berlin to label him as politically suspect and threaten his incarceration.[26]

The next month, Senator Douglas came to Lincoln's hometown to open the state fair on October 3. People from around Illinois attended the annual event to exhibit their crops and animals, to exchange useful information, to socialize, and to politic. Just returned from Washington, the senator used the occasion to explain his proposals for the Kansas and Nebraska territories to fairgoers. From this largely rural and Democratic audience, he hoped for a sympathetic if not enthusiastic reception. The previous night in Chicago, a hostile audience of 8,000 people had pelted him with eggs and greeted his pro-Nebraska rhetorical points with jeers, eventually heckling the infuriated senator from the podium.[27] Even though his Springfield audience remained polite and engaged in no similar rowdiness, Douglas's message incited a more formidable opponent. After listening to the senator's justification of his policies, Lincoln announced to the departing crowd that anti-Nebraska Democrat Lyman Trumbull or he would respond the next day.

As he had promised, the following afternoon, Lincoln spoke to a packed chamber in the state legislature. Judging from newspaper reports, correspondence, and speaking invitations, anti-Nebraska constituencies received his words most favorably. Political antislavery activists now invited him to attend a meeting for the organization of a new, antislavery party in the state. In an age when political loyalties were deep-seated and usually lifelong, the cautious Lincoln declined for fear of restricting his political appeal. At this moment, a strong antislavery stance in Illinois would have alienated conservative Whigs and Democrats. He needed votes from these sources to satisfy his ambitions, which had expanded to include election by members of the upper house of the Illinois state legislature to the U.S. Senate. He hoped that the legislators would elect him to represent Illinois when its senate, presumably with an anti-Nebraska majority, reconvened in the first days of 1855.

Energized by Lincoln's powerful speech in Springfield, Whigs realized that Lincoln might reverse the sagging fortunes of their party. They urged the talented orator to follow Douglas around the state to rebut his message at each campaign stop. Lincoln did exactly this on October 16 in Peoria and planned an encore at Lacon on October 17. Probably for reasons of exhaustion, Douglas reneged on his speaking commitment in that town, allowing Lincoln the opportunity of returning to his home and family in Springfield before traveling to Urbana one week later for the beginning of the fall court term. By the end of the month, he was in Chicago.[28]

Horace White, a reporter from the *Chicago Journal*, which opposed Senator Douglas, had lured Lincoln to his city with the promise of an audience for a speech of eight to ten or even fifteen thousand. Lincoln followed the bait, in hopes of gaining the support of legislators in northern Illinois to his senatorial ambitions. The site at North Market Hall on October 27 held even more appeal. Lincoln would speak from the same stage from which the audience had hounded Douglas almost four weeks previously.[29]

Before the hour for the speech arrived, Lincoln dined with Isaac N. Arnold, a Democrat who was running in 1854 for the Illinois legislature under the banner of the recently formed Free-Soil Party, and George Schneider, owner and editor for the last three years of the *Illinois Staats-Zeitung*, the major German-language daily in Chicago and the voice of the Forty-Eighters. Through the *Staats-Zeitung* and other German-language papers, this ethnic community defined its identity in cultural, political, and economic matters. The previous March the newspaper had summoned its readers to a rally in opposition to the Kansas-Nebraska Act. Following several rousing speeches, enraged audience members had marched to Court House Square and ignited an effigy of the detested Illinois senator.[30] Subsequently, Schneider severed his allegiance to the Democratic Party and joined the recently founded Republican Party. The presence of Arnold and Schneider at the dinner as well as another event of that day demonstrate that Lincoln was now courting German-American voters directly.

After dinner the evening of the speech, most likely at the urging of Schneider, the trio dropped in to the photography studio and gallery located nearby the *Staats-Zeitung*, where Schneider's friend Polycarpus von Schneidau, another opponent of the Kansas-Nebraska Bill, created a memento of the occasion. The photographer posed the rising politician with a newspaper in his hands. Because the presence of reading materials in photographs of this time period is usual, not much significance resides in this selection of props. The name of the paper does hold significance.

Although scholars dispute the identity of the newspaper in Lincoln's hands, his holding of the *Staats-Zeitung*, the *Chicago Democrat*, or the *Chicago Press and Tribune* suggested political alliances in the making. Democrat Arnold and the Forty-Eighter Schneider accompanied Whig candidate Lincoln into the German-American photographer's studio. Lincoln and Schneider had attended the Decatur convention as had a representative of the *Chicago Press and Tribune*. At the meeting, delegates had affirmed the principles of the Declaration of Independence and that freedom was national "and slavery sectional."[31] If the *Chicago Democrat* was the photographic prop, then Lincoln posed with a newspaper owned by John Wentworth of Chicago, Democratic representative for Illinois's Second Congressional District. The previous March, his German-American constituents had pressured him to oppose the Nebraska bill. No matter which of the three newspapers appeared in Lincoln's hands, its presence still signaled that he was seeking support from German Americans and that he opposed the Kansas-Nebraska bill and the extension of slavery throughout the lands of the United States. Douglas's bill had promoted formation of a powerful anti-Nebraska coalition as Whigs, anti-Nebraska Democrats, and German Americans crossed existing party lines to make common cause.[32]

Lincoln's speech that October evening earned his auditors' enthusiastic approbation.[33] Historians believe that he delivered much the same address that he had made first at Springfield and repeated on October 16 in Peoria. Anti-Nebraska reporters, including the one who had lured Lincoln to Chicago, raved that it was a masterpiece "of argumentative power and moral grandeur, which left Douglas's edifice of 'Popular Sovereignty' a heap of ruins."[34]

When analyzing Lincoln's Peoria address of that fall, most historians of the contemporary period focus on Lincoln's reasons for opposing slavery, the Nebraska bill, and popular sovereignty. With foreknowledge of Lincoln's attention to his German-American constituency, this analysis addresses Lincoln's global message and appeal. From Lincoln's first publicly expressed criticism of the bill in his Scott County speech for Yates through his Bloomington speech, he had explained his opposition by rehearsing the history of congressional legislation with regard to U.S. territories from the Northwest Ordinance of 1787 to the present day. From his Springfield address on September 4 through the one at Chicago on

October 27, he added a second section that elevated the issue above politics and expressed his moral opposition to slavery and its extension. Since he did not mention once the words "German" or "immigrant" in any of these speeches, at least in their extant versions, he did not appeal directly to German Americans. They must have recognized implicit affirmation of their convictions, as the plaudits in German-language newspapers attest.

These affirmations appear after Lincoln finished with his usual thorough account of the territorial extension of slavery in U.S. territories. Then, he explained whether the admission of slavery to the Kansas and Nebraska territories through popular sovereignty, or whether, as he said, "the repeal, with its avowed principle, is intrinsically right."[35] To Lincoln's mind, Douglas's proposal of popular sovereignty for the new territories and the principles upon which it was founded was intrinsically wrong.

First, Lincoln disputed Douglas's contention that transporting slaves into the territories was no different from transporting farm animals to new lands. Although slaves were living property, he acknowledged, like horses or cows according to the laws of slave states, congressional legislation had abolished the Atlantic slave trade and imposed the penalty of death for its violation. Since the federal legislature had not enacted similar legislation for farm animals, the comparison proved that congressional legislators and most people, Lincoln argued, recognized the enslaved people as human beings.

Second, slavery itself violated the core principle of the Declaration of Independence: that government should depend on the consent of the governed. As Lincoln said in words that paraphrase vitiates,

When the white man governs himself that is self-government; but when he governs himself, and also governs *another* man, that is *more* than self-government – that is despotism. If the negro is a *man*, why then my ancient faith teaches me that "all men are created equal;" and that there can be no moral right in connection with one man's making a slave of another.... [N]o man is good enough to govern another man, *without that other's consent.* I say this is the leading principle–the sheet anchor of American republicanism.[36]

Lincoln's words thrilled his German-American auditors. They had left their homelands to make new homes in a country with a government to which they could give consent.

Three passages, only one of which is quoted frequently, show that by October 16, 1854, Lincoln thought globally because of conviction and because he had learned that this conviction would win votes. When discussing consent of the governed, he applied the principle "to communities of men, as well as to individuals."[37] If the Clayton amendment had remained in the Nebraska bill, the community of recently emigrated German Americans would have been disenfranchised in the new territories. Lincoln's choice of words affirmed to Forty-Eighters and their followers that this Whig would countenance no legislation that compromised the Declaration of Independence. Immigrants would retain their right to self-government.

Next Lincoln referenced a popular argument prevalent among proponents of Free Soil. He deemed the existence of slave labor and free labor in a territory as mutually exclusive. From the experience of his youth, he knew that poor whites in slaveholding states, such as the Thomas Lincoln family, had chosen to relocate in states that banned slaveholding. In his words about the Kansas-Nebraska territories, "We want them for the homes of free white people. This they cannot be, to any considerable extent, if slavery shall be planted within them. Slave States are places for poor white people to remove FROM; not to remove TO. New free States are the places for poor people to go to and better their condition."[38]

Finally, Lincoln demonstrated that he had become attentive to the transatlantic political community. He warned: "the liberal party throughout the world, express the apprehension 'that the one retrograde institution in America, is undermining the principles of progress, and fatally violating the noblest political system the world ever saw'." He had read these quoted words earlier in the fall in the *New York Times*, which had reprinted an editorial from the London *Daily News* critical of recent moves by southern Democrats, supported by the Franklin Pierce administration, to acquire Cuba from Spain. If Douglas could extend slavery via the agency of popular sovereignty into Kansas and Nebraska, as current diplomatic maneuvers by the Democratic administration suggested, Cuba might be next. These initiatives were soiling, as Lincoln put it, the nation's "republican robe." He called for a return to the principles of the Declaration of Independence so that the country would earn the respect of "lovers of liberty," in the United States and throughout the world. Concluding with a paraphrase of a psalm that his audience knew well, he declaimed, "the succeeding millions of free happy people, the world over, shall rise up, and call us blessed, to the latest generations."[39] The anti-Nebraska cause was larger than the United States or the current day. It mattered both to European liberals and to the God of the Bible.

Between the tumultuous election year of 1854 and Lincoln's run for the presidency in 1860, his commitment to the principles of the Declaration of Independence and to the constituencies attracted by that commitment continued to develop. In 1855, he explained in a lengthy letter to his great friend Joshua Speed, a pro-Nebraska Democrat residing in Louisville, Kentucky, his opposition to Douglas's bill as well as his revulsion at current political developments, especially at the growing anti-immigrant sentiment. His letter drew together his previous opposition to Russian intervention in Hungary and his sympathy for his newfound political allies: the German Americans of Illinois. He reasoned:

I am not a Know-Nothing. That is certain. How could I be? How can any one who abhors the oppression of negroes, be in favor of degrading classes of white people? Our progress in degeneracy appears to me to be pretty rapid. As a nation, we began by declaring that *"all men are created equal."* We now practically read it "all men are created equal, *except negroes."* When the Know-Nothings get control, it will read "all men are created equal, except negroes, *and foreigners, and Catholics."* When it comes to this I should prefer emigrating to some country where they make no pretence of loving liberty – to Russia, for instance, where despotism can be taken pure, and without the base alloy of hypocracy.[40]

He made his position public when he attended the February 22, 1856 convention in Decatur, Illinois, of anti-Nebraska editors, including John Nicolay of the Pittsfield *Free Press*, who were dedicated to forming a new political party that would be pro-immigrant and against the Nebraska bill.[41] After Lincoln's friend George Schneider proposed a resolution condemning the nativism of the Know Nothings, his fellow editors charged him with extremism. Chiming in to exonerate Schneider, Lincoln reminded his critics that the resolution reiterated the principles of the Declaration of Independence, which they celebrated.[42] Lincoln easily had recognized the parallel since Schneider was repeating the position that his friend had made in his Chicago address and 1854 campaign speeches. When Lincoln endorsed Schneider's resolution, the link between the German-American editor and the politician snapped shut. The coalition of the new party, the Republican Party, had coalesced.

Instead of oblique references to "communities of men" that Lincoln had made in his 1854 anti-Nebraska speeches, in the summer of 1858 and in the fall Senate campaign against incumbent Stephen Douglas, the self-identified Republican named names, especially those of immigrant groups. In late June, Anton C. Hesing and two other German-American politicians from Chicago's seventh ward invited him to their celebration of the Fourth of July. While declining the invitation, Lincoln offered "a sentiment" for the celebration. He greeted his *"German Fellow-Citizens,"* who stood "true to Liberty, not *selfishly*, but upon *principle* – not for special *classes* of men, but for *all* men."[43]

Appearing before a large crowd in Chicago on July 10, 1858, Lincoln delivered stirring words about the July 4 celebration of the previous week. He reminded the audience that recent immigrants to the United States – Germans, Irish, French, and Scandinavians – had not participated in the making of the Declaration of Independence. Yet, its central ideal, "all men are created equal," bound them to its propositions. This self-evident truth furnished, in Lincoln's words, "the electric cord...that links the hearts of patriotic and liberty-loving men together, that will link those patriotic hearts as long as the love of freedom exists in the minds of men throughout the world."[44]

Making a direct appeal to the more recent citizens in the audience, Lincoln told "you Germans" that his opponent in the race for the Senate seat had implied that the promise of the Declaration might not include them. Douglas's arguments reminded Lincoln, and would remind European immigrants, of "the arguments that kings have made for enslaving the people in all ages of the world.... [T]his argument of the Judge [Douglas] is the same old serpent that says you work and I eat, you toil and I will enjoy the fruits of it." If Douglas and slaveholders could say that the Declaration did not apply to African Americans, whom they called negroes, why could they not announce other exclusions? Either all men were created equal, or only some men were.[45] By implication, acceptance of Douglas's rhetoric would admit the serpent or the devil into the polity of the United States, or as many Americans then thought, the new Garden of Eden.

Several days later, Lincoln wrote his ally and supporter Gustav Körner that Douglas's endorsement of the Supreme Court Justice Roger Taney's Dred Scott decision had cost his opponent in the Senate race a few supporters. Douglas was trying to present himself as making "a triumphal entry into; and march through the country; but it is all as bombastic and hollow as Napoleon's bulletins sent back from his campaign in Russia."[46]

During August, Lincoln continued his campaign for the German-American vote with deeds and words. He told Körner that the response to his speeches had encouraged him and that he was ordering one containing his evocation of the Declaration printed or "done up" in German. On August 31, he criticized Douglas for implying that the Declaration of Independence did not include "the down trodden of all nations – German, French, Spanish."[47] At the next debate in Jonesboro, Douglas countered with ridicule of Lincoln's German-American allegiances. He flattered his native-born American supporters by averring that his opponent had but one friend, [Hermann] Kreismann. With this association the senator hoped to marginalize his opponent by linking him to a German American known for his extreme antislavery stance. Further, Douglas promised to extend the doctrine of popular sovereignty to new territories that the nation might acquire in Cuba, Canada, or South America.[48]

Even after Douglas bested Lincoln in the contest for a seat in the Senate when members of the Illinois legislature cast their ballots in January 1859, the defeated Republican continued to promote the cause of his new party. In the spring of that year, his German friends decided to test his adherence to the principles of the Declaration. Recently, the Republican-controlled Massachusetts legislature had amended the state constitution so that immigrants had to wait two years after their naturalization to qualify for the suffrage or to hold state and local office. In April, Lincoln had written Körner that the Illinois central committee of their party had concerns that the Massachusetts amendment would repel German voters from the party ticket in Illinois. Therefore, at their meeting, he had prepared a resolution to address those concerns. As confusion developed during the deliberations of the committee, Lincoln claimed, its members had neglected to vote on the document.

Several weeks later, Theodore Canisius, a German doctor from Springfield, who had previously founded a German-language paper in Alton, wrote Lincoln inquiring where he stood on the Massachusetts amendment. Canisius then published his response in his paper and forwarded it to Schneider's Chicago paper. Because newspapers at the time, even those with the largest circulations, reprinted stories, many Republican and German-language newspapers nationwide soon ran Lincoln's letter to the editor. During the 1860 presidential campaign, it also appeared in Republican campaign literature.[49]

Lincoln responded to Canisius's inquiry with his usual political tact, while his lawyerly mind discerned that in a federal union, the Massachusetts law could not affect and did not affect Illinois. The federal Constitution gave each state the power to define who could vote in its own elections. Election laws in Massachusetts pertained exclusively to Massachusetts.

His letter accomplished two purposes. It assuaged the worries of German Americans without insulting Massachusetts Republicans, and it accorded with the antislavery positions of both groups. Canisius and German Americans across the country now knew that Lincoln opposed the amendment's adoption "in Illinois, or in any other place, where I have a right to oppose it. Understanding the spirit of our institutions to aim at the *elevation* of men, I am opposed to whatever tends to *degrade* them. I have some little notoriety for commiserating the oppressed condition of the negro; and I should be strangely inconsistent if I could favor any project for curtailing the existing rights of *white men*, even though born in different lands, and speaking different languages from myself."[50]

When Lincoln and Canisius exchanged letters, they were scratching one another's backs. At the February Republican committee meeting, some delegates had thought that opposition to the Massachusetts amendment would carry more credibility if it originated from sources outside the party committee. Lincoln and his German-American friend assumedly had made a deal to bring about this result.

At the end of the month, the men signed a contract that suggested previous negotiation. Lincoln agreed to give Canisius use of a printing press that he had purchased. In return, Canisius consented to publish a German-language newspaper at least weekly in Springfield with an editorial policy that conformed to the existing platform of the Illinois Republican Party and the 1856 national Republican Party.[51] Consequently, the pact prevented Canisius from supporting either the Democrats on the one hand or, on the other, more extreme antislavery advocates. The radicals pressured for both immediate abolition in the slave states in addition to the more moderate position of slavery's exclusion from the territories. The paper, the *Illinois Staats-Anzeiger* (*Illinois State Advertiser*) began appearing weekly by July 1859. While keeping his relationship to the new paper secret, Lincoln sent samples or "specimen" copies to German-American officeholders and merchants, who might solicit subscriptions. To his benefit, Lincoln had gained the means of reaching potential German-speaking Republicans in the state capital and potential access to German-American voters across the northern states.[52]

While the Kansas-Nebraska Act impelled Lincoln into active opposition to the spread of slavery to the territories, it also impelled the development of Nicolay's and Lieber's careers. In the heated political climate ignited by debate over the legislation, Lieber found himself no longer able to keep private his antislavery and anti–states rights views, as the political mores of South Carolina required. The professor moved his family to New York City in 1856, and was appointed to the first chair in history and political science at Columbia College the following year.

Also in that year, Nicolay heard Lincoln speak at Bloomington and began to use his arguments in his anti-Nebraska newspaper articles. By 1857, Lincoln and nine others had contracted with the journalist to expand the anti-Nebraska coverage of the Missouri *Democrat* into southern Illinois, where Republicans needed to gain support in order to prevail in the statewide elections of 1858. Soon the journalist had gained employment as principal clerk for Ozias Hatch, who had been elected on the Republican ticket in 1856 as Illinois secretary of state. In Hatch's Springfield statehouse office, Nicolay and Lincoln saw each other frequently for games of chess, to discuss politics, and to review the election statistics contained in the secretary of state's official files. These meetings must have generated strong respect for Nicolay because in November 1858, Lincoln recommended him as a correspondent to Horace Greeley, editor of the *New-York Tribune*, as "altogether competent" and "trustworthy."[53]

By 1859, both Lincoln and Nicolay shared the articles of faith that drew German Americans to the newly formed Republican Party. The journalist often spoke of the foundation of the United States that he believed rested on the principle at the heart of the Declaration of Independence, namely "Liberty to all." At a Fourth of July celebration that year in Springfield, he delivered an address in German and declaimed that "the world had been striving for so long" toward the realization of this principle. Jefferson's words had become "a guide star of the world."[54] For Republican German Americans, allegiance to the words of the Declaration meant hallowing the phrases "all men are created equal" and "government depends on the consent of the governed." Opposition to the Nebraska Act and its Clayton amendment implied both opposition to slavery and its extension and support for immigrants' participation in citizenship, the suffrage, and the free land of the Kansas-Nebraska territories. The next year, at the Illinois Republican Party Convention, Nicolay later claimed, he had delivered the first speech in the state and nation to name Lincoln as the Republican Party nominee. He gave as the first reason for his advocacy Lincoln's belief in the Declaration of Independence.[55]

This document supplied the foundation for Lincoln's political thinking. During his career, he continually referred to the Declaration's words when explaining his core commitment. As the future president pronounced at Independence Hall, Philadelphia, while journeying to his inauguration in 1861, he had "never had a feeling politically that did not spring from the sentiments embodied in the Declaration of Independence."

He was right. Twenty-three years before, in 1838, he had cited the centrality of the Declaration's words to the promise of the United States in his address to the Young Men's Lyceum of Springfield. Fourteen years later in his eulogy to Henry Clay, the young politician expanded his interpretation of the phrase "all men are created equal" to include African Americans, and he decried how pro-slavery spokesmen recently had interpreted the document's words. Starting with South Carolinian John Calhoun, Lincoln charged, some Americans now thought that the Declaration was exclusively "the white-man's charter of freedom." Lincoln disagreed. From 1854 onward, while opposing the Kansas-Nebraska Bill and then Stephen Douglas in their 1858 debates, whenever Lincoln declaimed "all men are created equal," he thought globally. Not only did his understanding of the Declaration include both African Americans and white native-born Americans; it also extended the promise of equality under the law to immigrants, and especially to German Americans.[56]

# 5

## English Lessons

In 1961, the first year of John F. Kennedy's short presidency, the First Lady initiated a project to refurnish and refurbish the White House by reviving the historical presence of its interior decor. Jacqueline Kennedy wanted visitors to the mansion to view furniture and decorative arts with relevance to U.S. presidential history. She intended to restore to the public rooms objects and paintings associated with the mansion's previous residents. To assemble pieces with historical connections to the thirty-three men who had preceded her husband, she approached collectors of American furniture and decorative arts for donations of works with presidential associations. In the White House itself, Mrs. Kennedy and Lorraine Pearce, the newly hired White House curator, conducted so-called spelunking expeditions to its seldom-visited territories. Amid cobwebs and dust on rarely cleaned shelves in basements, storage rooms, and attics they discovered stacks of treasures.

Identification and restoration of some objects redeemed them from the status of junk. Mrs. Kennedy's team recovered, for example, the gold and silver flatware service that President James Monroe had ordered from France after British troops burned the White House in 1814 during the War of 1812, and the gilt-edged dinner service that Mrs. Lincoln had purchased and for which the press and public had found her guilty of profligate spending.

In search of forgotten masterpieces, Mrs. Kennedy and Miss Pearce also investigated those artworks that had accumulated on the shelves, walls, and windowsills in the mansion's sixteen bathrooms. In a powder room adjacent to a downstairs restroom they assembled marble busts of notable men that previously had dignified various mansion locations, both prestigious and humble. These included George Washington, Christopher Columbus, Amerigo Vespucci, Martin Van Buren, and John Bright.

The First Lady and the curator certainly recognized the likenesses of the Italian explorers and George Washington instantly. Identification of the bust of the less-well-known Martin Van Buren, Andrew Jackson's vice president and then president from 1837 to 1841, probably required some research.[1] Finally, only intensive investigation could have identified the likeness in Italian marble by British artist John Warrington Wood of John Bright, the orator for liberal causes and Member of Parliament. The Library of Congress archives letters telling of the arrival of the Bright bust at the White House in June 1866. A lawyer in Manchester, England, had commissioned the artwork as tribute to the relationship that had developed between the British MP and President Lincoln during his first term, 1861–1865. He was intending to present it to the president in the weeks following his inauguration to a second term in March 1865. (See Figure 5.1.)

Before arrival of the portrait bust at the Executive Mansion, the Confederate sympathizer and acclaimed actor John Wilkes Booth intervened. The shot from his derringer at Ford's Theatre on April 14, 1865, changed the course of U.S. history and the destiny of the bust. The donor then directed that the artwork be a gift to the nation "with whose future the name of Abraham Lincoln will be forever inseparably connected." From its delivery to the White House until 1902, the bust was displayed in the Cross Hall on the Executive Mansion's State Floor.[2] (See Figure 5.2.)

To Americans of the present day, John Bright is an unknown figure of unknown historical significance. No more than a few Americans familiar with nineteenth-century history, especially the diplomatic crisis between Britain and the United States during the last month of 1861, recognize his name. Surprisingly, during the first months of Barack Obama's presidency, his name surfaced once again in public discourse. A few commentators then suggested that the portrait bust of John Bright should be promoted from its current location in the White House to a place of prominence in the Oval Office. When personalizing his new office in 2009, Obama had ordered removed the bust of Prime Minister Winston Churchill by the noted British sculptor Jacob Epstein. The Churchill bust had occupied a place of honor in the presidential office since Great Britain had loaned it to President George W. Bush after the attacks of September 11, 2001. Its presence signified that fifty-six years after the end of World War II, Britain continued to stand by the United States. Instead of

FIGURE 5.1. Reputedly, Mrs. Kennedy found these marble busts in a White House powder room. Here the five portrait busts stand in the mansion's basement, with George Washington in the rear and, proceeding clockwise, Martin Van Buren, Amerigo Vespucci, John Bright, and Christopher Columbus. Photograph by Nina Leen/The LIFE Picture Collection/Getty Images.

honoring this country's special relationship with Great Britain, President Obama chose to personalize his office by recalling the history of emancipation and civil rights. He selected for display portrait busts of Abraham Lincoln and Martin Luther King.[3]

FIGURE 5.2. In the Kennedy White House, the bust of John Bright was displayed in the East Wing Visitors Foyer, where it flanked a portrait of Abraham Lincoln by William F. Cogswell. On the other side of the portrait stood a bust of President Martin Van Buren. Robert Knudsen. White House Photographs. Courtesy of John F. Kennedy Presidential Library and Museum, Boston.

Despite John Bright's current obscurity, from 1843 through the rest of the nineteenth century, he enjoyed a reputation for good deeds and good causes that extended from his homeland of Great Britain to the United States, Europe, and the British colonies. Americans knew Bright for his advocacy of free trade, support for extending the suffrage for Parliament, opposition to British involvement in the Crimean War against Russia, advocacy of emancipation, and support for the U.S. government in the Civil War. By 1864, the *New-York Tribune*, a paper with columns that reached a national audience, proclaimed that Bright stood as "the most indefatigable and influential British vindicator of our National struggle for existence."[4]

In the 1840s and 1850s, U.S. newspapers from coast to coast and from New England to New Orleans reported his doings and positions on these and other British issues. In the 1840s, he campaigned for abolition of the Corn Laws. Their taxes on imports of food grains severely affected low-paid British working families whose meager incomes barely covered the price of necessities. In the 1850s, his opposition to his country's war against Russia won positive comments from American Whig or Republican newspapers. Negative comments appeared in Democratic papers in the South and the North as well as occasionally in antislavery newspapers that condemned him for not opposing British manufacturers' purchases of slave-raised cotton.

Newspapers in the United States discussed or reprinted, sometimes in their entirety, his many speeches, especially when he favorably mentioned their own country. Bright frequently urged British politicians to learn from the example of their former colony, specifically its policies on suffrage and officeholding. Newspaper readers in the United States, especially Whigs and Republicans, would have known of Bright and his views even before his direct intervention in British-American relations during the Civil War.

Bright's speeches in the 1850s so lauded the United States that his critics in Britain accused him of wanting to Americanize their country.[5] He retorted that the United States originally had followed its mother country's lead by instituting a system of representative government. Then the newer nation had extended representation beyond that of Britain. By the middle of the nineteenth century, white male citizens of the United States twenty-one years or older enjoyed suffrage. On the other side of the Atlantic, suffrage excluded all but about 15 percent of males, especially urban, manual workers, until the Second Reform Act of 1867 doubled the electorate but still excluded poorer rural and urban workingmen. Despite the divergence of suffrage policies in the two countries, convergences increasingly prevailed in industry as technology advanced. On this score, Bright freely admitted that his country was Americanizing. From the United States, British manufacturers and farmers had imported inventions including the steam-powered printing press, the reaper, and improved brick fabrication methods.[6]

While Bright's pro-American statements received criticism in his own country, the press in the United States cheered. It applauded his praise for the accomplishments of its country's men of letters, including historians George Bancroft and John Lothrop Motley and poets William Cullen Bryant and Henry Wadsworth Longfellow, and appreciated when he favorably compared the statesmanship of U.S. presidents to that of British prime ministers from Lord North in the late eighteenth century through Lord John Russell in the nineteenth century.[7] Bright's appreciation of things American contrasted with his ridicule of the taxes that British workingmen paid to support their nation's standing army and the Church of England. With the rhetorical tactics of laud and shame, Bright sought to extend the franchise to his many countrymen who did not yet qualify to vote.

This chapter recounts why the bust of this Englishman, whom few in our generation recognize, came to reside in a White House powder room and be a candidate for placement in President Obama's Oval Office. It will look first at Bright's intercessions into the *Trent* Affair, a diplomatic crisis of the last months of 1861 and the first months of 1862, and then into British workingmen's reaction to the Emancipation Proclamation in 1863. During both these periods, the primary British exponent of American exceptionalism taught global lessons to the president of the United States.

Much evidence documents President Lincoln's strong admiration for John Bright, although the two men never met one another or even corresponded directly on any matter, including matters of national significance. Days before issuing the final Emancipation Proclamation on January 1, 1863, Lincoln had copied an extract from Bright's speech that borrowed from Thomas Gray's "Elegy Written in a Country Churchyard" to argue that the triumph of the slaveholding Confederacy did not belong in the destiny that he presumed God intended for the human race.[8] In 1863, Lincoln had placed a likeness of John Bright, probably a cabinet card, in the room he used as an office after receiving it as a gift from Joseph C. Grubb, a Quaker merchant from Philadelphia, who had been impressed by the Emancipation Proclamation.[9] Three months later, at Bright's behest, Lincoln pardoned Alfred Rubery, whose family resided in Bright's Birmingham constituency.

As a young émigré, the Briton had enlisted as a sailor on a vessel leaving San Francisco. Confederate President Jefferson Davis had issued a letter of marque to that vessel, thus permitting it to act as a privateer and to prey on U.S. ships and property. With advance knowledge of the privateers' plans, the Navy captured the ship immediately upon its departure from its harbor mooring. After the trial and conviction of Rubery and his fellow privateers, a federal judge sentenced them to ten years in prison and a hefty fine.

Upon learning of the sentence, Bright wrote Massachusetts Senator Charles Sumner, chairman of the Senate Committee on Foreign Relations, to request intercession on behalf of the imprisoned twenty-year-old, whom he called "wonderfully stupid." Sumner then contacted Lincoln, who, noting the youth and "highly respectable parentage" of the convicted privateer, granted a pardon with the condition that the young man promptly exit the country. Issuing the pardon gave the president an opportunity to emphasize the "public mark of the esteem held by the United States of America for the high character and steady friendship" of John Bright.[10]

On or soon after April 14, 1865, when the pockets of President Lincoln's blood-stained clothes were emptied, several objects were discovered in his brown leather wallet. (See Figure 5.3.) He had saved a five-dollar CSA banknote with an image of President. Jefferson Davis, in the lower right-hand corner. Additionally there were nine newspaper clippings reporting events of the last six months: emancipation in Missouri, Sherman's field orders for the march to Savannah, the 1864 National Unity Party (Republican) and Democratic Party platforms, and a letter from John Bright to Horace Greeley, editor of the *New-York Tribune*, recommending the president's reelection. On October 7, Greeley had republished Bright's prediction that Lincoln's victory in November would signal to the world that "Republican institutions, with an instructed and patriotic people, can bear a nation safely and steadily through the most desperate perils." Although Bright conceded that the president's first term had not been error free, he found that Lincoln had performed faithfully and admirably while showing "a brightness of personal honor."[11]

Lincoln folded Bright's words into his wallet and pinned his image onto the wall of his White House office for both immediate and underlying reasons.[12] During the diplomatic crisis of November and December 1861 with Britain, known as the *Trent* Affair, Bright had acted as a strong advocate for peace through a negotiated settlement of both nations' differences. Two years later, Lincoln had forwarded to Bright through Sumner his hopes for the resolutions that workingmen's associations in England

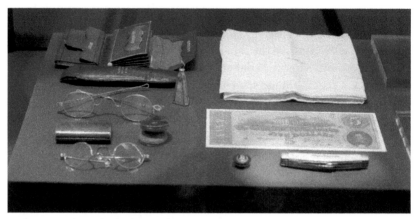

FIGURE 5.3. Lincoln had stored a clipping of a speech by John Bright in his wallet. The clipping advocated the president's reelection, and the wallet was among the objects found in his pockets after his death. The other objects were: two pairs of spectacles and a lens polisher, a pocketknife, a watch fob, a linen handkerchief, and a brown leather wallet containing a five-dollar Confederate note and newspaper clippings. "Contents of Abraham Lincoln's pockets on the night of his assassination on exhibit at the Abraham Lincoln Bicentennial Exhibit. Library of Congress Thomas Jefferson Building, Washington, 2009." Courtesy of Library of Congress, Prints & Photographs Division, photograph by Carol M. Highsmith [reproduction number, e.g., LC-USZ62–123456].

might adopt at public meetings in support of the Emancipation Proclamation. These events brought Bright and Lincoln into immediate cooperation and created the bond of affection that led to the gift of Bright's bust to the United States.

In late November 1861, the United States and Great Britain came as close to armed conflict as they ever would during the American Civil War.[13] On the eighth of that month, the *San Jacinto*, a U.S. sloop of war commanded by Captain Charles Wilkes, fired two shots across the bow of a British mail steamer in the Caribbean Sea and forced it to halt. (See Figure 5.4.) The ship was carrying James Mason and John Slidell, Confederate emissaries, to their posts in England and France. Jefferson Davis recently had appointed the first man to represent the CSA in London and the second as its representative to the court of Napoleon III in Paris. The diplomats had started their voyage in Charleston, South Carolina, on the *Theodora*, a vessel small enough to navigate in shallow coastal waters and avoid the Union naval blockade, currently attempting to close the harbor. With the benefit of a shallow draft and a foggy night, the ship had hugged the coastline and skirted Fort Sumter, which

THE " SAN JACINTO " STOPPING THE " TRENT."

FIGURE 5.4. "The *San Jacinto* Stopping the *Trent*." This steel engraving, which appeared in a British periodical, shows the USS *San Jacinto* firing on the HMS *Trent* and launching its boats to inspect the cargo of the mail ship.

guarded the harbor entrance and had been in Confederate possession since
April 14.

After evading the Union vessels enforcing the blockade, the *Theodora*
sailed to Havana, Cuba, a preferred port for Southerners, since the laws
of the Spanish colony maintained the institution of slavery. In Cuba,
the British consul entertained the diplomats before they boarded the
British mail ship *Trent*. Their intended destination was St. Thomas, Vir-
gin Islands, from where they would embark on the final leg of their
transatlantic voyage.[14]

Learning of the capture of the commissioners and their incarceration in
Fort Warren, a federal prison on George's Island, defending the entrance
to the harbor of Boston, Massachusetts, practically all residents of the
northern United States hurrahed. The military defeats in 1861 at Bull
Run in July, Wilson's Creek, Missouri, in August, and, most recently
Ball's Bluff, Virginia, in October had rendered despondent supporters of
the Union war effort. Now, they celebrated ecstatically that their navy
had seemingly won a victory, albeit one that involved the capture of just
two diplomats and their secretaries from a mail ship not armed for war.
Further, Mason and Slidell could serve as hostages to forestall the execution of captured pro-Union privateers that CSA President Jefferson Davis
had promised. After delivering the prisoners to a spacious and comfort-
ably furnished cell in Fort Warren, Captain Wilkes was feted in Boston at
a Faneuil Hall reception followed by a gala dinner attended by the leading
merchants and politicians of the state. Before a demonstrative crowd, the
governor, the mayor of Boston, and many other officials toasted Wilkes
and his crew. The celebration continued in New York City, where the
historical society honored Wilkes with a medal, and the City Council
with a reception in his honor.[15]

In the nation's capital, a crowd amassed to serenade Wilkes when the
captain returned to his home on H Street.[16] The Congress and members
of the Lincoln administration initially joined the celebration. The House
of Representatives adopted a joint resolution lauding Wilkes for "his
brave, adroit and patriotic conduct."[17] Suddenly, the formerly arcane
topic of international law commanded attention from the popular press
and the general public. The loudest voices in the public discussion lauded
the captain and justified his taking the Confederate envoys from their
ship and delivering them to military prison. International law in 1861
permitted contraband to be seized from a ship as it traveled between
neutral ports when it carried the flag of a neutral power in wartime,

such as that of Great Britain during the Civil War. If Wilkes's adversaries argued that diplomats were not contraband, the loud voices contended that the United States should not conform to international law because it should not apply in this instance. Among Lincoln's cabinet members, similar enthusiasm prevailed with few exceptions.

As news of Captain Wilkes's grand and giddy reception by the American press, public officials, and people reached Great Britain in late November, the British press and people responded severely. Diplomatic relations reached a fraying point. Along with titled Britons, merchants and manufacturers had caught the contagion of war and spread the fever throughout their country with the aid of anti–United States newspapers. Charles Francis Adams, the American minister in London, noted in his diary that the newspapers were becoming "more and more ferocious" and that the London populace were "all lashed up into hostility." British journalists termed the episode an outrage and ridiculed the heroic receptions with which Americans had feted the captain, pointing out that he was no Lord Nelson, who had triumphed over the Spanish and French fleets at the Battle of Trafalgar in the Napoleonic wars. The fever especially gripped members of the aristocracy, congregants of the Church of England, and manufacturers affected by the blockade. By early December, British anti-Americanism in the press became so intense that Minister Adams stopped reading the articles.

In response to the incident and the outcry by the public and the press, the British government promptly ordered more troops and warships to North America. Its war plans called for invading Maine and blockading key ports from Boston to Wilmington, Delaware. Having heard that a U.S. agent had purchased the country's entire reserves of saltpeter (a crucial ingredient in gunpowder), the British cabinet ordered an export ban on that commodity and subsequently issued an Orders in Council prohibiting the export of arms and munitions.[18]

In mid-December, five weeks after Captain Wilkes had detained the Confederate emissaries, news of the furious British reaction to the seizure of the Confederate diplomats and preparations for war halted the celebrations in the United States and turned jubilation to concern. Shocked by the possibility of war, investors in the northern states feared a precipitous decline in the stock market. They exchanged their paper shares in U.S. companies for gold coin and bullion. Responding to the high demand for hard currency, American banks moved to conserve their reserves of coin and precious metals by suspending exchanges of paper money and notes for gold. Foreign investors shared the Americans' fears. The French Rothschild's bank repatriated its American holdings to eliminate the possibility that the federal government would confiscate them. By the last two weeks of December, the question whether war soon would ensue with Great Britain, and consequently with France, dominated public debate.[19]

Informed Americans realized that the short-term interest of British commercial and manufacturing investors and business interests drove the British clamor for war. As 1861 ended, the Union blockade of Confederate ports and the Confederates' burning of their existing cotton supplies, approximately 2.5 million bales, had started to force slowdowns in British factories. In 1860, Britain had imported that amount of cotton from the United States; in 1862, the Confederate embargo had reduced cotton imports by 97 percent.[20] With British manufacturers' stockpiles acquired in the abundant harvests of the late 1850s now nearly depleted, by late 1861 the price of cotton had started to rise. Manufacturers could not accommodate that increase by increasing the price of their finished cotton products because a glut of these goods already met market demand. Facing lower profits, British manufacturers cut their costs. They reduced the employment of cotton workers, who accounted for about one-fifth of the British labor force, to four- and sometimes three-day weeks. John Bright, whose family owned textile factories, predicted that his cotton-spinning operation would close at the end of 1861. Many workers in his hometown of Rochdale would lose the means to support their families.[21]

The King Cotton strategy of President Davis suddenly appeared potent. In the first nine months of combat between the Union and Confederate armies, the military might of neither adversary had done much to end the conflict. Neither side had yet won a telling victory. The diplomatic crisis occasioned by Wilkes's taking of the Confederate emissaries now combined with the need of French and British textile factories for raw cotton to suggest that the major European powers might intervene to end the contest between the American states. To protest the detention of Mason and Slidell, cotton-hungry Britain now might declare war on the United States. As a consequence, its navy could break the blockade, divert the Union army to defend the border with Canada, and most likely encourage other European countries to extend diplomatic recognition to the Confederate States of America. Whether two Confederate diplomats remained in Fort Warren or proceeded on their mission to Europe could determine the future of the United States as a united country.

Even before mid-December, when news of the British reaction to the *Trent*'s seizure reached the United States, President Lincoln probably had realized that Captain Wilkes's capture of the Confederate emissaries called for deliberation and not celebration. His response resembled that of the majority of cabinet members. Initially he asserted that the United States would not release Mason and Slidell to complete their transit to Great Britain. A day or two later, he started to modify his opinion. Reputedly, he walked into Attorney General Edward Bates's office and lamented that worries about the diplomatic crisis had rendered him sleepless at times. Lincoln expressed his conclusion that his administration must determine what international law had to say. At that point, Bates was fully convinced that Captain Wilkes had the right to take the Confederate diplomats from a vessel of a neutral nation. Nonetheless Lincoln purportedly had begun to think, according to one memoirist, "If Wilkes saw fit to make that capture on the high seas he had no right to turn his quarter-deck into a prize court." This memory may be an exoneration of the president after the fact because it so closely resembles the wording of instructions subsequently sent to the British envoy in Washington.[22]

As Lincoln came to interpret the international laws governing seizures of vessels at sea, Wilkes would have been justified in stopping the ship of a neutral power with a cargo of contraband goods if he had left the contraband materials aboard and then escorted the ship to a prize court, presumably in the United States, where its fate could have been determined. Accordingly, the captain had violated international law when he removed Mason and Slidell from the *Trent* and then permitted the mail ship to proceed to its destination. Had Wilkes detained the Confederates, the *Trent*'s crew, and the vessel itself, he would have conformed to prevailing understandings of international law. When he removed only Mason and Slidell from the *Trent*, he took too little action and incited too much of a result.[23]

The president immediately responded to the counsel offered by Senator Charles Sumner, one of the few residents of Massachusetts who had not joined in the initial exultation over the Confederate diplomats' capture. The senator had both experience in conducting foreign affairs and direct knowledge of British attitudes through his correspondence with John Bright, who had sent him condolences after his near fatal caning in the Senate Chambers by South Carolina Representative Preston Brooks on May 22, 1856. To learn British views of American affairs, he also relied upon other leading members of the British Emancipation Society including Richard Cobden, a leader of the anti-Corn Law campaign, and the Duchess of Argyll, whose husband served in the British Cabinet. Meeting with the president nearly daily during the crisis period, Sumner reinforced the position of the more cautious cabinet members. Fearing the possibility of war with the world's greatest naval power, with them he advised the return of the Confederate commissioners. Sumner based his counsel on advice that he recently had received from John Bright, who had direct knowledge of British Cabinet meetings. He reported that the British Foreign Office would be mollified if it knew that Wilkes had acted independently and that the Lincoln administration had not authorized the seizure of the commissioners. Disturbed by the British government's dispatch of 11000 troops to Canada and suspension of shipment of war goods, Bright cautioned that such actions "point to trouble."[24]

To avert a catastrophic outcome, Lincoln first sought to persuade members of his cabinet that their interpretations of international law should yield to considerations of power. Some cabinet secretaries disagreed. Influenced by the outburst of American support for Wilkes, the secretaries of War, the Navy, and the Interior demurred in expectation of a loud protest from the public if the administration yielded to British demands. Faced with a British deadline of December 30 for releasing the Confederates, the cabinet met on December 25 and 26. In attendance at the first four-hour meeting, Sumner read his latest letters from Bright and their mutual friend Richard Cobden, Bright's ally in both the anti-Corn Law crusade and campaign for free trade. In the letters, Bright repeated his earlier advice to release the prisoners and seek international arbitration while noting that anti-American passion was receding from the intensity reached immediately after news had arrived of Wilkes's adulation. Despite this trend, he cautioned that "this Government is ready for war if an excuse can be found for it. I need not tell you that at a certain point the <u>moderate</u> opinion of the country is borne down by the passion which arises, and which takes the name of patriotism."[25] Further, Thurlow Weed, whom Seward had dispatched to Britain as an unofficial emissary and lobbyist for the United States, had confirmed Bright's warning. He had written Seward and warned Senator Sumner, in early December, that British manufacturing interests supported war with the United States in the belief that it would help them secure cotton for their factories and reopen markets for their finished goods.[26]

Although historians argue that Bright's warnings ignored the complexity of opinion toward the United States found among British Cabinet members, Sumner could not benefit in 1861 from these contemporary investigations into the nuances of opinion. He related Bright's alarmist concerns to the president and his cabinet.[27] Letters from the French foreign minister and the United States minister to France closed the case; they reported that no European country would support the United States if it decided to persist in detaining Mason and Slidell.[28] Reflecting upon the dire situation, Treasury Secretary Salmon P. Chase complained that the release of the emissaries made him taste "gall and wormwood." Still, the diplomats' release would send "to England and the world signal proof that the American people will not, under any circumstances, for the sake of inflicting just punishment on rebels, commit even a technical wrong against neutrals."[29]

Before the British deadline, Secretary of State Seward delivered to the British ambassador in Washington a lengthy diplomatic note that acceded to British demands for the prisoners' release and offered an apology. On the last day of the year, a tugboat collected the Confederate emissaries and their secretaries from Fort Warren and ferried them to Provincetown, Massachusetts, where they transferred to the British ship of war *Rinaldo* and continued on their mission to the capitals of Britain and France. Some reports suggest that the Confederate diplomats were unwilling to depart and had to be compelled to exit Fort Warren. Mason and Slidell realized that when an American prison no longer held them, the crisis in British-United States foreign relations ended.[30] Consequently, the tensions that could have prompted Britain to declare war against the United States would subside. No longer could the Confederacy count on this incident to bring victory through international diplomacy. Victory would have to be won on the battlefield, barring another international incident. (See Figure 5.5.)

As news of the diplomatic resolution to the *Trent* Affair leaked into newspapers in the United States during the last two weeks of the year, investors regained confidence, the stock market rose, and gold prices declined to pre-crisis levels. In late January, the British government removed the ban on sales of saltpeter and munitions to the United States. On the western side of the Atlantic Ocean, the British troop transports dispatched by the foreign office to defend the Canadian border against invasion by the United States reached the North American coast. With freezing winter weather, ice now choked passage of the vessels up the St. Lawrence River to the Canadian cities. In need of an alternate route, British officials asked Secretary Seward for permission to dock the transports in Portland, Maine. From there, the redcoats planned to proceed on the British-owned Grand Trunk Railroad, which ran from Portland to Quebec. Although the so-called British incursion across U.S. territory

FIGURE 5.5. Showing the British Foreign Secretary, Earl John Russell, on the left, James Mason and John Slidell in the ship, Secretary of State Seward on the shore, and a peeved-looking Jefferson Davis in the background, this cartoon (New York: E. Anthony, 1862) is entitled "The Great Surrender." On its reverse side, the subtitle: "American surrenders the Great Commissioners–Jeff. Davis surrenders his great expectations." Courtesy of Library of Congress Prints and Photographs Division.

troubled some Americans, reportedly Seward smiled when he granted the British soldiers permission for their travel through U.S. territory.[31]

A little noticed action by the Congress gave the diplomatic episode a dénouement. On February 19, three months after Captain Wilkes's so-called naval victory, the Senate "postponed indefinitely" consideration of the joint resolution to honor him, which the House had passed on December 2.[32]

In the calm following the storm of the *Trent* crisis, Bright reported in January that "the whole spirit of our Parliament and press and people is changed." Sumner learned, "There is now no disposition to interfere with you, or with the blockade, or to recognize the South."[33] Bright continued to warn against maintenance of the blockade of the southern states. While some influential pro-American Britons, such as Richard Cobden, recommended that the United States instantly raise its blockade of southern ports, Bright urged the capture of key southern harbors, namely Savannah, Georgia; Mobile, Alabama; and New Orleans, Louisiana. With their fall, he imagined that cotton, being grown and prepared for shipment even in wartime, could be exported from the United States to his country's factories. With maintenance of the blockade, he worried, the British government of Lord Palmerston might feign sympathy with the plight of workers thrown out of employment and then "join France in the vile attempt to ensure your permanent disruption."[34]

For Bright, the abolition of slavery promised both an end to the war and a means to win the war. As he explained to Sumner, with the abolition of slavery neither Britain nor France would dare intervene in the war or undertake mediation between the federal government and seceding states. To do so would be to contravene public opinion as the European powers would seem to be restoring slavery to areas where it previously had been abolished, thus committing a "horrible and shameful" crime "in the eyes of the world." In early 1862, he recommended that the federal government first undertake a program to compensate slaveholders in the border states of Delaware, Maryland, Kentucky, and Missouri who emancipated their slaves. If Congress failed to pass an act to provide for compensated emancipation, he worried that the Constitution would not permit abolition by the legislative process. Certainly, he wondered, a deviation from Constitutional action would be justified if that action saved the Union.[35]

During the winter and spring of 1862, the advice that Bright had offered Sumner in January became reality because it coincided with Union military operations. Several weeks after Sumner read Bright's letter, the naval campaign to capture the mouth of the Mississippi River began. After a successful assault in late April by ships commanded by David Farragut, U.S. land forces led by Major General Benjamin Butler captured New Orleans.

Additionally, the Lincoln administration took several other steps to put the Union conspicuously on the side of antislavery. Seward negotiated an agreement with Great Britain to suppress the African slave trade, which the two countries signed on February 17. The agreement, which Britain had wanted even before the war, permitted each country the right of search of the other's ships off the African coast and Cuba, where slavery still was legal, if a vessel was suspected of carrying a cargo of slaves. Then, the trial of the alleged slave-traders would be held in British or American courts that judges from both nations would staff.[36]

This treaty held both diplomatic and military significance. First, it showed that the two nations had stepped back from the threshold of war. It also signaled to the Atlantic world that the United States, although presently not fighting to abolish slavery, was taking action to stop the trade in humans, a necessity for the continuation of slavery as an institution. Militarily, the treaty relieved the U.S. Navy of patrol duty against slave ships active off the African coast. The navy could reduce its presence in Africa while increasing the number of ships enforcing the blockade of the CSA. Reinforcement of the blockade was crucial to its effectiveness. According to international law, nations did not need to respect a so-called paper blockade. If actual naval presence remained inadequate to close ports of the CSA, the ships of European nations might continue commercial relations with the CSA. The new treaty helped forestall that possibility.

In late November 1862, as the *Trent* Affair was beginning, Attorney General Bates had the opportunity to issue an opinion on whether free African Americans were citizens of the United States. Secretary of the Treasury Chase had raised this question previously when he queried whether African Americans active in coastal trade as ships' officers should be considered citizens when detained by the U.S. Navy. In reply, Bates's lengthy opinion argued that no provision in the Constitution determined the color of U.S. citizens. Given that the Constitution stood as the supreme law of the land, no state law could overrule its contents. Therefore, "a freeman of color," according to Bates, "if born in the United States is a citizen of the United States." As a London paper explained to its readership unfamiliar with the significance of this ruling, "The opinions in the Dred Scott case are pronounced to be of no more authority than the *obiter dicta* (words said in passing) of eminent lawyers, as the question before the Supreme Court in that case only involve the jurisdiction of the Circuit Court." Now free African Americans, if born in the United States, were entitled to all the rights and privileges of citizenship such as passports, which had been denied them until this ruling. Bates's ruling did not affect political privileges such as voting because the federal Constitution relegated matters of suffrage to the states.[37]

Additionally, acts of Congress during the winter and spring of 1862 began to shift the war from one to preserve the Union as it was. The states would be united but their union would be quite different with regard to race and slavery. In early February, Sumner introduced a bill to Congress that authorized the United States to send diplomatic representatives to the countries of Haiti and Liberia and to receive representatives from them. The president had recommended such action in his message to Congress of the previous December. Before 1861, U.S. senators and representatives, mostly from the seceded states, had objected to receiving black-skinned diplomats from those countries and thus thwarted their diplomatic recognition by the United States.[38]

Seward also wrote a telling letter to Charles Francis Adams, the U.S. minister to Great Britain, in February in hopes that he would convey his message informally to ministers of the British government. He reminded Adams of the diplomatic initiatives that the United States recently had taken with Great Britain, Haiti, and Liberia. Although admitting that the war was not being waged for slavery, he bragged that the army had turned the conflict into "an emancipating crusade." He drew attention to the flight of enslaved people into the lines of Union troops; he estimated 5,000 slaves in Virginia and 9,000 on the South Carolina coast. The crusade, he averred, had begun the previous May at Fort Monroe, Virginia, when Major General Butler had deemed three slaves who had fled their master "contraband" (a topic discussed at length in the next chapter). The Lincoln administration had not announced this crusade, Seward confided, because to do so would forfeit the support of Unionists not opposed to slavery.[39] These Union initiatives favorably impressed Europeans. By March, Henry Boernstein, the U.S. consul for the Port of Bremen, reported that Great Britain, France, and Russia had abandoned completely their plans for intervention. People had recognized that the United States had taken the first steps toward a "gradual emancipation," and these, Boernstein rejoiced, had "gained for us the sympathies of the civilized world."[40]

In Congress, Representative Isaac Arnold from Illinois, a longtime ally of Lincoln and foe of slavery's expansion into American territories, continued the Republicans' antislavery campaign when he introduced a bill on March 16 that would ban slavery from all places, such as arsenals, forts, the high seas, and territories, governed by federal laws and power. This bill would apply the antislavery and Republican credo "freedom national" across the United States and the areas such as waters bordering a state where state laws prevailed. Worried that some party members would oppose a bill that prohibited slavery in federal forts in slave states, including those that had not seceded, Republicans guiding the bill through House committees and floor debate edited it down to its essence. It would prohibit slavery exclusively in federal territories. On June 19, the president signed the bill into law that Congress had approved two days earlier. As historian James Oakes says, the one sentence of the act recalled the Northwest Ordinance and anticipated the wording of the Thirteenth Amendment. From the day that Lincoln approved the new law, it said, "there shall be neither slavery nor involuntary servitude in any of the Territories of the United States now existing, or which at any time hereafter be formed or acquired."[41]

On April 3, 1862, Congress took another notable step to abolish slavery in an existing area of the United States by passing an act to establish a program of compensated emancipation in the District of Columbia.[42] Lincoln's signing of this act into law on April 16 completed the initiative toward emancipation that he had made initially thirteen years previously during his congressional term of 1847–1849. A bill for emancipation in the district could win a majority of votes in Congress because many representatives who had previously lobbied against it had represented seceded states. After secession, the representatives of these states had withdrawn from Congress. Not surprisingly, some senators and representatives from the border states as well as peace Democrats, like Clement Vallandigham of Ohio, continued to oppose the emancipation bill, which passed the Senate 29 to 14 and the House 92 to 39.

Unlike Lincoln's 1849 emancipation bill, this one enacted immediate emancipation, did not depend on a vote of free people of the district, but did establish a fund for the colonization of freed slaves and African Americans. Similar to Lincoln's earlier bill, this one continued the established method of emancipation with compensation. In this instance, the federal treasury paid slave owners a maximum of $300 for each human possession. By the following year the federal treasury had spent less than $1 million, the sum that the bill had appropriated, in payment for 2,989 slaves. Three days after enactment of the emancipation bill, April 19, African Americans throughout the capital celebrated with a festive parade. In succeeding years, the date of the bill's passage became a day for annual celebration in the Washington African-American community.[43]

Despite the success of these initiatives, Lincoln's plan for compensated emancipation in the rest of the United States went nowhere after its announcement in his annual address to Congress in December 1861 in the midst of the *Trent* crisis. In mid-July 1862, border state congressmen met to consider the president's proposal. A majority responded, in the words of historian Eric Foner, with a "scathing rejection" of Lincoln's plan, which would effect, they thought, "radical change" in the current social system and its racial hierarchy. The refusal of border state legislators to endorse emancipation, compensated or not, gradual or not, forced Lincoln to initiate a new plan for emancipation in the war zone.[44]

As explained in the next chapter, he moved toward a plan for emancipation that relied on his powers as commander in chief rather than on congressional legislation. On July 22, he read a draft of his plan to his cabinet. Following the advice that Secretary of State Seward offered at that meeting to wait for a military victory before issuing the

Proclamation, Lincoln delayed its public announcement and spent the next two months waiting.[45]

On September 17, 1862, at Antietam Creek in Maryland, that victory came. There, the forces of General George McClellan turned back the 39,000 invading Confederate soldiers under the command of General Robert E. Lee. The battle is remembered as the bloodiest single day of fighting in the history of the United States with 23,000 casualties. Even so, the Union soldiers who died and shed their blood that day unknowingly did so for a greater cause. Five days after the Union victory, on September 22, President Lincoln invoked the powers that he possessed as commander in chief to promise emancipation to the more than 3 million enslaved people still held in areas under the control of the seceded states. That promise would become effective on January 1, 1863, if the slave owners in the CSA had not by then sworn their loyalty to the United States.

Lincoln had not expected that the Emancipation Proclamation would produce an outpouring of support from foreign governments or their peoples for the Union cause, as Americans committed to antislavery were hoping. The week before the crucial battle at Antietam Creek, a delegation of Chicago ministers had urged him toward emancipation with the argument that freeing the enslaved people in the Confederacy would capture Europeans' moral sympathies and avert their countries' intervention. The president demurred by projecting that emancipation would have limited potency in discouraging Britain and France from their intentions to intervene.[46]

In fact, the foreign reaction to the Proclamation during the three months after Antietam proved the Chicago clergymen wrong and even the president overly optimistic. In the ensuing months, Weed reported to Sumner that Napoleon III was distraught. The Proclamation meant that he had to change his arguments in order to reach his goals for France of increased military and commercial influence, extending even to territorial empire in the western hemisphere. He no longer could argue for intervention on the basis that the Union was fighting against the right of the southern states for self-determination. Emancipation as a cause trumped the cause of slaveholders fighting for a government that depended on their consent. With the Union now standing for emancipation, Louis Napoleon and his diplomats focused on the economic harm to the people of France that the closure of Southern ports caused. They also took offense at the increased import duties that the Republican-controlled Congress had imposed in the Morrill Tariff of 1861. Consequently, during the fall of

1862, France proposed to Great Britain and Russia that the three nations intervene in the American conflict.

To gain allies, the French government deployed a new argument. It contended that humanitarian concern about the sufferings of their own unemployed and the carnage of battles such as Shiloh in April and Antietam in September justified European intrusion into American affairs.[47] Their mediation between the United States and Confederate States would bring peace, stop the bloodshed, and return prosperity to the continent and its working classes.

In London, the leaders of Great Britain considered the French proposal.[48] The withdrawal of McClellan's troops from their assault on Richmond in the spring of 1862 and the defeat in December of the army under the command of General Burnside at the Battle of Fredericksburg, Virginia, showed that the Union Army might be able to repel a Confederate invasion into Maryland but that it remained incapable of making significant military advances into the territory of a seceded state, at least on the eastern front.

Even more terrifying to white Europeans, the promise of emancipation now portended a catastrophic race war such as had occurred in Europe's Asian and American colonies. British and French government figures feared that the American Civil War would become as catastrophic as the Indian Rebellion of 1857 – then known as the Sepoy Mutiny – or the bloody and vicious Haitian Revolution at the turn of the previous century. On both sides of the English Channel, leaders supposed that Lincoln had issued the Proclamation to paralyze Confederate military efforts in order to encourage a slave revolt. Indeed, in the third paragraph of the Preliminary Proclamation, the president had ordered that "the executive government of the United States, including the military and naval authority thereof, will recognize and maintain the freedom of such persons, and will do no act or acts to repress such persons, or any of them, in any efforts they may make for their actual freedom."[49] With the federal government's disavowal of the use of force to suppress slave rebellion, the promise of emancipation seemed ominously to encourage racial violence. Combined with these fears of race war, economic woes intensified and encouraged British involvement in the American conflict.

During the last months of 1862, British factories finally exhausted the bumper crops of cotton stockpiled from prewar days. Unemployment in the cotton textile industry rose toward 40 percent and poor relief roles were growing. Consequently, cotton workers in a few communities began to hold protest meetings that endorsed intervention.[50] The deliberations of the British cabinet on whether to intrude in the American Civil War became public in October. In a speech in Newcastle, William Gladstone, a Liberal party member of the cabinet who had for some months been predicting the un-uniting of the United States, propounded that no doubt remained that "Jefferson Davis and other leaders of the South have made an army; they are making, it appears, a navy; and they have made what is more than either – they have made a nation."[51]

Almost immediately, John Bright wrote Sumner that Gladstone had given "a vile speech" in which he became "the defender and eulogist of Jeff. Davis [sic.] and his conspirators against God and man."[52] In concert with European nations, the British government tried to end the conflict in North America. Numerous meetings and diplomatic exchanges between the French, Russian, and British governments in the first half of November produced no plan for joint action. Without such agreement, Britain would neither intervene nor present an offer to arbitrate the conflict, at least until after fighting resumed in the spring. When fairer weather arrived, either clashes between the two armies would make obvious the potential victor or a slave revolt would make obvious the need for European intervention. During the winter months no uprisings of freed slaves occurred to encourage European forebodings, although the Emancipation Proclamation did swell the stream of fugitives fleeing northward.

In Washington, Lincoln, cabinet members, and the military leadership fretted. They hoped that advances by the troops of Generals Grant and Rosecrans on the war's western front would convince the British leaders that the Union was progressing toward victory. General-in-Chief Halleck explained that Rosecrans's campaign to drive Confederate forces from middle Tennessee might be "the very turning point of our foreign relations."[53] Shortly after Halleck made this observation, the distressing slaughter and defeat of Union troops at Fredericksburg, Virginia, in mid-December placed additional weight on the foreign policy implications of the next battle.

A fortnight after Fredericksburg, from December 30 to January 2, Halleck's turning point happened at the Battle of Stones River, just west of Murfreesboro, Tennessee. When Rosecrans led his troops to the victory that won control of middle Tennessee and caused the Confederate army to retreat, the leaders in Washington could exhale in relief, and some British papers responded as expected by concluding that the recent battle "has shown that the Federals, if decently led, can fight as well as their antagonists, and can almost gain a victory." Subsequently, the commander in chief assured his general, "you gave us a hard earned victory which, had there been a defeat instead, the nation could scarcely have lived over." Lincoln feared that support for the war would have evaporated.[54]

After the Battle of Stones River and during the first six months of 1863, military progress or the lack of it kept the eventual outcome of the war in doubt. In the western theater, troops under the command of Brigadier General Grant had laid siege to Vicksburg, Mississippi, the last barrier to reestablishing Union control of the Mississippi River. Meanwhile, in the eastern theater at Chancellorsville, Virginia, the Army of Northern Virginia had once again routed the Army of the Potomac. As they had the previous September, General Lee and his soldiers were marching northward in search of a decisive victory on northern soil. That campaign would end at Gettysburg, Pennsylvania, during the first week of July.

As European plans to intrude into the American conflict lessened in the last two months of 1862, American merchants and businessmen took action to relieve the food shortages that unemployed Lancashire cotton mill workers were experiencing. Noting earlier efforts to organize a relief program, Bright had advised Sumner that the sending of food to relieve the want of unemployed textile workers, some of whom Bright's mills had employed, "would have a prodigious effect in your favour here. Our working-class is with you and against the South; but such a token of your good will would cover with confusion all those who talk against you."[55]

Food relief from New York City began to flow to England in the first months of 1863. In early December, leading merchants and businessmen of the city had formed a committee to collect and organize the relief, and by mid-January, three ships had sailed filled with at least 25,000 barrels of flour and other relief supplies.[56] Contributors emphasized not only that they sympathized with the sufferings of the British textile operatives but also that the textile operatives were true friends of the United States. As Seward's foreign emissary Thurlow Weed, who had witnessed the suffering caused by unemployment in the textile districts of England, wrote when he made his substantial contribution of $1,000 to the cause, the workingmen and their representatives had resisted numerous efforts of the British commercial classes and cotton manufacturers "to secure their cooperation against the blockade and in favor of intervention."[57] By late February, Weed began to hear reports of "better feelings" toward the United States. Sensing encouragement, he wrote Seward about the shift in public opinion. He now felt "nine-tenths of the English people would rejoice to see us successful." Possibly, he had heard of meetings in Lancashire. In Bury and Rochdale, Bright's hometown, unemployed cotton workers and their families had met to offer thanks for the relief supplies and their approbation of the president's emancipation announcement. By March, Minister Adams in London was confiding to his diary that a revolution in opinion had occurred and neutralized the British "desire to meddle."[58]

Optimism in the United States rose as the economic distress in Great Britain occasioned by the King Cotton strategy dissipated. Harvests from India and northern Africa had begun to replace previous imports to the Continent from the United States and supplied about half of the 3 million bales previously consumed annually by British manufacturers. The deficit of raw cotton called forth more production of flax and wool and brought increased prosperity to the producers of those crops across the English countryside. Further increased demand from the United States for war matériel stimulated British industrial prosperity and increased trade.[59]

Simultaneous with American relief efforts for the unemployed Britons, British antislavery societies, nonconformist ministers, Quakers, and, of course, Bright encouraged pro-Union meetings and expressions of sympathy. Minister Adams soon wrote Seward that efforts were in progress for "a more effective organization of the antislavery sentiments" to promote his country's interests. In early February, Protestant clergy in France sent their British brethren a missive lamenting that success of the South "would cause the angels in heaven to weep." They urged the English clerics to pray and petition so as to stir up a "great and peaceful demonstration" until every black man was free and "upon equality with the white."[60] During the spring of 1863, the London Emancipation Society and the Union and Emancipation Society sponsored meetings and submitted pro-Union petitions to Parliament. These petitions addressed multiple issues, including the construction of ships for the Confederate navy then in progress.[61]

Alongside these middle-class liberals and antislavery activists' strong support for an anti-Confederate campaign, workingmen's support for Lincoln and the United States arose independently and prolifically.[62] Starting in late December 1862, British laborers organized themselves to praise Lincoln's intended signing of the Emancipation Proclamation on January 1. They affirmed their previous support for the president, free labor, and the United States while confirming their opposition to Davis, slave labor, and the Confederate States. Over the next five months, they held meetings in numerous cities throughout Britain and Scotland, among them London, York, Halifax, Birmingham, Sheffield, Coventry, Bristol, Bath, Glasgow, Cobham, Carlisle, and Chesterfield.[63] At these meetings, workingmen assembled, debated, and approved resolutions and sent delegations to deliver their petitions to the U.S. minister to Great Britain, Charles Francis Adams.

At these meetings, resolutions sometimes were presented that criticized the motives that their authors supposed had motivated the Emancipation Proclamation. These anti-Lincoln resolutions generally followed the editorial line of the *Manchester Guardian* or the *Times* of London. It had called the Emancipation Proclamation a farce because it freed no slaves immediately and promised freedom to slaves only in areas not yet controlled by the Union military while allowing slaves to be held in states loyal to the Union.[64] At some assemblies of workingmen, such arguments were repeated and embodied in proposals. At a meeting in Scotland, a motion criticized the motive behind the Proclamation as ignoble because military necessity had been the force behind it. As further proof of Lincoln's base motives, the motion pointed to the laws in northern states that discriminated against African Americans. The critical resolution did not pass because a majority of the workingmen present supported motions that praised Lincoln's "firm resolution" in offering a proclamation of freedom. They predicted that the Proclamation would make "the name of Abraham Lincoln to be revered by posterity."[65]

In Manchester, at the first and most famous pro-Union meeting of British workingmen on December 31, 1862, the workingmen of that city, sent through their mayor to Minister Adams an address that expressed their support for the "decisive steps" the United States had taken toward making real the well-known phrase of the Declaration of Independence: "all men are created equal." They expressed sympathy with the Union because of their positive conviction that the victory of the Union would "strike off the fetters of the slave."[66]

After Lincoln had received the first two petitions from British workingmen, he responded with public papers, the first to the workingmen of Manchester, on January 19, and the second to the workingmen of London. These letters received widespread notice with many, if not most, British newspapers publishing them. The president assured his petitioners that he knew of and deplored the sufferings caused by the cotton drought in their city and throughout Europe. In his interpretation, the actions of disloyal citizens who wished to erect a government based on human slavery had brought about the workers' hardships. He presumed his country had earned the "forbearance of nations" during the war because it was "generally regarded as having been beneficent toward mankind" in its past behavior. In the current war it stood for preservation of its foundation of "human rights" – the only reliable basis for free

institutions throughout the world. He concluded that a great duty had
devolved to the American people; they had to prove "whether a government, established on the principles of human freedom, can be maintained
against an effort to build one upon the exclusive foundation of human
bondage."[67]

Besides these public letters, Lincoln also communicated his appreciation and views that the United States was fighting a universal crusade
through his diplomatic intermediaries, Secretary Seward and Minister
Adams. His petitioners learned of his sympathy with the plight of working people having to endure "the interruption of industry" and his belief
that the maintenance of the United States' government and its free institutions held great importance "to all other nations."[68]

After still more petitions arrived from England, the president must
have realized their publicity value as he attempted to direct the sentiments that the workingmen expressed. In April, he sent through Sumner
to Bright a model proposal that future petitioners might adopt. It proposed that no state that adopted as its "fundamental object to maintain,
enlarge, and perpetuate human slavery . . . should ever be recognized by,
or admitted into, the family of Christian and civilized nations." These
words referenced CSA Vice President Alexander Stephens's well-known
speech of March 1861, in which he propounded that the cornerstone of
the new country rested "upon the great truth that the negro is not equal
to the white man; that slavery – subordination to the superior race –
is his natural and normal condition."[69] This extraordinary, precedent-
breaking effort of a U.S. president to influence another country's domestic events appears to have been superfluous. No evidence exists to prove
that any British workingmen's organization ever explicitly recognized
and followed Lincoln's lead.[70] Still, after reading Lincoln's message,
Bright responded, "nearly every meeting held here has been in accordance
with it."[71]

Even before Lincoln's attempt to shape British public opinion, workingmen had been voting for resolutions with sentiments similar to those
that he had suggested, although they held less global import and sometimes implied self-interested motives. At a March meeting, British workingmen congratulated the North for maintaining "the interests of freedom
and humanity by preventing the establishment of a military power in the
South, based upon slavery, and whose existence must not only prove
inimical to free labour, but seriously endanger the peace and tranquility
of our West Indian colonies."[72] For their part, workingmen sometimes
selected John Bright to chair their meetings, and he was chosen to lead

a delegation that presented a petition supporting the United States to Minister Adams in May.[73]

R. J. M. Blackett, a historian who has analyzed British sentiment toward the United States and the Confederacy, asserts that presentation of pro-Union petitions carried immense "politically symbolic weight." Because they were disenfranchised, the workingmen could not influence politics directly by their votes. They possessed only a few peaceful ways in which to express their opinion. Their most important means was the public meeting at which they debated and approved petitions that their delegation subsequently presented to an official in a public ceremony. Unlike meetings of Confederate adherents that usually were closed to the public, the presentations of workingmen's antislavery petitions to Minister Adams were public and widely covered by newspapers.[74] Confederate supporters in England attempted to diminish the impact of such meetings by accusing Adams of promoting them, a charge that the minister denied, even assuring Seward that he was doing everything in his power to avoid the appearance of sponsorship.[75]

Attending the pro-Union meeting of workingmen at Exeter Hall in London in late January 1863, Minister Adams found the enthusiasm for the union "most extraordinary," and noted that the moment had arrived to "checkmate" the aristocracy. *The Illustrated London News* confirmed Adams's impression by reporting that when someone in the packed audience cried "Emancipation and Union... there broke forth the most tremendous outburst of popular enthusiasm it has ever been our fortune to witness. It could not stop, but went on and on, the whole audience having leaped to their feet with hats and handkerchiefs waving, having apparently only waited for some such signal to relieve themselves from the almost painful because suspended enthusiasm with which they overflowed."[76]

Impressive material evidence of workingmen's sentiment for Lincoln and Emancipation exists at the National Archives and Records Administration, which houses the petition to Lincoln from the workingmen of Birmingham, Bright's parliamentary constituency since 1858. The huge scroll contains a minimum of 13,500 signatures and extends (I estimate) 21 feet in length. The signatures were collected on columned ledger sheets glued end-to-end and rolled into a mammoth scroll for delivery to the president.[77]

Presenting the petition to Minister Adams in London on February 27, the Birmingham delegation suggested that more than twice as many signatures would have been collected if additional time had been allotted for the project, if more than one hundred posters had advertised it, and if notices had appeared in the city's newspapers. The message to which the signers added their handwritten names expressed their abhorrence of the Confederacy. Even before Lincoln's suggestion, the Birmingham petitioners referenced Stephens's cornerstone speech, which previously had been widely reprinted in pro-Union British newspapers. In the petitioners' minds, the Confederacy deserved condemnation as the first nation in world history to place at its basis "slavery and the extension of slavery." One Birmingham petitioner, Charles Vince, emphasized the message of the resolution by penning a denunciation after his name, "in utter and perpetual detestation and abhorrence of the South."[78]

Responding to the Birmingham petition via intermediaries, Lincoln took special notice of its message, perhaps because John Bright represented the petitioners in Parliament. He also had to have been impressed by its size, although he noticed merely its words in his response. The men of Birmingham, he praised, had seen the current war in its proper light, as testing whether labor should be "free and compensated" or "involuntary and unpaid." Lincoln effusively thanked these petitioners "so well known to all the world by their genius, their arts, their industry, their political sagacity, and their indomitable devotion to freedom, in support of his judgment upon a question that affects so deeply the interests of our country and the prospect of civilization throughout the world."[79]

In response to the Emancipation Proclamation, several U.S. ministers currently serving in Europe noticed a shift. After a debate in the House of Commons about the government's position on war cruisers being built in British shipyards for the Confederacy, Adams remarked that the American struggle was dividing that country's opinion on the war in a "horizontal manner." James Pike, minister to the Netherlands, developed that point on what he termed "the American question" by observing its danger for the ruling classes. When secession had first occurred, European liberals saw its cause as a misrepresented or unrepresented people breaking away from "some form of oppression. But everybody can understand the significance of a war where emancipation is written on one banner and slavery on the other."[80]

On July 4, 1861, five months before the *Trent* crisis, President Lincoln had explained to the Congress why the United States was fighting to maintain the Union. In that address, he famously declared that the present war was "essentially a People's contest. On the side of the Union, it is a struggle for maintaining in the world, that form, and substance of government, whose leading object is, to elevate the condition of men – to lift artificial weights from all shoulders – to clear the paths of laudable pursuit for all – to afford all, an unfettered start, and a fair chance, in the race of life."[81] He continued by elaborating one of his major reasons for issuing this statement. No "common soldiers" had left their posts to fight for the seceded states. In contrast, their officers in the Army and Navy had turned on their nation "in large numbers," the most notable of whom was Virginian Robert E. Lee.[82] Among the many lessons offered by British reaction to the capture of Mason and Slidell and the Emancipation Proclamation was the demonstration that the working people of Great Britain, its common people, understood as did the common soldiers of the United States that a war was being fought for a cause larger than reunification of the United States. It was being fought for free labor. As Lincoln had said on July 4, 1861, the fight to preserve the Union was a people's contest.

Because of the British reaction to the Proclamation, by the spring of 1863 President Lincoln had learned that supporters of the Union cause lived on both sides of the Atlantic. During the *Trent* Affair, John Bright had described to Lincoln the forces in Britain that supported and those that opposed the United States. Subsequently, the petitions of British workingmen and antislavery advocates had demonstrated that the struggle for free labor transcended national boundaries and possessed global significance. In Lincoln's responses to his British supporters during the winter and spring of 1863, he rehearsed his conviction that the United States was engaged in a conflict with worldwide import. The speaker who proclaimed at Gettysburg that the Union was fighting so that a government of free men should "not perish from the earth" had received eleven months previously petitions from British workingmen. They had expressed the same hope for the future of the globe.

As Bright had predicted to the residents of Rochdale, his hometown, many of whom derived their income from cotton manufacturing, in August 1861, a month after the disastrous battle of Bull Run, "the people of England... will have no sympathy for those who wish to build up a great Empire on the perpetual bondage of millions of their fellow men."[83] John Bright's strong advocacy of the Union cause lay behind the arrival of his portrait bust at the White House. His counsel also promoted the cause of emancipation that Lincoln officially endorsed on January 1, 1863.

If the bust of Lincoln now sits in the President of the United States' White House office because of the Emancipation Proclamation, then indirectly, John Bright helped ensure that placement. While **the special relationship** between Great Britain and the United States grew from those nations' collaboration for the defeat of the Axis Powers in World War II, the presence of Lincoln's portrait bust perpetuates the commemoration of a special relationship that originated some seventy-seven years before World War II.[84] It was formed during the Civil War, when a government based on republican principles might have disappeared from the globe. As President Lincoln wrote to the workingmen of Manchester in response to their letter praising the Emancipation Proclamation, "whatever misfortune may befall your country or my own, the peace and friendship which now exist between the two nations will be, as it shall be my desire to make them, perpetual."[85]

# 6

# Lessons from International Law

In August 1863, a month after the decisive Union victories at Gettysburg, Pennsylvania, and Vicksburg, Mississippi, John Hay, Lincoln's private secretary, felt sufficiently confident to predict: "the rebellion is nearing its close."[1]

Heartened by those battlefield successes, artist Francis Bicknell Carpenter dreamed of a monumental painting to commemorate a pivotal event in United States and world history. (See Figure 6.1.) It would depict the moment, almost a year previously, on July 22, 1862, when, he believed, a "new epoch in the history of Liberty" had begun. When Lincoln announced his plans for emancipation to his assembled cabinet members, Carpenter projected, the Union started toward its triumph and slavery's end. The ardent antislavery supporter, who had voted for John Frémont in 1856, recalled that he always had thought that victory over a rebellion "with slavery at its corner-stone" required the Union to strike "a death-blow at the institution itself." When Lincoln composed and read the Emancipation Proclamation to his cabinet, Carpenter believed that the Lincoln administration had armed itself to strike such a blow.[2]

The artist envisioned the conflict with the Confederate States in apocalyptic, Christian terms as the battle between the rebel angel Lucifer and the loyal angels of God. Carpenter located the moment of right, when the evil angel had to face his inevitable defeat, with Lincoln's first reading of the Emancipation Proclamation to his cabinet, in the cabinet room at the Executive Mansion. By naming July 22 as the date when the federal government embraced the cause of right, or the side of the angels, Carpenter moved the story of the Emancipation Proclamation away from battlefields, the agency of the enslaved people themselves, and the actions of

FIGURE 6.1. Francis Bicknell Carpenter, "First Reading of the Emancipation Proclamation by President Lincoln" (1864). Oil on canvas, 274.3 cm by 457.2 cm. Courtesy of U.S. Senate Collection, U.S. Senate. In color at http://www.senate.gov/artandhistory/art/common/image/Painting-33_00005.htm.

Congress. Moreover, he minimized the role of Congress, the military, and the Lincoln administration as it proceeded during its first fifteen months in office to surround the slave South with areas of freedom, for example by joining with Great Britain to end the slave trade. By centering the painting on Lincoln and his cabinet in the Executive Mansion, Carpenter created a visual polemic awarding the Emancipation Proclamation and its author the central role in the ending of human slavery in the United States. His painting helped mythologize Lincoln as the "Great Emancipator" while leaving unnoticed, as this chapter will show, crucial events of 1861 and 1862.

Carpenter benefited from his strong friendships in the community of antislavery activists and Republican legislators to transform his apocalyptic vision into the material reality of oil paint on canvas. First, he persuaded politicians in the Washington antislavery network to lend their efforts to win the president's cooperation. After they succeeded, Carpenter, by his telling, fortuitously encountered a wealthy former acquaintance who simply happened to appear one day outside the artist's Manhattan studio. This serendipitous meeting clinched financial backing for production of the commemorative painting. Having gained both presidential cooperation and funding, the artist arrived at the Executive Mansion on February 6, 1864, to begin his project.

Six months later, on July 12, 1864, in the state dining room, where Lincoln had permitted Carpenter to set up a temporary studio, the artist unveiled to the president his completed, huge (108 × 180 inches) work. Responding to pressure from a curious public desirous of viewing the monumental work, Lincoln and the artist displayed the "First Reading of the Emancipation Proclamation of President Lincoln" in the mansion's East Room on July 26 and 27. Examining the artwork, Lincoln told Carpenter, "there was little to find fault with." Seeking to root out those "little" faults, the artist encouraged the president to scrutinize the details.[3]

The top section of the painting contains portraits of the president and his seven cabinet members assembled around a rectangular table with a draft of the Proclamation in the president's left hand and a white feather quill in his right one. Facing the painting, we see that Carpenter sat Lincoln in the left foreground at the head of the cabinet table. The left-hand two-thirds of the canvas contain the principal cabinet members, who also took leading roles in the drafting and presentation of the document. Secretary of State Seward sits across from the president while a copy of the Constitution lies between the two men. With his right hand extended on the table toward the two documents, Seward directs his attention toward the chief executive and subtly points. Carpenter depicted him possibly in the midst of suggesting to the president that he delay the Proclamation's issue until the Union army won a military victory. Anticipating foreign reaction, the secretary had wished that France and England should not be allowed to conclude that the Proclamation was issued as a means to rescue a losing cause. With Seward's gesture, the artist created a visual narrative link between the Constitution and the Proclamation.

Secretary of the Treasury Salmon P. Chase stands to the president's right across from Secretary of War Stanton, who is seated. Behind the table to Lincoln's left sits Secretary of the Navy Gideon Welles, while the remaining three cabinet members – Attorney General Edward Bates, Postmaster-General Montgomery Blair, and Secretary of the Interior Caleb B. Smith, who played supporting roles in this particular drama – occupy positions that form a triangle, thereby accentuating the significance of Seward in the foreground. Two of these cabinet members opposed the Emancipation Proclamation. Both officials resigned their positions before Carpenter had completed his painting: Smith in December 1862, and Bates on June 30, 1864.[4]

Carpenter eagerly solicited the president's opinion on his masterwork. He recalled that Lincoln deemed the portraits of his cabinet members and himself "absolutely perfect." The artist appreciated his effort as more than a collection of portraits. He had aimed at accuracy as he visually narrated how Lincoln had come to issue the Proclamation. So he was curious about the president's response to his representation of the cabinet room and its contents. By their presence and positioning of these contents, the painter had added detail and narrative to the composition. Newspapers, books, and folios of maps rest against the cabinet table legs and the chairs surrounding it. Carpenter's selection of objects to include in his painting, especially his choice of two particular books, tells a crucial story about Lincoln's global education and how he came to understand the presidential powers that conferred the authority for him to emancipate the enslaved people in Confederate-held territory.

Carpenter assigned these objects in the painting's lower third to the role of supporting characters in his historical composition. The narrative told by these significant objects leads us to understand how Republican party adherents, including Lincoln and the artist, wanted to create a history of wartime emancipation that placed the chief executive in its starring role, an especially significant role in the election year of 1864. After constructing the story suggested by these objects, we will investigate in greater depth the executive powers that these books assigned to the president.

When viewers face the canvas, the objects in its lower third reside in an approximate triangle extending from the bottom left corner of the painting to its bottom right corner. Selecting the mid-point of the triangle base and extending a vertical line through it, perpendicular to the floor and the ceiling, our eyes follow a line passing upward through Seward's foot, behind Welles's shoulder, and through the left side of the frame around an image of President Andrew Jackson.

In Lincoln's office, the portrait, reputedly an "old discolored engraving," did hang over the mantel, as Carpenter depicted. He positioned the people and the objects in his painting to accentuate Jackson's image in its center. After all, Jackson belonged to the Democratic Party, is considered its founder, and owned slaves. His likeness seems an odd choice for inclusion in a monumental painting commemorating emancipation, even though the globes of the gas lighting device suspended from the ceiling somewhat veil his image.[5] Still, they do not totally obscure Jackson's being at the center of things.

During the Civil War years, viewers of the painting knew what the presence of Jackson meant. On January 8, 1861, while president-elect Lincoln remained in Springfield and maintained his office in the Illinois State House, the Democrats in the Illinois legislature proposed a resolution to honor General Jackson for his victory in New Orleans on that day in 1815 and to adjourn in his honor. In response, the Republican legislators added an amendment to the resolution praising President Jackson for his "resistance of nullification and secession in 1832."[6] Surely after adjournment, Republican legislators regaled the president-elect with stories of their poaching the reputation of the Democratic Party's founder and hero.

After Lincoln's November victory, President James Buchanan had not dealt with the secession of South Carolina as President Jackson had done during his first term (1829–1833). Throughout the earlier crisis, which began with the Palmetto State's political leaders' opposition to the Tariffs of 1828 and 1832, President Jackson had countered threats from South Carolina officials that its legislature would nullify the federal tariff law. He sanctioned the state by taking action to ensure the loyalty of federal troops stationed there. Additionally, he recommended that Congress pass a Force Bill, which would make federal authorities responsible for collection of the tariff's import duties in South Carolina as well as enforcement of the national tariff law. In a famous and often repeated toast that

President Jackson gave at the Democratic Party's Jefferson birthday dinner in 1830, he summed up his policy of enforcing federal supremacy. Raising his glass, the president showed that he would countenance no state opposition to federal law. He toasted: "Our Federal Union," and declaimed, "it must be preserved."[7]

Thirty years later, after the surrender of Fort Sumter and the vicious riots in Baltimore, Maryland, that had impeded the transport of militia from loyal states to the national capital for its defense, Lincoln savored his Jackson moment. Fearing more bloodshed if pro-secessionists continued to mob U.S. soldiers in transit to the national capital, a delegation from Baltimore visited the president on April 22 and requested that federal troops no longer travel through their state. In effect, its members asked that the preservation of the federal union be made subordinate to maintenance of civic order in their community. The recently inaugurated president responded: "you would have me break my oath and surrender the Government without a blow. There is no [George] Washington in that – no Jackson in that – no manhood nor honor in that."[8]

The presence of Andrew Jackson's image in the cabinet room also conveyed a second meaning most obvious to viewers who supported abolition sentiments and who possessed deep knowledge of political lore. On more than one occasion during his presidency in the 1830s, Jackson had asserted the power of the presidency over that of the Supreme Court or Congress. Two decades later in 1858, as a contender for a seat in the U.S. Senate, Lincoln had referred to his predecessor's interpretation of the chief executive's duty to follow the Constitution. To confound Senator Stephen Douglas, his Democratic Party rival in their senatorial contest, Lincoln had summoned Jackson's words to explain his opposition to Supreme Court Justice Roger B. Taney's opinion in the *Dred Scott* case of 1857. When Douglas and other Democrats criticized Lincoln's hope that the decision would be overturned, the Republican candidate reminded them, "General Jackson once said each man was bound to support the Constitution 'as he understood it'."[9]

Carpenter's centering of the general's image over his visual portrayal of the Emancipation Proclamation demonstrated to viewers that Democrats and Republicans had acted together in the past and could act together in the future to preserve the Union and to oppose the Supreme Court decision. To overturn the Dred Scott decision, which said that no African American could be a citizen of the United States and that the federal government had no power to ban slavery from U.S. territories, a president might recommend constitutional initiatives to guarantee that the future of the country would include no extension of slaveholding to its territories. This future would become real only if Lincoln and his cabinet interpreted the nation's founding document as they understood it. Three documents that Carpenter placed in the lower third of his painting suggest that the artist composed his painting to illustrate how Lincoln and his cabinet understood the Constitution and especially its treatment of slavery.

Tracing from the left corner of the frame around the Jackson image to the floor below reveals that Carpenter placed two folio volumes of the *Congressional Globe*, which contains records of debates and votes in the national legislature, against the table leg closest to Lincoln and behind Seward's feet. The presence of the *Globe* points to the substantial, while subordinate, role that the national legislature played in the emancipation process.

By July 22, 1862, Congress had passed two Confiscation Acts. After the president signed them, the bills became law, the first on August 6, 1861, and the second on July 17, 1862. The earlier Confiscation law empowered the military forces to seize property of persons in rebellion against the United States when that property was employed "in aiding, abetting, or promoting such insurrection or resistance to the laws" of the United States. Further, it maintained that rebels lost claim to persons, namely slaves, employed in service of their rebellion. The second law increased pressure on the rebels. It confiscated their property if they did not swear allegiance to the United States within sixty days. As for slaves, if they belonged to rebels and fled into Union lines, or if they lived in lands held by U.S. troops, they were "deemed captives of war, and shall be forever free of their servitude and not again held as slaves." Neither Congressional Act referred to the enslaved people as property; in both Confiscation acts, the lawmakers placed the disposition of property and slaves into separate paragraphs with distinctive provisions for each.[10]

Moving to the left and toward the foreground of the painting, we find, lying next to Stanton's chair, rumpled pages of the *New-York Tribune*, edited by Horace Greeley, at times a Lincoln supporter and, at other times, a critic of his administration. When the president moved on emancipation, the actual act of emancipation occurred by presidential action and rested on presidential power – exclusively.

On August 20, 1862, Greeley's newspaper printed an editorial as an open letter to the president entitled "The Prayer of Twenty Millions," with the millions representing the citizens of the Union holding antislavery sentiments. In his protest letter, Greeley criticized the president for not executing the laws, especially the Confiscation Acts. They permitted enslaved African Americans who fled into Union lines to be held as contraband of war and, according to the Militia Act of July 17, 1862, to be employed as laborers by the Army. The second Confiscation Act also prohibited Union forces from sending fugitives from their lines back to rebels claiming to own them.

A report that Greeley had received from an abolitionist about the fate of fugitive slaves in Louisiana prompted his stern letter. The correspondent described a dispute between Union generals over the military role of African Americans. During July 1862, General Benjamin Butler, whom many residents of New Orleans called "Beast Butler," refused to transfer military supplies to General John W. Phelps, who had raised three companies of black soldiers without his commander's knowledge. Butler denied Phelps's request to arm and provision his recruits because he reasoned that his superiors in Washington had sent the supplies to provision white troops and that no presidential order had authorized the arming of black troops. Rather than obey his superior officer, Phelps resigned his commission.

Upon hearing of the debacle, many abolitionists who favored the arming of blacks expressed their indignation to Greeley. Purportedly, "in obeisance to the Slaveocracy," General Butler had commanded Phelps to return the blacks not needed as laborers to Southerners who claimed to be their owners and established so-called slave pens in Union encampments where owners could claim their property. Greeley's informant lamented how people who "came miles, wearing iron yokes and with marks of brutal cruelty, were sent out from us" while voicing "agonizing prayers for protection." They reported that "to kill them" was far less cruel than to "drive them into the revengeful huts of their masters."[11]

So inspired, Greeley published his open letter to the president exhorting him to execute federal laws, at least the Confiscation Acts. Motivated by the charges against Butler, the antislavery editor also complained of the disregard and disobedience of Union officers who returned enslaved people to Southerners who claimed to own them. Going further, Greeley urged Lincoln to act on the supposed fact "that every hour of deference to Slavery is an hour of added and deepened peril to the Union."[12]

Two days later, Lincoln answered Greeley in a public letter printed in a rival newspaper. He assured his "old friend," as well as millions of newspaper readers, that he intended to save the Union by "the shortest way under the Constitution." As for slavery, its demise, or not, would be a means to this desired end: "if I could save it by freeing some and leaving others alone I would also do that. What I do about slavery, and the colored race, I do because I believe it helps to save the Union; and what I forbear, I forbear because I do *not* believe it would help to save the Union."[13]

With these famous words, Lincoln retracted the avowals he had made seventeen months previously, in March 1861. In his inaugural address, he had reassured the nation, "I have no purpose, directly or indirectly, to interfere with the institution of slavery in the States where it exists." Referring to his interpretation of the Constitution, he averred that he had "no lawful right to do so," and further that he had "no inclination to do so."[14] During the first sixteen months of his presidency, Lincoln repeated those remarks or their substance frequently in addresses to Congress and to the public.

Even as Lincoln tried to address the fears of proslavery Democrats and citizens of the seceded states and border states, his estimate of his constitutional powers with regard to slavery was changing markedly, as was his inclination to direct the future of human slavery. As the open letter to Greeley demonstrates, he was admitting that he no longer promised not to interfere with the institution of slavery where it presently existed. He conceded that he would touch it if by doing so he could restore the Union. With these words, Lincoln put in play the future of slavery in the United States.

In August, when Greeley read the president's response to his accusations, he did not possess information about recent events in the Executive Mansion. The president and his cabinet members knew in July 1862 that one month prior to receiving the newspaper publisher's accusations, Lincoln had prepared an executive order that proclaimed the emancipation of slaves held within the seceded states. He had said: "I, as Commander-in-Chief of the Army and Navy of the United States, do order and declare that on the first day of January in the year of Our Lord one thousand, eight hundred and sixty three, all persons held as slaves within any state or states, wherein the constitutional authority of the United States shall not then be practically recognized, submitted to, and maintained, shall then, thenceforward, and forever, be free."[15]

With this inside knowledge of events in July, we can interpret the president's response far differently than did nearly every member of the newspaper-reading public in August 1862. Besides reneging on his promise to the seceded states, Lincoln also assured everyone anxious for an end to the war and slavery that he would "adopt new views so fast as they shall appear to be true views." In fact, the document that he read to the cabinet on July 22 showed that his adoption of new views the month before he wrote his reply to Greeley in late August. Now Lincoln was prepared to act on his understanding that the Constitution gave him the power to abolish slavery among those rebelling against the authority of the United States.

Those views continued to develop until he signed the final Emancipation Proclamation on January 1, 1863. They originated in the books stacked at the right-hand end of the semicircle of objects in Carpenter's painting. Benefiting from the twenty-twenty hindsight of the artist who understood the import of those books, we can plot Lincoln's course toward the first reading of the Emancipation Proclamation.

Moving out from the center of the lower third of the painting where the *Congressional Globe* resides, we first find a book resting against another. Supreme Court Justice Joseph Story's *Commentaries on the Constitution* lies open before William Whiting's *War Powers of the President*.[16]

Both books played crucial roles from the spring of 1861 to the summer of 1862. They brought Lincoln's understanding of his presidential emancipating powers in accordance with the "new views," to which he had referred in his response to Greeley. Additionally, they moved Lincoln from an approach to emancipation based on global experience and influenced by Riley's narrative to an understanding of international law and the powers that it conferred upon the president when he acted in his capacity as commander in chief during wartime.

Before publication of Whiting's volume in the spring of 1862, supporters of a strong national government consulted Story's *Commentaries on the Constitution* as the must-read book for legal advice on the meaning of that document. From 1812 to 1845, Story served on the Supreme Court, where he was its recognized expert on international law. Most famously, he wrote the opinion in the *Amistad* Case in 1841, which applied the Somerset precedent. Story held that people who rebelled on ships proceeding outside the waters of nation states were free and could not be re-enslaved when reentering the waters of a country that recognized slavery and disembarking there.

While an associate justice of the Supreme Court, he also taught law at Harvard College, where his students included Wendell Phillips, the abolitionist; Charles Sumner, chairman of the Senate Committee on Foreign Relations during the Civil War; and William Whiting, whose influential book we will shortly consider. First published in 1833, the *Commentaries* originated from Story's Harvard law school lectures and went through numerous editions between its publication

and the Civil War. Story's book contains significant sections on federal war powers and the right of slave owners to retrieve their fugitive
slaves.[17]

Story contended that the Constitution held that slaves were not mere
property but "moral person[s]," because laws protected their "life and
limbs against the violence of others," as well as holding slaves "punish-
able for all violence committed against others."[18] Harvard law students
learned that the congressional power to declare war included the "ordinary rights of belligerents" such as the seizure of property.[19]

At the same time, the professor recognized that the Constitution
acceded to the "peculiar interests of the south." Thus it called for multiple
"sacrifices of opinion and feeling" from "the eastern and middle states,"
when it provided for the return of fugitive slaves to their owners.[20] Moreover, he recognized that, according to the law of nations, "no nation is
bound to recognize the state of slavery." Referring to the Somerset Case
of 1772, Story found that "the state of slavery is deemed to be a mere
municipal regulation founded upon and limited to the range of the territorial laws."[21] In other words, slaves who managed to reach a country
other than the one in which they were held as property were free. The
country of asylum had no obligation to return the fugitive persons to their
former owners. Nevertheless, in the United States, a state did not possess
the power to overrule the Supreme Law of the Land, or the Constitution.
Since the Constitution included its fugitive slave clause, a non-slave state
would violate the Constitution if it declared slaves free when they fled
into its free territory.[22]

In the *Commentaries*, Story argues that the Somerset precedent had
made the fugitive slave clause necessary in the Constitution. Had the
British precedent not existed, citizens in one state of the United States
would incur no obligation to return slaves across state lines to an owner
who resided in a different state. Because the United States comprised
states, each one with its own laws on the topic of slavery, the state's laws
to which the enslaved person fled determined whether that enslavement
was legally recognized.[23] The provision in article 4, section 2 that persons
"held to labor" in one state had to be returned on demand of the person
to whom that labor was due set aside the Somerset precedent and thereby
gave Congress power to enact laws requiring the return of fugitive slaves.

When Story first made this observation in his textbook, he could not
predict that constitutional commentators and U.S. military officers would
draw on his interpretations during the Civil War to argue that the federal
government had wartime powers to free slaves held in belligerent areas.

In the spring of 1862, Justice Story's student William Whiting did just that when he published his *War Powers of the President*.[24]

His contribution to the president's thinking on emancipation received visual acknowledgment with Carpenter's positioning of the slim first edition of approximately 143 pages against the leg of an empty chair in the bottom right corner of his painting behind his teacher Story's text. Whiting said, in the introduction to the second edition of his book, that he had started to contemplate the relationship of the president's war powers to the Constitution in the early months of 1862. During the spring and fall of the preceding year, warfront events both on U.S. soil and on the high seas had made these connections salient.

During a war, international law governs the combatants and their commanders. As constitutional authorities, preeminently Story, argued, that document sets forth both explicitly and implicitly the powers the federal government possesses in domestic affairs. In the realm of international affairs, the Constitution says nothing. In 1861, no national constitution, including those of the United States and the Confederate States, enumerated the duties and rights that nations possessed in the extra-domestic realm. In the 1860s, nations recognized that international law originated from rules established by international convention or agreement. To determine international law, American jurists conventionally consulted eighteenth-century European authorities on the topic, most frequently the Swiss Emmerich de Vattel's *Principles of the Law of Nature, Applied to the Conduct and Affairs of Nations and Sovereigns* (1758). In English translation, editions of the treatise appeared in American editions throughout the entire nineteenth century. Beginning in the 1830s, American scholars addressed the topic with jurist and diplomat Henry Wheaton's *Elements of International Law* (1836, new. ed. 1855) becoming the standard work until Whiting's text superseded it.[25]

Until Whiting's book appeared, most scholars and diplomats concluded that when the Lincoln administration implemented blockades, schemes of prisoner exchange, and periods of truce for clearing battlefields of the wounded and dead, it was following the laws of war and, by implication, recognizing the CSA as a foreign nation. When the administration implemented those laws, it had created an apparent conundrum. Many statesmen and diplomats believed that when the United States used the laws of war to justify its actions, it implicitly was recognizing that the Southern states had seceded and established the Confederate States of America, or a foreign country. Of course, the Lincoln administration and its supporters denied that it had done so. If it had recognized the CSA as a foreign nation rather than as a collection of rebellious states, then it also had recognized the constitutional right of states to secede. President Lincoln devoted his presidency to proving that contention wrong. In his inaugural address, he had contended, "the Union of these States is perpetual."

The actions of European powers seemed to confirm the Constitutional interpretation that establishment of a blockade implied, namely that the Confederacy possessed the status of a nation instead of a collection of seceded states. After President Lincoln declared a blockade of Southern ports on April 19, 1861, European powers recognized that belligerency existed among the previously united states. Consequently, they accorded the CSA belligerent status under the internationally accepted laws of war. Great Britain acknowledged the belligerent status of the Confederate States and declared itself a neutral power in the conflict on May 13, with news reaching the United States on May 29. Brazil, France, the Netherlands, and Spain soon followed Britain's lead.

According to international law, these declarations meant that ships carrying the flag of these nations would respect the U.S. blockade and not carry goods to the ports of the belligerent CSA. Merchants from the seceded states still could buy goods in neutral countries and transport them where they wished except to the CSA in ships of the neutral nations. Neutral nations also gave to CSA vessels in their ports the same rights and imposed the same limitations on them as they did on ships of the United States. Additionally, international law theoretically prevented citizens of a neutral country from joining the armed forces of a belligerent power or from supplying it with warships.[26]

As foreign policy experts debated whether the Confederacy was or was not a nation during April and May 1861, a related issue arose, especially among abolitionists. In a war, would slave property be secure or not?

Antislavery advocates turned to the constitutional arguments of Joseph Story, which had become articles of faith among them, especially as former president and Congressional representative John Quincy Adams deployed them. Three years after publication of Story's law school lectures, Massachusetts Congressman Adams reiterated the jurist's arguments in an 1836 congressional debate. After the recent war in Florida with the Seminoles, members of the House were discussing relief measures for refugees, of whom many were fugitive slaves. During the debate, Adams described the war powers of the president with regard to emancipation. Echoing Story's *Commentaries*, Adams maintained that when the slaveholding states became theaters of war, the war powers of the federal government "extend to interference with the institution of slavery."[27]

Following this first instance, the congressman often repeated his views on the powers of the federal government with regard to slavery in wartime, most notably in 1842. By the time of Adams's death during Lincoln's congressional term, Story and his constitutional arguments had become well known among politicians and among members of the anti-slavery community, especially among followers of Boston-based aboli-tionist William Lloyd Garrison, readers of his newspaper, *The Liberator*, and Congressional allies of Joshua Giddings, Adam's friend and ally and Lincoln's messmate at Mrs. Sprigg's boardinghouse.[28]

In congressional debates, Giddings frequently referenced Adams's anti-slavery arguments. In January 1849, the representative told fellow House members that under the war power, a military commander "may do any-thing in the power of man to accomplish; may command any sacrifice of the people, or of any portion of them, in order to secure the safety of the Government, and of the subjects generally. It is that power which authorizes the military commander, in short, to do whatever he deems necessary for the security of the public."[29] Given the lively discussions that occurred around the boardinghouse table at the so-called Abolition House where Giddings and Lincoln rented rooms in Washington, the younger representative most likely learned a great deal about presidential wartime powers.[30]

During the 1850s, discussion of the power to emancipate under the war powers receded in political and public discussion, even among anti-slavery activists such as members of Garrison's American Anti-Slavery Society.[31] National consciousness of the war power of military comman-ders first reappeared among longtime antislavery advocates in the fraught first two weeks of April 1861 as the Lincoln administration was deter-mining whether it would surrender or would provision and defend Fort Sumter.

Chair of the Senate Committee on Foreign Relations Charles Sumner, who considered Story, his law professor, as his mentor, recalls visiting President Lincoln in the Executive Mansion in the days immediately after the president's decision to provision Fort Sumter and before the resulting bombardment. The senator counseled the president that when the federal government should provision the fort, "the War Power will be in motion, and with it great consequences." Throughout the spring and summer of 1861, the senator returned to the topic of emancipation that he had raised during the Fort Sumter crisis during his frequent visits to the president's office or while accompanying him on carriage rides. Despite Sumner's persistence, his arguments did not answer Lincoln's concerns. The president still held to his position that he had neither the power nor the inclination to emancipate the enslaved people in the combatant states.[32]

In the days following the shelling of Fort Sumter, General Butler did not feel the same political and constitutional constraints as did the president. He first applied the international laws of war to the institution of slavery in May 1861. A Democrat by political affinity and Massachusetts lawyer by profession in pre-war days, Butler commanded the Union-held Fort Monroe on the coast of Virginia from May 22, 1861, through most of the remaining months of the year. By summer 1862, he had assumed command of the Union occupation of Louisiana, where his conflict with a subordinate would inspire Greeley's letter of protest to Lincoln. His by-the-book response to the plight of fugitive enslaved people in that instance incited abolitionist ire and prompted Greeley's letter.

A little more than a year before the New Orleans controversy in April 1861, Butler had earned his appointment to major general of federal volunteers due to his initiative in securing Annapolis and Baltimore when pro-secessionist Marylanders confronted federal soldiers. After the surrender of Fort Sumter, CSA sympathizers had destroyed railroad routes necessary for movement of troops to Washington. In command of the first militia brigade that Massachusetts Governor John Andrew had dispatched to the beleaguered national capital, Butler led the 8th Massachusetts in a circumnavigation of secessionist-held Baltimore, arranged for sea transport of his troops to Annapolis, and then directed the soldiers' repair of the vital railroad tracks leading to the nation's capital.[33]

Rewarded with his major general appointment by his commander in chief, Butler took command of Fort Monroe and of the military department of Virginia and the Carolinas. After his arrival at the fort, troops from the fortress proceeded to reconnoiter the land around the nearby town of Hampton, where they encountered uniformed Virginians belonging to a domestic police force, and some enslaved people. Delighted to see the Union troops, the slaves presumably spread word of the soldiers' whereabouts. One evening, three of them took advantage of the confusion prevailing among Virginia whites by the presence of U.S. troops at Fort Monroe, eluded the watchful eyes of their taskmasters, and escaped to the Union picket lines outside the fort. Guarded and directed by soldiers in the 115th Virginia regiment, the three men – Frank Baker, Shepard Mallory, and James Townsend – belonged to the labor gang constructing an artillery position on the dunes of Sewell's Point, a site across the water from the fort. Safely inside the Union stronghold, the escapees brought General Butler intelligence about the cannons and the Confederates' plans to fortify the point.[34]

Rather than the three enslaved men's patriotism for the Union, their master's dedication to the Confederate cause had inspired their flight. Word had reached the trio that their master, Colonel Charles Mallory, commander of the Virginia militia near Hampton, intended to send them to the deep South, where the CSA needed laborers to build fortifications. Facing separation from family, friends, and the community that they knew and that knew them, the three African Americans fled.[35] Coincidentally, on May 23, the day of Baker, Townsend, and Mallory's flight, the state legislature of Virginia declared secession. Had the men sought refuge in the Union lines on May 22, Virginia still would have been one of the United States, and the Constitution would have obligated the officers in charge to return the fugitives to their bondage under the provisions of the Fugitive Slave Act.

About nine weeks earlier, Lincoln had delivered his inaugural address. He tried to reassure the seven southern states still in the Union that he would not touch the institution of slavery in the states where it already existed. As he had stated many times, the Constitution gave no power to the federal government to end slavery. If his listeners did not fully comprehend his opening statement, he quoted article 2, section 4 of the Constitution requiring that property, implying enslaved people, escaping from one state to another "shall be delivered up on claim of the party to whom such service or labor may be due."[36]

As a savvy lawyer, General Butler knew that Virginia's secession on May 23 had changed everything. Prior to the war, the Massachusetts citizen had participated in partisan politics, held a seat successively in both houses of the state legislature, served as an officer in the state militia, eventually reaching the rank of general, and actively engaged in the presidential campaign of 1860. At the national party nominating convention of that year, he spoke in favor of the candidacy of Jefferson Davis, the future president of the CSA.

Butler's transformation from supporter of Davis to champion of fugitive slaves began when the Confederates shelled Fort Sumter. That conflict set in motion the events that propelled the Massachusetts lawyer from civilian employment and service as a volunteer in his state's militia to the general in command of Union forces at Fortress Monroe, Virginia, on May 24. His decision that day repercussed over the next eighteen months, eventually affecting the purpose of the war.

As Butler tells the story of his use of the war powers, a representative of Baker, Mallory, and Townsend's master approached Fort Monroe under a flag of truce to request an audience with its commander on May 24. Not wanting to permit the enemy within the fort where he might see its vulnerable points, Butler arranged for a meeting at his picket line. Having ridden there, he exchanged pleasantries with the slave owner's representative, a Confederate major, who had previously met Butler at the 1860 Democratic convention in Charleston, South Carolina. The officer first inquired whether Butler would permit sea transport past the fort – he would not – and next whether the general would allow Virginians to travel by rail to the northern states – he would, but he said that the decision about whether they could traverse Washington did not lie with him.

These queries held trifling import compared to the one that the Confederate officer posed next. After informing the Union general that he acted for the owner of the three men, the major inquired, "What do you mean to do with these negroes?"[37]

At this point, Butler had to reach into his familiarity with current events and legal experience to retrieve an answer. If he had familiarity with British government publications or discussions of the slave trade, he would have remembered that their usage of the term supplied some guidance. The word "contraband" had a meaning other than that used in discussions of war powers. It could connote illegal commerce. So an author would describe seventeenth-century Dutch merchants pursuing "a contraband business in Negro slaves and European merchandise," or a report to the British Parliament would mention that "a considerable contraband Traffic in Negroes" continued in Turkey.[38]

Further, General Butler's immersion in the political debates of Massachusetts, including its heated antislavery debates, had familiarized him with the relationship between slavery and war powers as explained by Massachusetts representative John Quincy Adams. After the surrender of Fort Sumter, the word "contraband" suddenly had surfaced in newspaper reports as the national government began to act as a belligerent power. When federal agents seized cargoes in northern cities such as Philadelphia and Pittsburgh destined for southern depots, newspaper reports of the seizures labeled the goods contraband.[39]

Butler later said that he had held no intention in 1861 to return the escaped men. At the time of the parlay with his CSA interrogator, he replied that the laws of war justified his actions. He refused to return the men and claimed that the Fugitive Slave Law no longer applied. As he explained, "I mean to take Virginia at her word as declared in the ordinance of secession passed yesterday. I am under no constitutional obligations to a foreign country, which Virginia now claims to be." Although the Confederate officer countered Butler's arguments by pointing out that Union supporters, including the president, contended that the Southern states could not secede according to the Constitution, Butler did not relent and release the three fugitives. He explained, "but you say you have seceded, so you cannot consistently claim them. I shall hold these negroes as contraband of war, since they are engaged in the construction of your battery and are claimed as your property. The question is simply whether they shall be used for or against the Government of the United States."[40]

In subsequent analysis of his impulsive words with his fellow officers at Fort Monroe, Butler conceded that established international law did not address whether fugitive slaves might be considered contraband property. Among the many items that author Henry Wheaton, the reigning authority, listed as contraband in his *Elements of International Law*, no mention of slaves as contraband existed. The absence of justification in published material did not deter Butler. As he observed to his fellow officers at Fort Monroe, anyone who swore allegiance to the CSA constitution could not deny that slaves were property. Further, by the fugitives' own testimony, secessionist forces had impressed the African Americans into service to build fortifications and batteries. Because contraband referred to property used by a belligerent power, the former slaves certainly seemed to qualify when Butler followed the slave owner's logic.[41] The general's superiors in Washington agreed. On May 29, Lieutenant-General Winfield Scott responded to Butler that his account of the reception of the fugitives held "much to praise ... and nothing to condemn"; Secretary of War Simon Cameron concurred and gave "his entire approval."[42]

Despite the unsettled nature of his legal argument, Butler was absolutely correct when he claimed in his memoirs, "The effect on the public mind, however, was most wonderful."[43] Within a week, newspapers across the country publicized the major general's defiance of CSA demands. By May 28, the *New York Herald* proclaimed that if other commanders would follow Butler's precedent, "very short work will be made of this whole Southern rebellion."[44]

Within another month, the word "contraband" had acquired a new meaning for the northern, media-informed public. Members of antislavery churches and societies as well as readers of daily newspapers and antislavery periodicals had learned of General Butler's novel

One of the F. F. V's after his Contraband.
General Butler "can't see it."

FIGURE 6.2. On this envelope, the cartoon pictures General Butler defending a fugitive slave or, as Butler said, "a Contraband," from capture by an F.F.V., or a member of the First Families of Virginia, who wields a cat-o'-nine-tails and restrains a fierce dog. Image courtesy of the Library Company of Philadelphia.

interpretation of the international laws of war. They now understood that the word referred to both material property seized by U.S. military forces and human property who reached the Union lines from Confederate-held territory. By mid-June, the abolitionist paper *Douglass' Monthly* reported that nearly 500 formerly enslaved people had found sanctuary in Fort Monroe. Their claim to be "the happiest fellows in the world" undermined pro-slavery forces of their argument that masters treated their slaves so kindly that they would never leave.[45] By August, the number of people seeking sanctuary in the fortress had reached between 700 and 800, and their fellow enslaved people in Florida, northern Kentucky, and the Carolinas were following their example by seeking refuge in Union strongholds.[46]

Soon the people seeking contraband status and General Butler became celebrities in American popular culture.[47] Decorative and often humorous imprints on envelopes sold by stationers and bookstores throughout the North incorporated images of them into their design repertoire. During the Civil War, consumers purchased paper and envelopes imprinted with topical themes for one or two cents. Among the 15,000 or more patriotic imprints supporting the Union cause published during the war, more than 20 celebrate Butler's invention of the term "contraband." (See Figure 6.2.)

FIGURE 6.3. On this mailing envelope, a cartoon portrays fugitive African Americans running toward Fort Monroe and refusing to heed a slave master brandishing a whip. Image courtesy of the Library Company of Philadelphia.

For example, in one design topped by the national flag, Butler extends his sword to protect an African-American man, probably a fugitive, clinging to his leg from the pursuing slave owner who carries a cat-o'-nine-tails and restrains a snapping dog. The title pokes fun at the slave master by saying, "One of the F.F.V's [First Families of Virginia] after his Contraband." (See Figure 6.3.) Another envelope, published in Cincinnati, showed a pair of barefoot black feet with the title: "The Peculiar Institution," and the caption: "Secession's Moving Foundation, Tendency due North – via 'Monroe'." From the images on these envelopes, buyers had to be impressed with the cruelty of slave owners and the determination of the enslaved people to reach freedom. Even while celebrating the independence and agency of the fugitives, the images descended into racist caricature. Many envelope imprints portrayed the fugitives with kinky hair and legs and arms akimbo. They utter responses to their pursuers that would evoke smiles from a white audience. For example, to his pursuer's demand to "Come back here, you black rascal," the fugitive responds, "Can't come back now, massa; dis chile's contraban," as he runs with a group of fugitive men, women, and young children into Fort Monroe.[48]

Musicians also discovered General Butler and the contrabands as subjects. Sheet music for the parlor organ and piano-forte featured them. We can imagine either families and friends gathered in their parlors or raucous groups assembled in saloons singing along to piano-forte accompaniment about the contrabands and the general. (See Figure 6.4.) Reputedly, the chaplain at Fort Monroe, R. C. Lockwood, heard the contraband people singing the spiritual currently known as "Go Down Moses" or "Let my People Go" shortly after their arrival in May at the Virginia fortress. After he recorded their words, music publishers in New York and Philadelphia released versions of the original song plus a parody adapted to the war situation in 1861.[49]

While trying to replicate the vernacular of a slave, another song expressed the enslaved people's desire for freedom. "Old Shady," a ditty published in Boston, cheered, "Good bye to work and wid never any pay,/Ise a gwine up North the good folks say,/White bread and a dollar a day/ Are coming." Its Boston publisher dedicated the ditty to "Columbia's Noble Son, Maj. Gen. Benj. F. Butler."[50]

During 1861, all sorts of publications such as the *Atlantic Monthly*, the *Ladies Repository*, and humorous pamphlets lampooning Confederate chivalry retold stories about Butler's smart words or the slaves' defiance of their owners by invoking contraband status.[51] Antislavery newspapers reminded their readers yet again of Adams's interpretation of federal war powers. Garrison's *Liberator* published multiple blasts in its pages, while antislavery lecturers such as Wendell Phillips trumpeted the message to lecture audiences in New York City and other antislavery centers.[52] The prevalence of the contraband argument as it was now applied to people attained such popularity that Union commanders tried to find new applications. With knowledge of its ubiquity, it should come as no surprise that a Union officer might stretch application of the word "contraband" too far.

No direct evidence confirms that Captain Charles Wilkes, commander of the *San Jacinto*, directly recalled General Butler's innovative use of the term when he encountered the British mail ship *Trent* in November 1861 six months after the incident at Fort Monroe. Yet, the captain might have drawn from his knowledge of Butler's actions and the accolades that they gained in the North when he justified his removal of Mason and Slidell from the *Trent* as they sought transportation to their diplomatic posts. In this instance, neither Lincoln, Wilkes's commander in chief, nor the secretary of the navy found that the emissaries of the CSA qualified as contraband of war. Despite that term's having no applicability in the *Trent* Affair, Captain Wilkes's use of the term "contraband" refreshed awareness among Northerners that during wartime commanders might

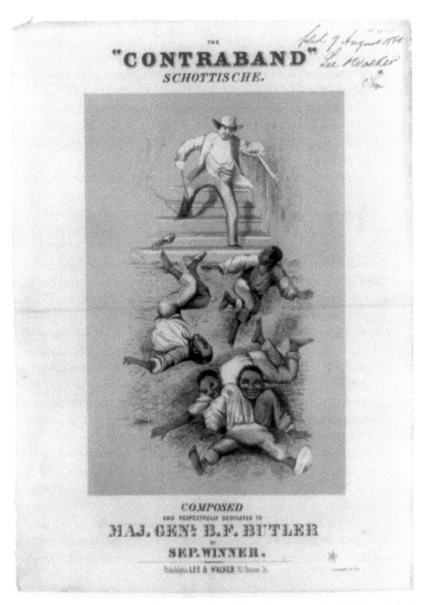

FIGURE 6.4. This cover to sheet music entitled "The 'Contraband' Schottische" shows caricatures of a slave master with his whip pursuing enslaved people. In 1861, Septimus Winner composed this country dance and dedicated it to General Butler. Courtesy of Library of Congress Prints and Photographs Division.

deem enemy property contraband according to the stipulations of international law.

The popularization of the word "contraband" also inspired legal scholars. In Massachusetts, lawyer William Whiting began to compose the short book that would find a place in Carpenter's historical narrative. His *War Powers of the President* appeared in print close to a year after Butler's innovation and six months after Captain Wilkes had made a triumphant tour through Boston immediately following his interdiction of the *Trent*.[53]

To prove that the United States could free slaves held in the CSA without recognizing that the CSA had status as a foreign country, Whiting offered a precise, closely reasoned argument. He contended that the Constitution gave the president certain powers in wartime and certain powers in peacetime. He argued that the Constitution required "the President, as an executive magistrate, in time of peace to see that the laws existing in time of peace are faithfully executed – and as commander in chief, in time of war to see that the laws of war are executed. In doing both duties he is strictly obeying the constitution."[54]

Whiting's exposition moved beyond the claims of abolitionists who cited Adams's congressional speeches. Whiting's reasoning possessed greater utility: it justified the constitutionality of the president's wartime powers within the domestic framework of constitutional law. In other words, implementing the laws of war did not imply recognition of the Confederacy as a nation. War powers established by international law were not an absolute alternative to domestic constitutional powers. When a nation suffered from a domestic rebellion, it suffered from a war. The initiation of internal combat, in this case by the shelling of Fort Sumter, had activated the president's war powers and permitted him to act as commander in chief. A state of war existed in such an instance; Congress did not have to declare war. It began as soon as the nation was attacked. Drawing on common sense, Whiting maintained that the Constitution "never leaves the nation powerless for self-defense." If it had done so, British forces might invade the United States from Canada, while Congress was not in session, and proceed to capture the national capital before the Congress could reassemble to declare a state of war and permit the president to respond constitutionally. By application, after Fort Sumter, Lincoln's calling up of the militia and ordering a blockade of Southern ports constituted entirely constitutional actions because they derived from the president's reliance on his war powers during a state of domestic insurrection.[55]

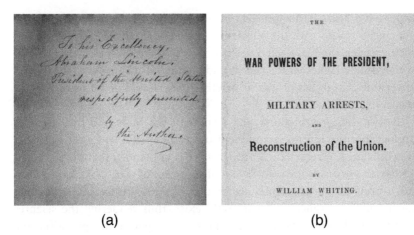

(a)                               (b)

FIGURE 6.5A, 6.5B. This inscription appears in the copy of *The War Powers of the President* (second edition, 1862), which William Whiting presented to President Lincoln. Courtesy of the Alfred Whittal Stern Collection of the Rare Book Division of the Library of Congress.

During the year following publication of *War Powers of the President*, a decision by the Supreme Court and an appointment by the Lincoln administration showed the positive reception of Whiting's words. Six months after publication of the volume, President Lincoln demonstrated his approval of Whiting's constitutional arguments by appointing him as solicitor and special counsel to the War Department. The reading public of abolitionists and legal scholars also must have agreed with the salience of Whiting's work. After the first edition rapidly sold out, the publisher issued a second edition in the same year. The author presented a signed copy of it to President Lincoln. By the end of the war, the book, lengthened with additions to address postwar issues of reconstruction, had gone through eight editions.[56] (See Figures 6.5a and 6.5b.)

The following year, a Supreme Court majority, including two justices whose appointment predated the Lincoln administration, repeated Whiting's arguments when the court ruled in the *Prize Cases*. These cases tested whether the president had the power to deploy an act of war, namely a blockade of a belligerent area's seaports, before the Congress had voted a declaration of war. During the spring of 1862, these legal cases had surfaced as Whiting was writing his treatise. Between April 19 and 27, 1861, when the president issued executive orders establishing a naval blockade of Southern ports, and August 8, when Congress ratified his orders, the Navy had captured numerous ships trying to run the blockade and to trade with the seceded states. Having seized these ships and their cargoes, the Navy referred their disposition to federal district courts, which decided whether the vessels and their goods belonged to the federal government as prizes of war or whether they should be returned to their owners.

Before these prize courts, the owners of the ships and their cargoes argued that the federal government owed them compensation or that it was obligated to return their property. They contended that the president had acted unconstitutionally by initiating an act of war, a blockade, without a previous congressional declaration of war. Without congressional sanction, they argued, no war could exist, thus rendering the seizures unwarranted. After the district courts ruled against the plaintiffs, the cases were appealed to the Supreme Court, which heard their arguments in February 1863.

Before the court, Richard Henry Dana, Jr., United States Attorney for Massachusetts and another pupil of Joseph Story, maintained that Congress need not declare war for a war to exist. Applying the arguments of Whiting, his fellow Bostonian and Harvard Law School graduate, Dana argued that Lincoln had acted constitutionally. A majority of the justices concurred and ruled that the president had not violated the Constitution when he had deployed in a civil war the powers of commander in chief without prior congressional declaration of war.

By implication, they also affirmed the position that Whiting had argued in his book that was published the previous year. He contended that the Constitution had not left the United States vulnerable to insurrection or attack by mandating that the president could do nothing to defend the country until the Congress had declared war. On March 10, 1863, Justice Robert C. Grier wrote for the Supreme Court majority that, according to international law, "it is not necessary that the independence of the revolted province or State be acknowledged in order to constitute it a party belligerent in a war." In other words, the Lincoln administration could have its way. A war existed after Fort Sumter, even though Congress had not voted for it, and because a war existed, the president had the power to institute a blockade of the ports of the belligerent entity. By implication, the president's resort to acts of war, in this instance a blockade, did not imply recognition of the seceded states as a nation. Belligerent acts against the United States, whether their origins were foreign or domestic, implied the existence of a state of war.[57]

Whiting also applied his legal reasoning to justify emancipation by presidential action in wartime. Because the United States was at war, the activation of the president's war powers meant that certain Constitutional guarantees of rights could be suspended. Specifically, during wartime, Amendment 7 of the Bill of Rights did not prevent the seizure of property. In a war, the war powers of the president superseded peacetime rights of citizens to have the federal government take their property only after following due process of law and providing compensation.

As commander in chief, the president could order the military to seize property without due process of *civil* law and provide no compensation without violating constitutionally guaranteed rights. The laws of war recognized property as subject to seizure if it were used to support or to prosecute a war. Therefore, since the Southern states had laws that established property rights in slaves, the commander in chief could order that property confiscated or emancipated since slave labor supported the maintenance of a belligerent power. As Whiting wrote, "It is in accordance with the law of nations and with the practice of civilized belligerents in modern times, to liberate enemy's slaves in time of war by military power."[58] Because similar phrases in Whiting's book justified the constitutionality of Lincoln's Proclamation of Emancipation, fellow abolitionist Francis Carpenter painted the *War Powers of the President* into a significant place behind the tome of Story, Whiting's teacher on the Constitution. In Carpenter's mind, both books played a key role in emancipation and deserved memorialization.

Had Captain Riley still lived in 1864, he might have asked Francis Carpenter why the artist gave his *Narrative* no place in the mammoth canvas. Indeed, Lincoln himself might have seconded Riley's query if we remember that he had conceded to Carpenter that his painting did have *a little* to find fault with. After all, the president's campaign biography of 1860 had claimed Riley's work as one of the most influential books in his early life. This book's chapter 2 explains Lincoln's claim by showing how the narrative of African slavery promoted Lincoln's understanding of the efficacy of compensated emancipation.

Even so, Carpenter chose to ignore the significant role of Riley's *Narrative*. If we follow the painter's lead, we remain blind to seeing that Riley's influence persisted even while the president prepared to issue the executive order that was the final Emancipation Proclamation of January 1, 1863.

In Lincoln's annual message to Congress of December 2, 1862, five months after the initial reading of the Emancipation Proclamation and about ten weeks after the release of the preliminary Proclamation on September 22, the president asked Congress to consider three new amendments to the Constitution. The first two continued the policy of gradual emancipation and compensation to slave owners. The first amendment proposed that any state emancipating its slaves before 1900 would receive compensation from the federal government. The second mandated that slaves enjoying freedom "by the chances of war" should remain "forever free." If their owners had remained loyal to the national government during the conflict, they too would receive compensation for their liberated human property. The third amendment would give Congress power to appropriate federal funds to pay for the colonization of formerly enslaved people "with their own consent" in locations outside the United States.[59]

Lincoln's recommendation of gradual compensated emancipation combined with the Emancipation Proclamation to provide his administration with a carrot-and-stick approach to end slavery, end the war, and restore the Union. The carrot, or the amendment plan that Riley's *Narrative* anticipated, proposed compensation to loyal owners for their human property who would be gradually emancipated and deportation to Africa for individual freed people who consented to their removal from the United States.

The second plan supplied the stick. The Emancipation Proclamation relied on theories of presidential wartime powers promoted by theorists from Joseph Story in the 1830s to William Whiting in the 1860s. Drawing on international law, these legal theorists sanctioned the Proclamation and unleashed the stick of emancipation. They explain why the Emancipation Proclamation contains these words: "I, Abraham Lincoln, President of the United States, by virtue of the power in me vested as Commander-in-Chief, of the Army and Navy of the United States in time of actual armed rebellion against the authority and government of the United States, and as a fit and necessary war measure for suppressing said rebellion. . . ." The depiction of Story's *Commentaries* and Whiting's *War Powers* demonstrate that the roots of the Emancipation Proclamation extended from the Constitution to international law. To mandate the demise of slavery in the war zones of the Confederacy, President Lincoln, as the nation's commander in chief, had exercised powers accorded by the internationally recognized laws of war.

To create narrative drama in "First Reading of the Emancipation Proclamation of President Lincoln," Francis Carpenter chose subject matter that raised to exclusive, exalted status the plan of emancipation that comported with his own abolitionist belief, one that Justice Story and his student William Whiting had made constitutionally palatable. By placing the two volumes in the lower right-hand section of his celebrated canvas, the artist helped create Lincoln's reputation as the Great Emancipator. Admirers of Carpenter's effort might not have realized that the painter had memorialized exclusively the lessons consistent with his abolitionist beliefs. Abraham Lincoln had extracted these lessons from international law as taught by Justice Story to his Harvard pupils, most notably to William Whiting, who taught them to a broader public through his *War Powers of the President*.

# 7

## German Lessons for Reelection

During the last days of August 1864, leading Republican Party figures in New York City attended a meeting where they discussed whether they might encourage Abraham Lincoln to resign as their party's presidential candidate in the approaching election. Most of them had supported the Republican in 1860, and some, such as David Dudley Field, had promoted his nomination at the tumultuous Chicago convention of that year.

Several days earlier many of these men, as members of the national committee of the Republican Party, had visited the president in Washington. Their "darkness doubt and discouragement" produced John George Nicolay's complaint that "they have got a stampede on that is about to swamp everything." Writing to his fiancée, he described their retreat. Referring to the rout of Union troops in the first major battle of the war, he saw his party experiencing "almost the condition of a disastrous panic – a sort of political Bull Run."[1] Military and political events from March through July 1864 had squashed the party leaders' faith. They now doubted that the president and his generals had the ability to lead the country in wartime and to end slavery throughout the United States.

Costly military advances had helped bring on the Republicans' despair. During the spring and summer, Lieutenant General Grant had sent the Union armies into a series of battles that had ended in stalemate near Petersburg, Virginia, where the Confederate Army had entrenched itself. Prior to that siege, the ocean of blood spilled during the Battle of the Wilderness in May, that of Spotsylvania Court House, and finally in June during the slaughter at Cold Harbor spread dismay among residents of the White House. The distressing outcomes of these engagements so afflicted Mary Lincoln, the president's staunchest supporter, that she adopted the disparaging term with which Confederate newspapers had labeled General Grant during the Virginia battles of earlier that spring. She complained that the Union commander was causing his soldiers to be butchered.[2]

In July, the Union army experienced another military embarrassment. To draw soldiers from Grant's siege of Petersburg, General Lee had ordered Lieutenant General Jubal Early to march his troops northward through the Shenandoah Valley into Maryland. East of Frederick, at the junction of the turnpike and railroad lines connecting Baltimore and Washington, the Confederate soldiers confronted on July 9 Union forces commanded by Major General Lew Wallace. Although defeated, Wallace's soldiers managed to slow the Confederate advance toward Washington. By the afternoon of July 11, some of Early's troops had progressed to the outskirts of the national capital, where they encountered resistance at Fort Stevens, one of the several forts connected by rifle pits that formed a continuous defensive line protecting approaches to the city from Maryland. Defense of the nation's seat of government depended on an unimpressive force of partially disabled veterans and inexperienced militia soldiers until regular soldiers arrived mostly from City Point, Virginia, and also from Baltimore and Fort Monroe. Thanks to these reinforcements, the capital's defenders prevailed in repulsing the Confederates' attack.

Although the city's residents initially celebrated the withdrawal of Early's forces, Washingtonians' relief and that of Lincoln administration members quickly dissipated. Discontent arose among the president's adversaries and even his supporters because the Union military, as at Antietam in 1862 and Gettysburg in 1863, had not pursued the retreating Confederate troops and punished them for the burning and pillage that they had inflicted. Benjamin French, Commissioner of Public Buildings in the capital, called the escape of Early's forces "humiliating," concluding, "my friend Abraham has to do something to retrieve this awful blunder or he is 'a goner!'" The July attack and the Confederates' subsequent escape fed the growing narrative of President Lincoln as an ineffective and indecisive leader.[3]

This chapter follows this decline in support to its nadir in late August and early September 1864 as it developed among Lincoln followers, especially among German Americans. It focuses especially on Francis Lieber's loss of faith in the president during the winter and summer of 1864. His discouragement is notable because in 1860, the German-American professor's support for the Republican ticket had alienated his son. The senior Lieber's backing of the Lincoln administration had continued through the first years of the Lincoln presidency. Crucially, from 1861 to 1863, his theories of warfare and military practice had justified and supported the administration's conduct of the war and helped thwart foreign intervention. As Lieber sensed Lincoln losing support among the larger German-American community in 1864, his support for the administration also ebbed. Then, in the fall of 1864, like a majority of the voting public, he reversed course to back the president's reelection. In conclusion, we briefly see how Lincoln's supporters in Germany greeted the president's reelection.

During the winter and spring of 1864, a presidential election year, the cords holding together the Republican coalition that had formed around Lincoln in 1860 unraveled almost completely. A small number of Forty-Eighters and radical abolitionists had met in New York City's Cooper Union on March 18, 1864, to discuss founding a third party and nominating a presidential candidate. It would have stood for extending emancipation to slavery everywhere in the United States, preserving civil liberties in wartime, and pursuing an aggressive war against the military forces of the seceded states. They invited Francis Lieber, a prominent supporter of the Union cause, to chair the effort, called the Frémont Campaign Club. Lieber declined. While criticizing a third-party effort as divisive and harmful to the war effort, he kept open the option of his backing its candidate, John C. Frémont, the Republican Party candidate in 1856 for whom Lieber had voted.[4]

These military and political setbacks at the national level, plus disagreement with Lincoln's patronage policy at the local level in New York City, had brought Lieber into the August meeting of disgruntled New York Republicans to discuss the president's deteriorating election prospects. Several days afterward, the professor wrote his longtime patron, Army Chief of Staff Henry Halleck:

There are but two things that could save us – a telling victory, or rather the taking of Richmond, and Mr. Lincoln's withdrawal. The first will not take place with our decimated army; the other will not occur.... All this is nothing necessarily against Mr. Lincoln; but individuals wear out quickly in revolutionary times, were it for no other reason than that familiarity with a name takes from it the enthusiasm.... We must have a new man against a new man, and we cannot have him without Lincoln's withdrawal. Oh, that an angel could descend and show him what a beautiful stamp on his name in history such a withdrawal would be![5]

During the summer of 1864, many Lincoln supporters agreed with Lieber and the New York City Republicans about the sure fate of their party's ticket if Lincoln was its candidate for the presidency. Disagreements over the war and emancipation policy had divided his administration. Three weeks after Lincoln's own renomination for the presidency in June, Salmon Chase had resigned his position as treasury secretary, thus making obvious both his long-standing disagreement with Lincoln on the emancipation issue and his current objections to patronage appointments to positions in the New York City Customs House.

Even German Americans, who had supported the Republican candidate in 1860, predicted that the president could not win in November. After General Early's attack on Washington in July, the *Ohio Statesman* reported that of the thirty-two usually pro-Republican German-language newspapers, twenty-six had declared against Lincoln and for Frémont, candidate of the third party, the Radical Democracy. It had been founded in late May 1864 by approximately 350 Forty-Eighters and Radical Abolitionists at its initial convention in Cleveland. The platform of the new party demanded immediate emancipation and an end to wartime restrictions on civil liberties. The *Statesman* estimated that with backing from German-American newspapers, Frémont would win close to 700,000 votes.

By early September, the disillusionment that radicals had shown with Lincoln had spread to Republicans generally and specifically to Lieber. A favorable electoral outcome in previously safe Republican states looked doubtful. The *Westliche Post* (St. Louis) agreed with Lieber's New York City Republican leaders. It reported that Indiana party members opposed Lincoln and that the state ticket would lose if he were not thrown "overboard."[6]

During August, pessimism about the Republican ticket's dismal electoral prospects afflicted the president as well. He penned a private memo to himself, folded the paper to hide his words, and had every member of his cabinet sign his name on the memo's exterior without knowledge of its interior message. It promised that President Lincoln would try to "save the Union" between his probable defeat in the November election and the inauguration in March of the next president, most likely Democrat George McClellan.[7] With gloom prevailing among Republicans, that Lieber should question Lincoln's electoral prospects seems unremarkable. His loss of faith in the president becomes remarkable given the enthusiastic support that he had given the Lincoln ticket in 1860, together with the assistance that he had offered to the administration from 1861 through the spring of 1863.

In 1860, when he decided to cast a Republican ballot, he had paid practically the highest price that any father possibly could. His political commitment came at the cost of his relationship with his oldest son, Oscar, who ceased corresponding with him. The son, who lived in South Carolina where he was pursuing a career as a geologist, had been deeply embarrassed after Southern newspapers castigated his father for his supposed enthusiastic participation in a pro-Republican rally in New York City in October. Publicity about the senior Lieber's speech at the event reached students at the South Carolina College, where his father previously had taught. Furious, they protested the politics of their former beloved professor. They jabbed knives into Professor Lieber's portrait, and members of the Euphradian fraternity deleted his name from its roll of honorary members and removed his portrait bust from their hall.[8]

Not sharing his father's hatred of slavery and states rights, the younger Lieber had fully acculturated to South Carolina and its political beliefs during his teen and college years, when his father had taught at the southern college and counted even the son of John Calhoun, the ardent states rights advocate, among his pupils. Oscar had not decamped for the North as his father did in 1856. Privately disgusted with the slave-holding states' advocacy of the Nebraska bill and the ensuing drive to extend slavery to federal territories, the elder Lieber had resigned from his professorship and moved to New York City when his antislavery sentiments became publically known and prevented his advancement to the college presidency. In May 1857, Columbia College appointed him to its professorship of history and political economy.[9]

In the weeks before the 1860 election and after the newspaper publicity of his Republican politicking, he responded with pain to Oscar's queries about which presidential candidate he would support. To salve his son's embarrassment over his public endorsement of the Republican ticket, Lieber assured him that he felt his grief. The political theorist deplored the current age as "an intensely political" one in which "a difference of opinion or conviction is instantly denounced as a crime or a shame." He asked his son to understand that he was "so made that I cannot otherwise than speak out what I hold to be unconditionally the truth."[10]

Oscar and his father never reconciled. After Fort Sumter, Oscar left a promising career as a skilled geologist to join the Confederate army. On May 7, 1862, during the early days of General George McClellan's Peninsular Campaign, he suffered a mortal wound as his unit covered the Confederate troops' retreat toward Richmond. The young soldier's last testament instructed that the location of his burial place "matters little," so long as his body did "not rest in Northern soil. May it never be moved there."[11]

Given the paternal suffering that Oscar's political apostasy and death must have caused, the decline of Lieber's enthusiasm for the Lincoln administration and the rise of his disapproval in the summer of 1864 are telling. After Lincoln and fellow Republicans had gained German-American support in 1860, during the next three years, the exigencies of waging war impinged on their idealism and diminished their commitment to the Lincoln administration.

In the campaign of 1860, the Republican Party and its candidate had attempted to win the German-American vote with political party platform planks and appointments. Before the Republican Party convention of 1860, their notable political figures had been chosen as delegates to the Chicago meeting. There, the delegates approved a party platform containing two so-called Dutch, or German planks. Further, once elected, Lincoln rewarded his German-American supporters with appointments.

Of course, not even a majority of German Americans had deserted the Democrats during the anti-Nebraska controversy of 1854 to join the new political party. Republicans found their greatest supporters among the urban and more political German Americans, while Catholic, rurally situated German Americans tended to retain their original loyalty to the Democratic Party. In Illinois, Wisconsin, Missouri, Indiana, Ohio, and Pennsylvania, many German Americans shifted their political loyalty to the Republicans. Among the more notable German-American delegates at the convention were Gustav Körner, whom Lincoln had nominated to the Illinois delegation, and Carl Schurz from Wisconsin, who intended to support William Seward because of his anti-nativist stands while a senator from New York. Both Körner and Schurz served on the platform committee.

To satisfy its German-American members, the Republican Party voted to include planks on which they had insisted. First, the platform put the party on record against "any change in our naturalization laws or any state legislation by which the rights of citizenship hitherto accorded to immigrants from foreign lands shall be abridged or impaired; and in favor of giving a full and efficient protection to the rights of all classes of citizen." This plank essentially labeled as renegades the Massachusetts Republicans who had proposed in 1858 a two-year delay in granting the suffrage to newly naturalized citizens. In 1860, Republican candidates would not have to hedge on the issue of suffrage for recently naturalized citizens as Lincoln had done in 1858 and 1859.

Second, the Republican Party platform offered its support to the homestead measure then pending in the Senate after having gained passage in the House.[12] It would permit both citizens and people formally declaring their intention of becoming citizens to acquire homesteads on designated areas of the nation's public lands, and to receive title to the land after working it for a specified number of years. If immigrants formally affirmed their intention to acquire citizenship, they had the same legal rights to public lands as did existing citizens. In this sense, all men were equal under federal law as the Declaration of Independence promised.

In 1852, 1854, and 1859, a majority of members of the House of Representatives had voted for a homestead bill while the majority of Senate members had voted against it, largely because of opposition from Democratic senators, who feared the admission of more non-slaveholding states and the consequent weakening of pro-slavery power in the Senate and the Electoral College. In the spring of 1860, a majority of both houses approved the bill, which President Buchanan, heeding the interests of southern Democrats, vetoed one month after the Republican convention.

The "Free Soil" unit of the Republican 1860 slogan "Free Soil, Free Labor, Free Men" sent a message designed to appeal especially to German Americans, who wanted inclusion in the Homestead Act. When they heard the term "Free Soil," they understood that the Republican Party would guarantee them access to public lands in the new territories and permit them to vote along with citizens on whether that land should exclude the institution of slavery. In the states belonging to the Union in 1860 and its territories – in other words, those lands that would become the states of tomorrow – immigrants would have equal rights and opportunity. The coded phrase "Free Soil" allowed Republicans to court German-American ballots without having to make an explicit pitch, thus offering no spoken offense to nativist members of their party.[13]

Historians and political scientists have conducted a prolonged debate about whether German Americans supplied the decisive votes in 1860 to swing the election to candidate Lincoln. To summarize the current consensus among them, they now believe that the German-American vote was significant and possibly decisive in Illinois, where the Republican won by 3.52 percent of the ballots, and was potentially important in a few other states.[14] From 1854 through the 1860 presidential election, no one could benefit from the sophisticated data analysis deployed by contemporary scholars. With the information at hand in those years, Lincoln acted as if this ethnic group was vital to his political career.

On his railroad journey to Washington as president-elect in February 1861, Lincoln refused to discuss in exact detail what actions he would take as president with regard to the seven states that already had seceded. As his train chugged its extended, roundabout route to the national capital, he made a significant exception. His speeches mentioned only one bill that he would support, and he endorsed that bill – the homestead bill – before only one group, an assemblage of German Americans. When the president-elect arrived in Cincinnati on February 12, the Association of German Workingmen presented a resolution stating: "You earned our votes as the Champion of free labor and free homesteads... the German free working men, with others, will rise as one man at your call, ready to risk their lives in the effort to maintain the victory already won by freedom over Slavery." Later, before the German Industrial Association of Cincinnati, Lincoln renewed his pledge to support "that thing" that would "advance the condition of the honest, struggling laboring man," and he bid "God speed" to any foreigners wishing to enter the country. He deplored "their shackles – the oppression of tyranny," while promising to "do all in my power to raise the yoke, than to add anything that would tend to crush them."[15]

Further evidence of Lincoln's indebtedness to his German-American supporters comes from the patronage he distributed once elected. He rewarded his longtime German-American advocates in Illinois. During the first days of the new presidency, Secretary of State Seward and Lincoln were discussing candidates for ministerial and consular postings. (See Figure 7.1.) Lincoln said that their choices looked "huddled up," meaning that they came from New England. To spread out the assignments, he asked Seward, "what about our german friends?"[16] Future appointments addressed this issue.

Illinois German Americans whose names appear throughout Lincoln's career, especially from 1854 onward, received diplomatic postings: Theodore Canisius consul to Vienna, Herman Kreismann secretary of the legation at Berlin, and George Schneider consul at Elsinore, Denmark. When an illness compromised his eyesight in 1862, Gustav Körner resigned his commission as a colonel of volunteers to which Lincoln had appointed him, and succeeded German-American Carl Schurz as minister to Spain. Except for Körner, each of these German Americans wore a beard.

OLD ABE AND HIS ELECTORS.

FIGURE 7.1. This cartoon appeared in [Frank Leslie's] *Budget of Fun*, April 15, 1861, to ridicule Republicans for their need to reward the party's constituency, caricatured here as immigrants and African Americans. The cartoonist pictured Seward perusing a list and Lincoln, astride an American eagle, standing to the left of Uncle Sam, who holds a sheaf of diplomatic posts. The president addresses office seekers: an Italian (organ grinder), a Frenchman (Napoleon III), an Irishman (caricature), a German (Carl Schurz), and an African American (caricature). Courtesy of Archives and Special Collections, Franklin & Marshall College, Lancaster, PA.

After the Republican-controlled Congress had been in session for nearly a year, both houses passed a homestead bill, the same in every significant respect as the one that President Buchanan had vetoed. As Lincoln had promised in the party platform and reiterated in his Cincinnati speech, he signed it into law on May 20, 1862, and it became effective on January 1, 1863.

Readers may recognize New Year's Day of 1863 as possessing great historical significance. It marked Lincoln's signing of the Emancipation Proclamation, thereby making active its promise of freedom. A second event on January 1, 1863, gives that date even greater meaning since the provisions of the Homestead Act then became effective. Both the Proclamation and the Homestead Act bolstered Republican Party support from specific interest groups in the United States and in Europe. During the following months, numerous people from Great Britain sent resolutions

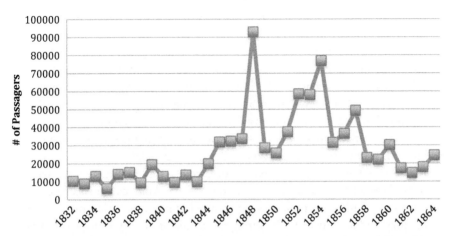

FIGURE 7.2. Passengers per year from Bremen, 1832–1864. *Source*: Consular Posts, Bremen, Germany, RG 84, Vol. 179. National Archives and Records Administration, College Park, MD.

to the Executive Mansion celebrating the Proclamation, as we have seen in Chapter 5. At the same time, in mainland Europe, thousands of Germans demonstrated their enthusiasm with their feet in support of the new Homestead Act. (See Figure 7.2.)

Emigration from the German states had fallen during the early war years to levels of the 1830s and early 1840s. At the busy North Sea port of Bremen, emigration had declined to 14,710 in 1862. During 1863, when the Homestead Act became effective, it increased 22 percent to 17,952 and in 1864 nearly 37 percent to 24,432. To prevent the 1862 decrease from repeating, Secretary of State Seward instructed consuls in Europe during the summer of 1862 to publicize that a labor shortage due to the war had raised wages to the point that only in the United States could the "industrious laboring man and artisan expect so liberal a recompense."[17] Early in February 1863, Seward promoted immigration again through a circular to foreign ministers and consuls. He informed them of the incredible natural resources of the country now open for mining by new settlers, especially newly discovered gold and silver deposits in California and the Rocky Mountain territories.[18]

In Prussia, U.S. diplomats arranged for publication of the Homestead Act in the leading journal that prospective emigrants consulted. Men wanting to enlist soon packed consular offices. The consul at Frankfort as well as Henry Boernstein from Bremen and Kreismann from Berlin reported that they could have raised "a few Brigades" or "at least a thousand men" if they had the funds to defray their fares. In Prussia, the government responded by cracking down. It prohibited importation from the United States of German-language newspapers from St. Louis and Cincinnati. From Paris, the consul reported that he could easily raise "whole regiments." The immigration lure reached even to northern Africa, where newspapers in Arabic, the consul in Tunis reported, reprinted articles about immigration from liberal Parisian journals.[19]

Conservative Europeans fretted. In Prussia, emigration could cause a labor shortage, demand for higher wages, and even labor unrest. Examining the new law, French newspapers detected "a fraud," while an Austrian paper labeled the Homestead Act and stories of American riches "a common lie." With false pretenses, the United States was luring men to the country and into its army.[20] Surely the revulsion felt by Europeans after they had read in 1862 about casualties at the battles of Shiloh in the spring and Antietam in the fall supported forebodings that the United States needed cannon fodder more than it needed settlers for its western lands. In spite of reports of bloody battles, the numbers of immigrants continued to increase.

Lincoln had responded to the favorable immigration news by recommending new laws in his 1863 annual message to Congress. He wanted both to encourage immigration and to prevent immigrants from using their status to avoid the draft. Fittingly, on July 4, 1864, the national legislature passed a bill establishing a commissioner of immigration. It also forbade the drafting of immigrants who had not declared their intention to become citizens, and it guaranteed the validity of labor contracts that immigrants might have made before their departures. This last measure addressed the issues raised by many consuls in Europe. These contracts might grant passage in return for payment, and immigrants could then satisfy their contracts with the bounties they would receive after enlisting in the Union army.[21]

Although Lieber in 1860 had not engaged in the Republican campaign energetically enough to be rewarded with a patronage position as many other German Americans had been, he still sensed opportunity when Lincoln moved into the Executive Mansion. In June 1861, he persuaded the administration at Columbia College to give him the honor of leading a college committee to Washington to bestow an honorary doctor of laws degree on the new president. Lieber remarked after the meeting with the honoree in the Executive Mansion that he was "far better than people think him, but oh! so funny." About ten days later they met again, and Lincoln indirectly thanked Lieber for the honorary degree. He confided to the professor that sections from his published lectures had anticipated two paragraphs in the president's July 4 message to Congress when he had made the case for retroactive approval of the war measures that he had instituted after Fort Sumter.[22]

A few days after awarding Lincoln with the honorary degree, Lieber accompanied Massachusetts Senator Henry Wilson and Republican operative and journalist Thurlow Weed to Fort Monroe, where, a month before, General Butler had deemed escaped slaves contraband of war. During the same month, in western Virginia, recently promoted Major General McClellan had assured residents that he not only would return escaped slaves but also would repress any rebellion by the enslaved people.[23]

Here were two generals in the same army with commands in the same state following two different practices with regard to fugitives from slavery. The discrepancy between McClellan's and Butler's treatments of fugitive slaves disturbed antislavery advocates. The disagreement prompted jurist William Whiting to compose his *War Powers under the Constitution of the United States*. In New York City, Lieber began to publicize his views in the *New York Times*.

The Columbia professor thought the actions of both generals did not comport with international law. On the one hand, Butler had erred because he had applied the term "contraband" incorrectly. His usage denoted that enslaved people were property. According to established principles, once enslaved people fled into territory where the law did not support slavery, they were free because local law alone had enslaved them. Slaves were not property, but people. On the other hand, McClellan had violated the same principle. His promise to return fleeing slaves did not recognize their humanity. A human could not be made a slave except through law. As Lieber explained to Sumner, a longtime friend and correspondent since their introduction by Justice Story, "our soldiers cannot see in a human being anything but his humanity."[24] Subsequently, the legal scholar began to lobby his contacts in Washington to have the federal government establish a uniform code of military rules – to make all soldiers follow the one drum played by their commander in chief.

A month after the first Battle of Bull Run on July 21, Lieber continued his efforts to promote himself among members of the Lincoln administration by applying his extensive knowledge of military and political history to current events. He attempted to cut through a conundrum presented by the conflict of international law with military usage occasioned by the aftermath of the July battle. When the federal government in April had announced its blockade of Confederate ports, critics on both sides of the Atlantic quickly had observed that the action implied invocation of international law. Such invocation, they argued, implied recognition that two powers were at war, and their being at war in turn suggested diplomatic recognition of the Confederate government. The Lincoln administration now delayed the usual practice of prisoner exchange.

In the July battle, both the Union army and the Confederate army had taken prisoners. Usual wartime practice now suggested that those prisoners be exchanged. For a while, the Lincoln administration did not know what to do with its captives. If it exchanged prisoners, that practice might suggest that the Union was following the procedures recommended by established international law. Unintended and undesired consequences would arise. The exchange would provide the administration's critics with further evidence that its wartime practices were extending to the CSA de facto recognition. According to the laws of war, a prisoner exchange occurred after a nation had declared war, and a declaration of war implied that the Union had recognized the Confederacy's existence as a nation. If the United States recognized the Confederacy as a nation, one might assume that the European powers soon would follow its precedent.

Consulting historical precedents, the Columbia professor suggested an exit strategy from the impasse. Several months before Whiting published his *War Powers of the President*, Lieber solved the problem for the Union with regard to prisoner exchange much as Whiting would do later with regard to the blockade. In a letter printed in the *New York Times* on August 19, the professor claimed that exchange of prisoners in a widespread rebellion implied no recognition of the rebel government by the established government. On battlefields, officers faced situations that made an exchange desirable. Because an exchange of prisoners existed solely as a battlefield practice, much like the use of a white flag of truce, it carried no larger significance.[25]

This public letter brought Lieber into correspondence with Attorney General Edward Bates. Combined with the publicity that the *Times* provided during the winter of 1861–1862 when it printed a condensed version of the professor's current Columbia Law School lectures on the laws of war, Lieber became known as an acknowledged authority and a sort of unofficial consultant to the Lincoln administration on the practice of war and the conduct of military personnel.[26]

In the spring of 1862, after being wounded in February at the Battle of Fort Donelson, Lieber's son Hamilton, a first lieutenant in the Ninth Illinois Volunteer Regiment, went missing. To locate him, his father went west and searched through military hospitals. For assistance, the senior Lieber renewed his acquaintance with Major General Henry Halleck, who had assumed command of the military department of Missouri after the president had dismissed Frémont. Lieber and Halleck shared interest and expertise in the fields of international law and military practice. Halleck's book *Elements of Military Art and Science* had appeared in 1846, and Lieber had encouraged the general as he composed his *International Law*, published in 1861. Although his two volumes totaled more than 1,350 pages, they provided insufficient guidance on the complex situation now troubling Union officers in Missouri with regard to guerilla warfare.[27]

Rebel commanders had sent soldiers in civilian clothes to penetrate civilian territory behind Union lines. There they destroyed bridges, houses, railroad lines, and other property. In retaliation, Union officers treated the captured Confederates as spies and ordered them punished, sometimes by firing squads. Confederate authorities, in opposition, considered the saboteurs as regular soldiers, who deserved treatment as prisoners of war according to military law. Regular soldiers could be imprisoned for the duration of the war but not executed. The Confederates threatened retaliation on their captured Union prisoners if Halleck did not agree that the captives were regular soldiers and not saboteurs.[28]

Lieber quickly composed a short brief on guerilla warfare that met with his friend Halleck's approval. Although Lieber declined to make a recommendation on the fate of the Confederates, his thorough definitions seemed to label them as marauders or brigands whom he thought unworthy of humanitarian treatment under the international laws of war. His concluding sentence stated, "no army, no society engaged in a war ... can allow unpunished assassination, robbery, and devastation, without the deepest injury to itself." In correspondence with Halleck, the professor also requested a noncombat assignment for his youngest son Guido Norman, who had been promoted for bravery after fighting in the Peninsular Campaign, the same campaign in which Oscar was killed. Simultaneously, Halleck arranged for Hamilton Lieber, whose arm had been amputated, also to be appointed as an aide de camp.[29]

Halleck's subsequent promotion to general in chief of the federal armies in July 1862 gave Lieber the opportunity for which he had hoped.

Once the general had relocated to Washington and been installed in his new position, Lieber proposed that Halleck convene a committee consisting of generals and himself to prepare a manual instructing soldiers on wartime practices. With such a manual governing the actions of an army in the field, theoretically at least, two generals in similar military situations would not issue different orders as had happened in 1861 with Butler's and McClellan's receptions of fugitive slaves. Although Halleck waited until the fall to act on his friend's idea, Lieber prepared the manual within weeks of his appointment. After some slight editing by committee members and approval by President Lincoln, it became in April 1863 his General Orders Number 100, or *Instructions for the Government of Armies of the United States in the Field.*

While prohibiting some brutal practices such as the torturing of prisoners or poisoning of water supplies, the General Orders did permit destruction of civilian property and "withholding of food" from areas under siege when called for by military necessity or enacted in retaliation for enemy transgressions. Unless military operations would be compromised, officers were required before attacking civilian areas or laying siege to a city to warn its resident civilians and to permit their flight. Thus, the Orders justified the starvation that civilians experienced during the siege of Vicksburg by General Grant's forces in 1863 and the destruction of Georgians' property by General William T. Sherman's troops in 1864.[30]

Even though the instructions permitted harsh wartime practices, Lieber himself did not recommend that Union officers employ the harshest military practices during the Civil War. When submitting the final draft of the *General Orders* to Halleck, he advised:

[I]t is now time for you to issue a strong order, directing attention to those paragraphs in the Code which prohibit devastation, demolition of private property, etc. I know by letters from the West and the South written by men on our side that the wanton destruction of property by our men is alarming. It does incalculable injury. It demoralizes our troops; it annihilates wealth irrecoverably, and makes a return to a state of peace more and more difficult. Your order, though impressive and even sharp, might be written with reference to the Code and pointing out the disastrous consequences of reckless devastation, in such a manner as not to furnish our reckless enemy with new arguments for his savagery.[31]

In the present day, General Orders Number 100 is known as the Lieber Code. When after the Civil War, Prussia, Great Britain, and France developed their own military codes, they followed its lead. In 1899 and 1907, participants in peace conferences held at The Hague consulted it as the basis for an international law of war. Subsequent meetings at Geneva in 1929 and 1949 to establish conventions for treatment of prisoners of war drew on it, even repeating in some instances Lieber's original wording.[32]

Several paragraphs of the thirty-six-page pamphlet compel attention. In paragraph #153, Lieber established the principle with regard to prisoner exchanges that he had researched in 1861 after Bull Run. Now, government policy held that while humanitarian concerns might encourage a country to adopt the rules of war to deal with rebels, such action did "in no way whatever imply a partial or complete acknowledgment of their government." Further, neutral powers had no right to make such a humanitarian act the grounds for recognition "of the revolted people as an independent power."[33] Thus, United States officers could arrange for the exchange of prisoners and declare periods of ceasefire or truce without triggering international consequences. Humanitarian practices in wartime did not and would not justify European intervention.

With regard to slaves who fled into Union lines, Lieber set as federal policy the views that he had previously expressed privately to his friend Charles Sumner. In paragraphs #42 and #43, he wrote that slavery throughout history had existed exclusively because of local laws. Where no governments existed – say, in a state of nature – all people were free. Therefore, if enslaved people escaped from an area where local laws established slavery and fled into a foreign country or from their country into the lines of an opposing power with no such laws, that country or power could and should recognize immediately their intrinsic humanity and not their former status as slaves. That status, of course, was invisible because it had depended on nothing but the law in the area from which the people had fled. "To return such a person into slavery," Lieber maintained, "would amount to enslaving a free person and neither the United States nor any officer under their authority can enslave any human being."[34] The Constitution of his country did not confer the power of enslavement because it neither established slavery as an institution nor mentioned in its text the words "slave" or "slavery." Antislavery adherents such as Lieber argued that the Constitution contained purely indirect references to slavery when it provided for representation of "those bound to service for a term of years" and their return across state lines to "the party to whom such service or labor may be due."[35]

At Halleck's urging, Lieber had added to the final draft of the Code a provision proclaiming that after enslaved people gained their freedom by fleeing into Union lines, their former owners could not reclaim them after the war.[36] By assuming the status of belligerents, owners had forfeited title permanently. Thus, the General Orders transformed the Confiscation Law of July 1862 into military practice, and just as important, the document predicted future Union policy. Lieber's code, which Lincoln approved, declared that fugitives who entered Union lines were forever free. Additionally, if Attorney General Bates's 1862 ruling on citizenship held authority in the postwar years, these fugitives also were citizens of the United States.

Lieber demonstrated the truth of his core premise – that the enslaved people were humans first and slaves second – by consulting European history back to Roman days. Lincoln had reached the same conclusion in 1854 by a mundane analogy to farm animals in the Peoria speech. Despite disparate logical strategies, the professor and the president agreed. And both positions accorded with the Somerset precedent, a foundational tenet of antislavery thought for at least three decades before the Civil War.

Lincoln might have argued that he founded his belief on universal principles of common sense whereas Lieber grounded his finding on the theory of international law and the historical practice of nations. No matter, both upheld the universal principle that the enslaved people were human and so entitled to the rights that they believed humans possessed. The common-sense thinking of Lincoln thus corresponded with the advanced, university-based thought of the mid-nineteenth century. The folksy wording of Lincoln could appeal to audiences in Illinois unschooled in antislavery thought and could reach across national borders where it would attract an audience throughout the Atlantic world.

Discerning readers will have noticed Lieber's insistence on the humanity of the enslaved people and denial that they were property. This position contradicts the argument that William Whiting made in his *War Powers* on which Lincoln based the Emancipation Proclamation. By issuing the Proclamation, Lincoln followed the practice of General Butler at Fort Monroe in May 1861 when he called the fugitives "contraband." Although Lincoln did not think that slaves were property and despite the Constitution's not recognizing them as property, he adopted opposite views when composing the Proclamation.

Lincoln had to accept what the seceded states maintained about themselves in order to eradicate what they themselves had mandated. To gain the power to abolish slavery, Lincoln implicitly recognized that the slave states' constitutions and codes of law had established human slavery as a legal institution and defined as property the population whom the Constitution referred to as "persons held to service or labour." By accepting that this definition existed in the slave states, as Whiting argued, the president gained the power to confiscate and destroy property in wartime, in this case the legal standing of slave property.[37]

Although Lieber disputed Whiting's contention about the war power to emancipate in areas not controlled by Union troops, he was not willing to express this opinion in public. As he explained in private correspondence, he kept silent because he vehemently opposed the Confederate cause and believed that slavery had to be abolished. During this civil war, circumstances might justify actions that in peacetime or even in foreign wars would have no sanction in the Constitution or its amendments. As he once explained, "The whole Rebellion is beyond the Constitution. The Constitution was not made for such a state of things; it was not dreamt of by the framers."[38] Even though Lieber considered the Emancipation Proclamation constitutionally questionable as an exercise of the president's wartime powers, this disagreement over the appropriate means to the desired ends of Union victory and slavery's abolition played no role in moving Lieber from support for the president.[39]

More than anything that Lincoln did, the factor that most influenced Lieber to oppose him as a Republican candidate in 1864 was the rise of an anti-Lincoln animus in New York City and among his fellow German Americans. Their criticism of the administration arose in the first two years of the Lincoln presidency. They complained of the military's treatment of German-American troops and officers, Lincoln's indecisive actions with regard to slavery, and troop call-ups.

Many German Americans admired decisive leaders, and Lincoln seemed decisive solely when enacting policies that they opposed, such as conscription and suspension of the right to habeas corpus. On July 1, 1862, the president had requested state governors to raise 300,000 more troops. When the governors acted during August and September, the call-up incited violence in German and Irish immigrant communities, especially in Pennsylvania and Wisconsin. The *Philadelphia Inquirer* reported active resistance in Meadville, Pennsylvania, and a "revolt" in Schuylkill County, Pennsylvania. In Luzerne County, four or five people were killed before the protest ended. Immigrants in Wisconsin engaged in the most violent and destructive acts. They hunted down the local official conducting the call-up and sacked six houses owned by Republican Party members who either opposed immigration or supported emancipation. After a day of violence, a militia force of 600 quelled the riot and arrested 70 culprits.⁴⁰

In response to the earlier protests, Lincoln had suspended the right to habeas corpus nationwide. Then, on March 3, 1863, Congress passed the Enrollment Act, the first federal military draft in history. When it became law, both Democrats and German-American Republicans reconsidered their support of the party and its pro-war stance. Violent protests ensued, including the infamous New York City Draft Riot of July 1863. Lieber, who lived in the midst of the rioting, wrote Halleck, "negro children were killed in the street, like rats with clubs."⁴¹

With the call-up for 300,000 volunteers from the states in June 1862 and with the Enrollment Act, moderate antislavery German Americans began to think that the United States had betrayed them. They ignored that the previous July, Congress had passed a law shortening the period of residency required for citizenship. Honorably discharged veterans now could become citizens with proof of one year's residence in the United States. Despite enthusiasm in Europe for this new regulation, immigrants in the northern states were more disturbed by the universal call-up to military service of men from eighteen to forty-five years old.⁴²

Male German Americans from Prussia had emigrated to escape conscription and arbitrary arrest by a strong central government. Now a nationwide draft ensnared the newly naturalized citizens and those immigrants who had declared their intention to acquire citizenship. Protest brought even more curtailment of rights. By election day 1862, Lincoln's United States seemed to promise less freedom. Unnaturalized German-American men could not escape the call-up even by returning to their homelands, where authorities quickly identified them and impressed them into their own militaries.⁴³

Despite Lincoln's and the military's strong response to draft resisters, Forty-Eighters thought him a weak president and leader, especially with regard to emancipation. They wanted a leader like John Frémont. He had acted decisively when serving as a general in command of the Department of the West in the summer of 1861. On August 30, he had put Missouri under martial law. To discourage opposition and resistance to federal authority, he ordered the arrest of armed citizens, their trial by court martial, and sentences of death. The orders proclaimed that enslaved people owned by those in sympathy with the rebellion were free. When learning of Frémont's decrees, Lincoln had not wanted to appear as subordinate to his generals or to alienate crucial support from Democrats in the border states. As commander in chief of military forces, he had overruled Frémont, removed him from command, and installed Halleck to assert his presidential authority and to restore conventional military practice to the previously disorganized department. Lincoln had demonstrated that generals in the field had to follow orders from Washington; as commander in chief, he held supreme authority.

When the president did act on his own authority with the Emancipation Proclamation, Forty-Eighters and radical abolitionists complained that he had not gone far enough. They groused that the Proclamation had insufficient geographic and temporal reach because it had not ended slavery throughout the entire United States. After peace came, because the Proclamation had been an action of the commander in chief, which had force in wartime exclusively, it would not apply. Slaves not freed during the war by fleeing to Union lines, recruitment by Union armies, or residence in an area of military occupation would remain in slavery. Laws in the border states and seceded states that established the institution of human slavery would remain in effect. Lincoln's critics placed first priority on emancipation of all the enslaved people and ranked its accomplishment more urgent than respect for the limits imposed by the Constitution on presidential power – even in wartime. With its limitations, the preliminary Emancipation Proclamation seemed indecisive and contrasted poorly with Frémont's forceful leadership in 1861.

At the other political extreme, Democrats opposed to the war's continuation and emancipation increased their opposition to the president and his policies as 1863 began and the Emancipation Proclamation took effect. Copperheads, or northern antiwar Democrats, formed an organization in February called The New-York Society for the Diffusion of Political Knowledge under the leadership of Samuel F. B. Morse, co-inventor of the Morse code. He damned Lincoln as a "Fanatic," who was determined to undermine the sovereignty of the people, and the Emancipation Proclamation as "unwise, unconstitutional and calamitous, productive of evil and only evil."[44]

To counter the publicity generated by Morse's society and to stem the anti-Lincoln sentiment roiling New York City, Lieber and other influential Republicans founded the Loyal Publication Society, which drew its membership from the city's pro-Republican intelligentsia, prominent merchants, and leaders in finance. Its publications counteracted the so-called misinformation propagated by Copperhead politicians and their

supporters in journalism and politics. As a leader of the Loyal Publication
Society, Lieber attempted to silence such discontent or at least to insert a
competing voice into public discussion. In its first year, the Society published some 43 titles and distributed 500,000 pamphlets, mostly in Ohio,
New York, Indiana, and Maryland to 649 Union Leagues, 474 Ladies
Associations, and 2,160 private individuals. In the succeeding years, its
operations extended to having pamphlets and broadsides reach military
hospitals and soldiers at the front.[45]

Shortly after the Enrollment Act became law in the spring of 1863,
the society staged at Cooper Union a "Great Mass Meeting," which the
*New York Times* called a "Monster Meeting."[46] Many of the pamphlets
appealed to ethnic and religious groups, including the Irish Americans,
Catholics, and German Americans. In 1863, just one pamphlet, *Einheit
und Freiheit* (*Unity and Freedom*), appeared in German. The next year
there were three, including Lieber's own *Lincoln oder McClellan? Ausrus
an die Deutschen in Amerika* (*Lincoln or McClellan? A Summons to
Germans in America*), which also appeared in Dutch.

The fall of the crucial city of Atlanta, Georgia, to General William
T. Sherman's army in early September 1864 ended Lieber's fears that
Lincoln and his party would fall to the Democrats and McClellan in
the approaching presidential election. The panic that the professor had
expressed in his September 1 letter to Halleck subsided. On the same day
that Lieber had whined for a new candidate and an encouraging military
victory, Confederate General John Bell Hood surrendered the Georgia
city and decisively reversed the series of disappointments experienced by
the Union army during the spring and summer of 1864. This battlefield
success allowed Lieber to disparage the leadership of Democratic candidate George McClellan. He soon asked whether voters would not prefer
a commander who brought an end to the war within sight over a general
"who did little more than hesitate."[47]

Additionally, Lieber's own close ties to the administration as well
as concern for the welfare of his two remaining sons probably influenced his political concerns. Both Hamilton, the amputee, and Norman, the younger son, now served as aides de camp. Norman had been
appointed an aide to General Pope in the Second Battle of Bull Run after
being brevetted a captain for bravery in the Peninsular Campaign. The
father's support of the Republican war may have kept his sons from
danger.[48]

Lieber's recommitment to the Republican ticket did not go the whole
way to an unqualified embrace of Lincoln. Neither his personal letters
nor his published political writings during the last months of the 1864

campaign contain any endorsement of the president's policies or his personal characteristics. As did Carl Schurz, another German American who campaigned for Lincoln in the 1864 campaign, Lieber based his advocacy of the Lincoln candidacy more on criticism of McClellan and the Democrats' 1864 platform, the so-called Chicago Platform.[49]

His arguments against the 1864 Democratic presidential ticket stem from his émigré sensibility and from his appealing to German-American voters' hopes and fears. First, he played to some German Americans' dread of political instability by finding parallels between the disastrous results of secession and the political turmoil in the German states due to the upheavals of 1848. The experience of the German states argued that the émigrés' new country of the United States would sacrifice its promise of great national strength if it agreed to its own partition. Since the Democratic platform of 1864 mandated negotiation to end the war with the Confederate States of America, a likely outcome would be two smaller, and weaker, countries.

Drawing on analogies from world history, he complained that disuniting the United States into two countries would bring a recurrence of the instability found in Europe of the Middle Ages, or the political and diplomatic impotence found in the current German states. He disparaged the seceded states' claim to sovereignty as "provincial pomposity." Recalling South American history since the 1810s, he cautioned that a dissolved United States would experience incessant revolutions. Further, with Napoleon III's recent installation of Maximilian of Austria as emperor of Mexico, the United States might stand to lose the extensive territories that Mexico had ceded after its defeat in the war of 1846–1847.[50]

Democratic triumph, he charged, would restore Southern landholders to power. Their dominion violated Germans' pursuit of civil freedom. He predicted that the ambition of slaveholders extended beyond control of African Americans to "using the working man, whether white or black, as the instrument of their power, their pleasure, and their arrogance."[51] Such criticism comported with German Americans' interpretation, especially the Forty-Eighters' interpretation, of Free Soilers' tendency to equate the North with their ideal state, one that promised land and freedom. In contrast, they portrayed the South as the North American incarnation of an old, illiberal Europe dominated by monarchy, aristocracy or oligarchy, and Junkers (Prussian landed aristocrats).[52]

After Union victories in Georgia and at Winchester, Virginia, during September 1864, Lieber hoped that German Americans would consider these large issues and march to their voting places with ballots for Lincoln.

The prize had become *Einheit und Freiheit* (Unity and Freedom) as an editor of the most prominent German-language newspaper in the United States explained. Compared with this prize, the grievances of the last four years were trivialities. German Americans should set aside their hurt feelings over abusive comments thrown at their soldiers in camp and on the battlefield. They should let go of the insults that they had felt when the press had charged German soldiers with cowardice after the disastrous battle of Chancellorsville in the spring of 1863. Instead of emphasizing the Lincoln administration's assignment of Major General Franz Sigel to a minor command in eastern Pennsylvania, Lieber counseled, proud German Americans should remember that Lincoln had restored General Sigel to command of the Department of West Virginia in the spring of 1864. Most important, the Emancipation Proclamation and other war policies had determined that free labor should prevail. In short, election of the National Union slate of Lincoln and Andrew Johnson, the vice presidential candidate, would promote the interest of German Americans.

Political events combined with Union military success to move the electorate toward support for the Lincoln-Johnson ticket. On September 22, Frémont announced that he was withdrawing from the presidential race, and he enjoined his supporters to vote for Lincoln, thus ending the threat of a third party draining votes from the president.[53] By mid-October, the military outlook brightened even further when General Philip Sheridan's forces expelled Confederate troops commanded by Jubal Early from the Shenandoah Valley.

Lieber concluded his argument for Lincoln with the hope that the election would bring a sufficiently large victory for Lincoln's party to vindicate the Union cause and impress Europeans. It did. Lincoln and Johnson won 55.03 percent of the popular vote and the electoral vote in every northern state but three: Delaware, New Jersey, and Kentucky. Despite the decisive national outcome, support for Lincoln declined in some states, thus reflecting the controversies of the last four years. In New York, the Republican ticket won by slightly less than 1 percent of the popular vote, whereas in 1860 it had won by about 7.5 percent. Contrary to the earlier projection of the *Westliche Post*, Lincoln carried Indiana, although his margin of victory decreased from 8.64 percent to 7.19 percent. Overjoyed with the election results, Lieber called it "the Great and Good Election of '64."[54]

When foreigners viewed the election results nationwide, the clear majority of voters who supported the president impressed them mightily. In Prussia, France, and Great Britain, working people and the liberal classes hailed Lincoln's victory on November 8. Henry Boernstein, a Forty-Eighter who had published a German-language newspaper in St. Louis and who now served as consul at Bremen, raved that general rejoicing prevailed "among all friends of freedom." Lincoln's victory, combined with the peaceful conduct of the election, moderated journalistic voices from Europe, even those from the southern German states that previously had stridently attacked the United States. German liberal newspapers, he reported, called the election "one of the greatest events of the times" and a "victory of republican and democratic institutions."[55]

In France, liberal newspapers that opposed Napoleon III agreed and touted Lincoln's reelection. It proved that republican government did not have to devolve to dictatorship, as had happened in their country. Further, victory for the Republican Party meant that slavery would no longer taint the freedom offered by the United States: "the reelection of Mr. LINCOLN is a pledge of abolition everywhere and in all things."[56]

A few weeks after the election, the president claimed in his annual state of the Union report to Congress: "the election has been of vast value to the national cause." It showed to Americans "one to another and to the world, this firmness and unanimity of purpose."[57] The president appears to have been right.

# 8

# The Last Lesson

On the morning of April 14, 1865, the fifth day of Passover in the Jewish calendar and Good Friday in the Christian one, residents of the city of Washington prepared for a final day of celebration after the tumult of the past two weeks. On April 2, General Lee's Army of Northern Virginia had evacuated the CSA capital of Richmond, Virginia. Seven days later, the general surrendered his forces to Ulysses S. Grant at Appomattox Court House, Virginia. The consequences of the surrender began almost immediately. On April 11, President Lincoln issued an executive order lifting the naval blockade that had closed ports in the Confederacy to the rest of the world. Two days later, the War Department announced that it would cease drafting and recruiting soldiers into the federal military. With combat winding down and the curtailment of the purchase of war matériel, the Department predicted that it would save a million dollars a day.

By the end of the week, celebrations with fireworks, bands, and cheering crowds had erupted across the northern cities, even in Baltimore, which had resisted the transit of Union soldiers through its streets in April 1861. As a former quartermaster of the Union forces remembered those days, "From Maine to California we belted the continent with bonfires, and rivaled the stars with the blaze of our rockets. Probably never again in this country will such scenes be witnessed; certainly never before in this hemisphere has there been such a saturnalia of rejoicing." If people had not lived through the Civil War years, he expected, they would find incomprehensible "the hight [sic] and depth and breadth of joy which welled up from the heart of the nation."[1]

In the nation's capital, the federal government celebrated after dark on Tuesday, April 11. Along streets illuminated with candles burning in the windows of its office buildings, crowds marched with flaming torches to the brightly lit Executive Mansion to hear the president speak. Light from the candle-filled windows extended an aura over the surrounding multitude and mansion grounds.

Greeted by cheers, Lincoln commenced by offering thanksgiving for the latest military developments that promised an imminent end to the conflict and by praising the soldiers who had won these victories, especially General Grant. Then, he reminded his attentive audience that they should not forget "He, from Whom all blessings flow." Following these introductory words, he presented a carefully reasoned defense of his policies for the reconstruction of the seceded states. Lincoln's lawyer-like, exhaustive justification probably disappointed most auditors; it certainly did not promote or prolong the jubilation of the evening.

The next day's newspapers took the president's words to a broader public, one eventually extending nationwide. Informed readers learned that the end to Civil War would not restore the status quo ante bellum. The conflict had imposed many social and economic changes on the states already occupied by the Union army where emancipation prevailed, and the defeat of Confederate armies would not end that process across the conquered territories. It would expand to include politics as recent events in Louisiana had demonstrated. Twelve thousand white male citizens in the state had sworn allegiance to the federal union and elected a new state government. Speaking to the crowd, the president lauded the Louisiana legislature for ratifying the Thirteenth Amendment and adopting a state constitution that conferred the "benefit of public schools equally to black and white."

Lincoln's words predicted continued change and the establishment of republican governments similar to that of Louisiana throughout the southern states as they resumed their relationship with the federal union. Although Lincoln recognized the republican achievement of Louisiana, he also knew that the republicanizing of the state had further to go. Its voters had not approved extending the vote to soldiers who served in the U.S. Colored Troops and "the very intelligent" civilian people of color. With these remarks on April 11, the president went public with his hope that eventually no state should deny the ballot to any male citizen on the basis of race. In his analysis of Louisiana's achievement Lincoln included the observation that the new constitution empowered the state legislature "to confer the elective franchise upon the colored man."[2]

As the president spoke to the crowd before the Executive Mansion, he did not know that he would enjoy merely four more days of life. Through these words on April 11 he demonstrated that he would continue in his second term to develop the republican results of the war after the remaining Confederate armies had surrendered. At the same time as Lincoln spoke, the Thirteenth Amendment was proceeding to ratification by the states after its passage by Congress the previous January. When that process was completed, the United States would be a union of free people. During the first months of 1865, the availability of free land, the stories of mineral wealth, and the country's vibrant labor market were luring laboring men and women from European countries in record numbers. In five years, after the presidential election of 1868, they could become citizens and the men among them would be able to cast ballots. Thus, both their state government and the U.S. government would rest upon their consent. Whether African-American men, whose citizenship had been established by former Attorney General Edward Bates's 1862 ruling, would have the right to vote remained less certain.

Before ratification of the Fifteenth Amendment by three-quarters of the states in 1870, the states could include in their voting regulations the stipulation that members of certain races or previously enslaved people could not vote. Such stipulations had existed in the former states of the Confederacy and still existed in eight northern states as Lincoln spoke on April 11, 1865. His words signaled that momentous change in the electorate of the country lay ahead.

John Wilkes Booth heard the words that Lincoln spoke from the second-floor balcony of the Executive Mansion on that night of celebration. He now understood the direction in which the Lincoln administration would steer the country. In a second term, the president would provide the leadership to transform the electorate from one of universal white manhood suffrage to one of universal manhood suffrage. Because Booth disagreed with that republican hope, the president would die.

The remaining pages of this chapter will show that Booth fired his lethal shot in a setting befitting a president with republican hopes for his own nation and the world. The content of *Our American Cousin* – the play that he saw that evening – sent a message that all men were created equal, whereas its performance in Ford's Theatre showed that the United States in 1865 did not promise social equality to all people. While most Washington theaters restricted admission of African Americans to their upper tier, or gallery, Ford's did not admit African Americans to any area of the theater, probably because the smallish theater had no gallery. Accordingly, among republicans of Lincoln's day, racist belief might coexist, and usually did coexist, with their opposition to slave labor and advocacy of free labor.[3]

Two nights after Lincoln uttered the words that incited his assassin to action, the city government of Washington sponsored an even grander celebration. On Thursday evening, municipal offices, federal offices, hotels, and private dwellings were illuminated with candles, lanterns, and torches. Banners of red, white, and blue adorned their facades. Store windows featured posters of Lincoln, General Grant, General Sherman, and George Washington. As a newspaper reporter exclaimed, the city dazzled with "a constant blaze of glory." Even the Asylum for the Insane, a journalist enthused, "looked like a palace of enchantment."

Across the Potomac River, Arlington House, the former home of Robert E. Lee and his wife, extended the visual spectacle. Occupied by the military since 1861 and confiscated from the Lee family in 1864 for nonpayment of taxes, the Arlington plantation had become the property of the federal government. Extending from Mrs. Lee's rose garden, graves of deceased soldiers radiated outward from the residence, thereby rendering unlikely the mansion's future domestic occupancy. On that Thursday night of celebration, as candles shone from the mansion's windows, the national flag with its stars and stripes flew brilliantly in the night sky. Atop the flagpole on the mansion's roof blazed the image of a star. The vision prompted the *National Republican's* correspondent to remark, "the star of freedom has arisen over his [Robert E. Lee's] house."[4]

To see the grand spectacle that Thursday night, the Lincolns had intended to enjoy a carriage drive through the city. Mary Lincoln had even written a note to General Grant inviting him, and not mentioning Mrs. Grant, to accompany them on the tour. The general regretfully declined, and the Lincolns did not take their carriage ride. Possibly, concerns for the first couple's safety amid the rowdiness of celebrating Washingtonians or the president's suffering from an intense headache canceled the outing.

The next morning the president was at his desk by seven. He was remarkably cheery, even happy. Never again would he read casualty reports like those of the Battle of Sayler's Creek in Virginia. After Lee had withdrawn his forces from Petersburg, this last major confrontation on April 6 between the armies commanded by Grant and Lee had produced more than 8,000 casualties. In addition, he may have observed the previous evening's fabulous display from the windows of the White House, and certainly the president had heard of it that morning from Nicolay,

Hay, or the people with whom he talked while walking to and from the War Department to read the most recent telegrams from the war front.

After returning to the Executive Mansion where he met with his cabinet and General Grant in the late morning, the president and Mary Lincoln took their customary late-day carriage ride, this afternoon to the Washington Navy Yard. There they toured the *Montauk*, a steam-powered steel-clad vessel with a revolving gun turret. Conversing in their carriage on that sunny but chilly spring day, the president and Mary together enjoyed moments of lightheartedness, rare occurrences for them during the war years. Their talk moved to their post-presidential life and ambitions.

The Lincolns wanted to travel in the United States and abroad. They would go to California, probably via the transcontinental railroad that the federal government had funded through legislation passed early in the president's first term and that would be completed during his second term. And, like many Americans, he wanted to travel to the Holy Land or the area of the world now known as the Middle East. For a well-informed American in tune with the trends of his day, such ambitions were unexceptional. For example, Fernando Wood, the former mayor of New York City, Democratic member of Congress, and a vocal opponent of the Thirteenth Amendment during the Congressional debates of the previous January, had sailed with his family for foreign lands, including the Holy Land, in late March, according to the April 3 Baltimore *Sun*.

During the 1860s, lecturers, authors, and publishers responded to the interest by featuring products that told or illustrated experiences in Palestine and the city of Jerusalem. Stereopticon slide collections let parlor spectators vicariously satisfy their curiosity about the region through visual images. If they wanted to know more, the advertising pages of newspapers touted the new books available in stores, including many histories and travelogues centered on the area. For instance, popular lecturer and author Bayard Taylor capitalized on Americans' curiosity with *The Lands of the Saracen; or, Pictures of Palestine, Asia Minor, Sicily and Spain* in 1854, as did Sylvanus Phelps in 1863 with *Holy Land with Glimpses of Europe and Egypt*.

Rather than a desire to be trendy, deeper, republican motives may have sparked Lincoln's interest. The French poet and politician Alphonse de Lamartine was among the first authors to popularize travel to the sacred Christian and Jewish sites with his *Voyage en Orient* (1835), subsequently translated and published in English as *De Lamartine's Visit to the Holy Land: or Recollections of the East . . . with Interesting Descriptions and*

*Engravings of the Principal Scenes of our Saviour's Ministry*. A leader of the 1848 revolutions in France and then a prominent politician in the first months of the Second Republic, Lamartine had advocated for, and won, the abolition of slavery in the French colonies. While a member of Congress in 1848, Lincoln had joined 173 of his colleagues to approve a resolution hailing "the efforts of France to establish civil liberties on the basis of a republican form of government [that] command the admiration and receive the warmest sympathies of the American people."

There also was Lincoln's search for understanding of the meaning of the war and its carnage. Having lost close friends such as Zouave commander Elmer Ellsworth, witnessing minie balls ending lives while visiting Fort Stevens on the northern edge of Washington, and viewing the devastation at the battlefields of Petersburg and Sharpsburg, Virginia, Lincoln might have pondered the effects of the attacks that he had ordered. The war had killed more than 700,000 men and women, about 2 percent of the population of the United States in 1860. God had spared the people of neither the Union nor the Confederacy. By 1864, devout people, especially those who had opposed slavery, had begun to realize that his goal seemed not the victory of one side and the defeat of the other, but the eradication of slavery altogether. As Lincoln eloquently explained in his second inaugural address,

If we shall suppose that American Slavery is one of those offences which, in the providence of God, must needs come, but which, having continued through His appointed time, He now wills to remove, and that He gives to both North and South, this terrible war, as the woe due to those by whom the offence came, shall we discern therein any departure from those divine attributes which the believers in a Living God always ascribe to Him? Fondly do we hope – fervently do we pray – that this mighty scourge of war may speedily pass away.[5]

Small wonder that Lincoln sought escape from the wartime world in the realm of humor.

Lincoln frequently took mental vacations from his presidential responsibilities by reading contemporary, popular humorists, especially Charles Farrar Browne, David Ross Locke, and Robert Henry Newell, who created the fictional characters Artemus Ward, Petroleum V. Nasby, and Orpheus C. Kerr. Reading books by these men to his visitors, who often laughed with him but sometimes privately grimaced at the president's so-called low taste, afforded Lincoln diversion and shifted his mind from focus on hordes of supplicants for federal patronage, casualty reports, and momentous issues awaiting his attention.[6] Before reading his draft of the Emancipation Proclamation to his cabinet on September 22, 1862, Lincoln read the assembled secretaries a chapter from Charles Farrar Browne's *Artemus Ward: His Book.*[7]

As they settled down to the business of that momentous day, Lincoln's cabinet members heard him read the recently published "High-handed Outrage at Utica." In this adventure, Artemus, a traveling showman, exhibits his oddities, including strange animals and wax figures or "statoots" of famous historical figures in Utiky (Utica). He recounts the misbehavior, sometimes vociferously, of one of its citizens, the son of one of its first families. During the show, an outraged Utikian walks up to Artemus's wax-figure display of the Last Supper, accosts the wax likeness of Judas Iscariot, and starts to pummel it. After some comical repartee, he protests: "Judas Iscarrot can't show hisself in Utiky with impunnerty (impunity) by a darn site!" Artemus has the last word by observing, "I sood him, and the Joory brawt in a verdick of Arson in the 3d degree."[8] Whether the excessive piety of the Utikian or the verdict convicting him of arson amused Lincoln, we cannot know. We can imagine slightly embarrassed or puzzled laughter greeting the president's utterances, and then amazement arising. Following his comical performance came the reading of a most serious document. Based on his powers as commander in chief, he would free 3 million people from bondage.

Such comic interludes in Lincoln's usual sedate behavior often struck his associates as frivolity, most seriously in the election campaign of 1864. A cartoonist then had pilloried Lincoln's supposed lightheartedness and used it to urge votes for Democratic candidate General George McClellan. In the cartoon, the president's frivolity morphed into contrast with the care and concern that his opponent, McClellan, had shown for his soldiers. In the *Harper's Weekly* cartoon, Lincoln and his friend Ward Hill Lamon stand among wounded soldiers. The commander in chief holds a Scottish tam (as discussed in Chapter 3 and shown in Figure 3.3) while encouraging Lamon to sing and provide comic relief.

The characters of Ward, Nasby, and Kerr transported the president to an oasis, where draughts of humor could refresh his mind. There he met, for instance, the fictional Kerr, a soldier in the Mackerel Brigade. He encountered German and Irish soldiers who speak with almost unintelligible accents, and locals who refer to kerridges, not carriages. Nasby, a pastor and both a Copperhead and a Democrat, dedicated his book to notable "Dimokrats" including "that Sterlin Patryot" "Fernandywood" (Fernando Wood) and "the grate Vallandygum, uv Ohio" (Clement Vallandigham). After various experiences with the military, including draft avoidance, Nasby founds a so-called Democratic church. During the service, the congregation and he read from:

One uv the follerin passages uv Skripter:– 9th chapter uv Jennysis, wich relates the cussin uv Canaan, provin that niggers is Skriptoorally slaves, and the chapters about Hayger and Onesimus, wich proves the Fugitive Slave Law to be skriptooral. (The rest uv the Bible we consider figgerative, and pay no attenshun to, watever.")

[A translation: One of the following passages of Scripture, the 9th chapter of Genesis, which relates the cursing of Canaan, proving that negroes is Scripturally slaves, and the chapters about Hagar and Onesimus, which proves the Fugitive Slave Law to be scriptural. (The rest of the Bible we consider figurative, and pay no attention to, whatever.)[9]]

Besides ridiculing Lincoln's political opposition, Nasby, along with Artemus Ward and the scheming Orpheus C. Kerr, poked fun at the language that cultured and educated Americans of the 1860s considered old-fashioned and quaint. They had abandoned their former folkways, either by emigrating from the old world or by rising from rural regional ways in speech and dress. As Lincoln enjoyed these humorists, while dressed in his usual black Brooks Brothers suit and sporting Kossuth-like facial hair, he could see how far he had come from his log cabin origins in Kentucky and Indiana. His chuckles connected him to this new community of wealth and taste. As he pushed the United States toward becoming a nation dedicated to free labor, he could enjoy the doings of the folk whom he had left behind.

After returning from his drive to the Washington Navy Yard with Mary on this final Friday, Lincoln greeted friends and admirers from Illinois in the Executive Mansion. During the early evening, he read to them *Petroleum Nasby*'s ridiculous account of his adventures during the war years. Finally, he yielded to repeated entreaties and sat down to supper with Mary. The first couple's light-humored day continued after their meal. Upon disposing of some final petitioners, including his longtime friend, Illinois Republican representative Isaac Arnold, Lincoln and his wife departed the Executive Mansion for Ford's Theatre.

Earlier that day, the Lincolns had decided to attend the last performance of Laura Keene's troupe at Ford's Theatre. It would feature *Our American Cousin*, a play popular in the United States since 1858 and in England since 1861. By late-afternoon editions of city newspapers the theater owner had rushed advertising announcing their presence at that evening's performance. (See Figures 8.1 and 8.2.) Consequently, although

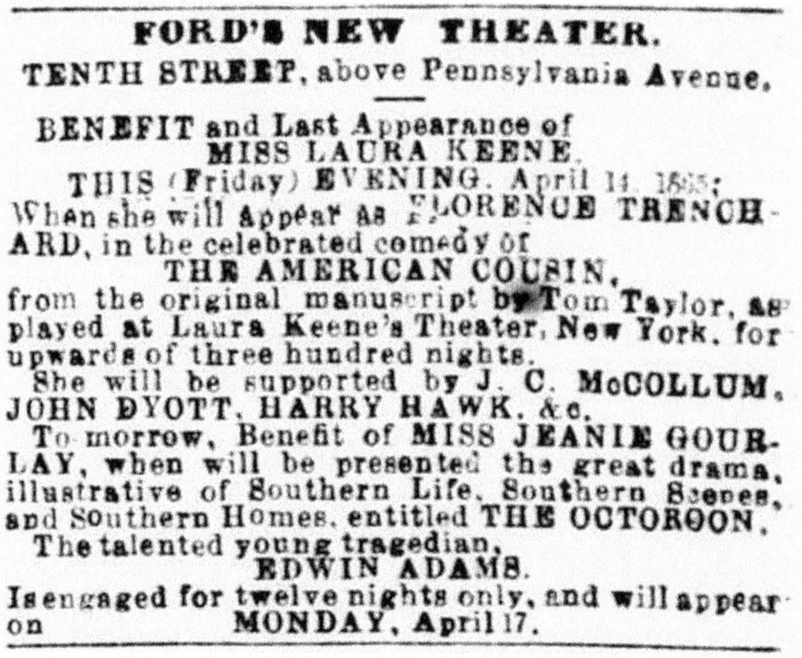

---

**FORD'S NEW THEATER.**
TENTH STREET, above Pennsylvania Avenue,

---

BENEFIT and Last Appearance of
MISS LAURA KEENE.
THIS (Friday) EVENING. April 14, 1865;
When she will appear as FLORENCE TRENCH-
ARD, in the celebrated comedy of
THE AMERICAN COUSIN,
from the original manuscript by Tom Taylor, as
played at Laura Keene's Theater, New York. for
upwards of three hundred nights.
She will be supported by J. C. McCOLLUM,
JOHN DYOTT, HARRY HAWK, &c.
To-morrow, Benefit of MISS JEANIE GOUR-
LAY, when will be presented the great drama,
illustrative of Southern Life. Southern Scenes,
and Southern Homes. entitled THE OCTOROON.
The talented young tragedian,
EDWIN ADAMS.
Is engaged for twelve nights only, and will appear
on                    MONDAY, April 17.

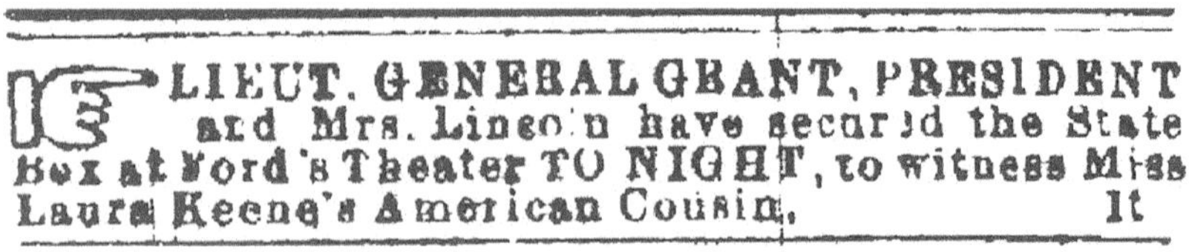

---

☞LIEUT. GENERAL GRANT, PRESIDENT
and Mrs. Lincoln have secured the State
Box at Ford's Theater TO NIGHT, to witness Miss
Laura Keene's American Cousin.                    It

FIGURES 8.1 AND 8.2. On Friday, April 14, 1865, starting with its first edition, the *Evening Star* (Washington) ran its usual column of ads for local theaters on page 1, including one for Ford's Theatre (Fig. 8.1), which announced the benefit performance for Laura Keene in *Our American Cousin*. In later editions, in column 1 of p. 2, a page made up later at many U.S. dailies, the Ford brothers inserted the news that General Grant and the Lincolns would attend the evening performance. Hearing this news in the early afternoon, Booth activated his assassination plot. The newspaper notice for the April 14 performance of *Our American Cousin* is reproduced as a courtesy of Archives and Special Collections, Franklin & Marshall College. With appreciation to James Cornelius for the clip from the *Evening Star*, taken from microfilm at ALPLM.

Mary tried to back out of the engagement, Lincoln felt committed. He persuaded his wife that they should attend the theater so that he could rest from the admirers and petitioners pressing for an audience with him in the White House.[10]

As usual at the theater, during the last performances of a play's run, the proceeds from ticket sales of that night were dedicated to the benefit of one of the stars. On the evening of April 14, Laura Keene would profit. Since emigrating from England, she had become a prominent actress, producer, and theater owner. On her New York City stage, *Our American Cousin* had enjoyed its first successful run in the 1858–1859 season and become the talk of the town. Running for more than 150 performances, it broke theater records. Currently, Keene toured *Our American Cousin* and had brought it to Ford's Theatre for a spring engagement in 1865.

That the Lincolns should choose to see *Our American Cousin*, a comedy contrasting American and British manners, American ways with the ways of a sharp lawyer and feckless British aristocrats, should not surprise given Lincoln's fondness for Kerr, Nasby, and Ward. Mary had enjoyed the comedy before, most probably in Philadelphia, where the show had become a staple offering, and possibly both Lincolns had seen the play previously in the capital city.

By 1865, the play had become thoroughly implanted in the national popular culture, and by the end of the century it would rank as one of the most performed plays in the United States. Theater troupes across the country had incorporated the melodrama into their repertoires.[11] A performance of the play in 1858 had benefited the Mount Vernon Ladies Association, which raised funds to preserve the first president's Virginia estate. Merchants profited from the show's popularity by selling sheet music for polkas inspired by either the New York or Philadelphia version of the play. Additionally, dramatists rewrote the play to extend its appeal. In 1859, New York theaters offered both *Our Female American Cousin* and *Our Yankee Cousin*. Between 1859 and 1865, the Stadt theater produced *Our German Cousin*, while *Our African Cousin* ran on another stage and *Our Irish Cousin* played on a third.[12]

As the Lincolns were well aware, the author of *Our American Cousin*, Tom Taylor, was a noted British playwright, especially of comedies of manners. The previous year, the president had purchased tickets for the January 23 performance of Taylor's *The Ticket of Leave Man* (1862) at Grover's Theatre, his most celebrated melodrama and a benefit for the Ladies' Soldiers' Relief Association.[13]

Best known in this century as a principal contributor to the British humor magazine *Punch*, Taylor possessed many talents. For a few years, he had taught language and literature courses at University College, London, while preparing for a career as a lawyer. Like many of his fellow Londoners, he had become fascinated by the American tourists, exhibitors, and business people who arrived in the city in 1851 for the great Crystal Palace Exhibition, the first international exposition of manufactured and agricultural products. It attracted Americans to London in droves, thus affording Britons extensive opportunities to observe how their former colonists had developed since independence. Their dress, speech, and behavior quickly became the subject of British humorists and a topic for conversation. Americans and their ways thoroughly amused well-to-do and mannered Britons. Finding the foreigners ludicrous, they started to say "I reckon" and "he calculated." They downed bourbon slings, munched peanuts, and savored pumpkin pie.[14]

Inspired by the fashion for things American, Taylor deployed his creative playwriting talents to popularize republican ideas such as the uselessness of rent-collecting aristocratic landowners and the true nobility of free labor. Following publication of *Uncle Tom's Cabin* in 1852, Taylor cowrote an adaptation of the antislavery and pro–free labor novel for the Adelphi Theatre in London. His connection with the Adelphi introduced him to Joshua Silsbee, a character actor from the United States, famous for his portrayals of the Yankee or Brother Jonathan.[15]

Seeing an opportunity to capitalize on the presence of Silsbee and the reigning interest in American corruptions of the English language, Taylor composed *Our American Cousin*. Like many of his dramas, it was adapted for the British stage from a French script that had been inspired by the political turmoil of the late 1840s. Besides translating the play, Taylor reset it in the English countryside and eliminated the most obvious risqué repartee to avoid offense to genteel audiences. In the case of *Our American Cousin*, he drew from *La Femme Forte* (1847), which featured an American Yankee, Silsbee's specialty.[16]

In Taylor's version, the starring role moved from the female protagonist to Silsbee, who played Vermonter Asa Trenchard. The villain of the piece became a lawyer scheming to steal his employer's property. He along with Lord Dundreary, a guest at the manor house on the estate, demonstrate the impotence of the British elite when faced with American energy, intelligence, and goodheartedness, the rising forces of the Atlantic world.

In the United States, the play began its successful run at Laura Keene's New York theater on October 18, 1858, after she had purchased rights to the work from the playwright following Silsbee's death in 1855. The actors then playing its central characters, Dundreary and the American Asa Trenchard, instantly rose to stardom. In the production, Dundreary appears to have no function in life other than to visit friends, to employ servants, to search for a spouse, and to produce an heir to Dundrearyness. Although the aristocrat does nothing of worth in life, for the melodrama he did a lot.

The actor E. A. Sothern, who portrayed Lord Dundreary during the play's first run, made the nobleman seem a relic of a bygone age, incapable of fitting either visually or mentally into the current bustling social and economic world. The Dundreary character sported a monocle, sideburns so long that they dangled below his chin, and an extravagantly long topcoat extending almost to his ankles. He spoke with a halting lisp while pretending to knowledge that he did not possess. In response to hoots of laughter from the audience evoked by Dundreary's affectations, the actor introduced even more stage business to accentuate his character's ridiculousness. He began to walk with a combination skip and hop that audiences found even more hilarious. Soon culturally literate Americans used the term "Dundreary" to imply a pretentious aristocrat. With his acerbic wit, George Templeton Strong, a New York lawyer and treasurer of the U.S. Sanitary Commission, dismissed the Marquis of Hartington, whom he had observed at a ball in New York City, as "a gaudy young English swell of the Dundreary type."[17]

In contrast to Dundreary stood Asa Trenchard. Like earlier stage Yankees, a stock character in Britain and the United States comedy since early in the century, Asa holds a high opinion of himself that he is not loathe to share. His words and phrases betray his less than genteel origins as he speaks in ways that his high-toned English relatives find ludicrous and incomprehensible. Although untutored in genteel ways, he is smart and resourceful. He has come to England to claim an inheritance willed to him by a relative, who had immigrated to the United States after dis-inheriting his British relatives, Asa's hosts. They envision their American cousin in terms that Romantic writers of earlier decades had popularized. A female guest at the Manor imagines him, an "Apollo of the prairie," and "the wild young hunter... with the free step and the majestic mien of the hunter of the forest."[18]

Asa's entrance and opening lines immediately show these words to be fantasy. Offending conventional polite behavior, he causes the Tren-chards, their guests, and their servants to gasp by referring to his shirt as a "buzzom," and offering to kiss his cousin on the cheek. He confidently introduces himself as "Asa Trenchard, born in old Vermont, suckled on the banks of Muddy Creek, about the tallest gunner, the fastest runner, the slickest dancer, and generally the loudest critter in the state." Shortly,

Asa offers to concoct drinks for his hosts and their houseguests: "Whisky Skin, Brandy Smash, Sherry Cobbler, Mint Julep or Jersey Lightning."[19] Upon sampling his Jersey Lightning, Dundreary collapses into the arms of Mrs. Mountchessington, another houseguest, who is stalking rich matrimonial candidates for her daughters.

Unlike previous stage Yankees, the Asa character in Tom Taylor's play possesses generous heart in addition to a sharp mind. In the dairy barn at Trenchard Manor, he discovers Mary, an impoverished direct descendant of the deceased émigré, who now supports herself as a milkmaid. Asa pronounces her far superior to "some pumpkins," a rating that flummoxes his hostess, Florence, the daughter of the Manor, whom Laura Keene portrayed.

Realizing Florence's confusion, Asa explains his terminology by comparing her to the industrious and modest Mary. Florence "can sing and paint, and play on the pianner"; consequently she merits the rank of "some pumpkins" because her social circle, centered in the parlor, valued those so-called genteel accomplishments. In contrast, Mary the milkmaid possessed useful skills for a family of working people. She "can milk cows, set up the butter, make cheese, and darn me, if them ain't what I call real downright feminine accomplishments." In short, she's no "small potatoes."[20]

Smitten with Mary, the Vermonter burns the document or will, which he had brought to England to prove his claim. It would have benefited him while disinheriting her. After the proof of Asa's right to inherit becomes smoke and ashes, she will inherit the estate of the deceased relative who had left his family years ago to find opportunity and wealth in the United States. Consequently, the audience learns that the bragging, rustic American possesses true nobility – that of the heart. Soon, Asa and Mary realize their mutual attraction and pledge their love.

At the conclusion of the melodrama, Asa and the milkmaid stand before the proscenium as the supporting characters line up in pairs behind them. All ends well for every character except the dishonest lawyer who sought to defraud the Manor owner. Asa's ingenuity and generosity have rescued the Trenchard estate and operated to produce a happy future. Overall, the play discredits aristocratic pretensions and both male and female conventions of gentility. Audiences learn that worth resides in truehearted and honest characters. A productive and good future lies ahead thanks to the United States and people on both sides of the Atlantic who dedicate themselves to attaining prosperity through their own efforts.

The bullet from John Wilkes Booth's derringer prevented President Lincoln from applauding this happy ending. Four scenes before the final curtain, the pistol shot penetrated Lincoln's brain, causing him to lose consciousness in the midst of the laughter elicited by Asa Trenchard's latest and most telling blast at Mrs. Mountchessington.

She has just discovered that Asa Trenchard has renounced the inheritance that would have made him a suitable candidate for her own daughter's hand. Rather crudely he tells the mother and daughter that he is "biling (boiling) over with affections, which I'm ready to pour out to all of you, like apple sass (sauce) over roast pork." Ordering her daughter to leave the presence of a boor who indirectly would suggest ejaculation to ladies, Mrs. Mountchessington harrumphs at Asa that he has no familiarity with "good society" and stomps off the stage. Famously, Asa retorts, "I guess I know enough to turn you inside out, old gal – you sockdologizing old man-trap."[21]

From the president, "sockdologizing" probably prompted the last laugh of his life. The word always evoked guffaws from the play's many audiences. Because of the word's linguistic absurdity, no one quite knew what it meant. In the context of Asa's exclamation, it implies a person who pretends to goodness while conniving and manipulating. In all probability, the playwright never had heard the word from an American visitor to England or read it in an American book. Bartlett's *Dictionary of Americanisms*, first published in England in 1848, when Taylor was still teaching at University College, defined both the verb "to doxologize" and the noun "socdolager." The first took the noun "doxology," a familiar word to nineteenth-century Christian audiences, and made it a verb meaning to give glory to their god. The noun "socdolager" referred actually to a gimmicky fishhook, which closed its two hooks after a fish had bitten one of them so that it was unlikely to escape, and figuratively to a conclusive argument or powerful blow.[22]

This manufactured word was among the last that Lincoln heard before he sank into the unconscious state from which he never emerged. We know that he liked a good laugh, especially at nonsensical words. Sockdologizing evoked humor in a way similar to Kerr's kerridges, Nasby's Dimokrats, and Ward's statoots. While these words sound ridiculous, the implications of Taylor's sockdologizing go further.

The playwright's sockdologizing does more than corrupt the standard pronunciation of an existing word into the vernacular. Rather, Asa coins the word in response to his antagonist's insult. By having Asa invent the term, Taylor deployed a theatrical convention familiar to audiences on both sides of the Atlantic in the 1850s and 1860s. For example, in the *Two Gentlemen of Verona*, Shakespeare creates a humorous moment when the character Proteus confesses to the innocent Julia that she has "metamorphosed" him. In the middle nineteenth-century decades, melodramas and minstrel shows also relied on this verbal convention for humor, and frequently it conveyed a verbal jab at aristocratic or genteel social norms, as *Our American Cousin* demonstrated.[23]

Taylor introduces his verbal fabrication to highlight the contrasting values of Asa and Mrs. Mountchessington. In the confrontation with the British society lady, the American proves his vitality and resourcefulness by abandoning conventional, polite formulations. To denounce her, he produces a hyperbolic new word. By doing so, he implies his country's break from class-ridden, English ways. The laughter from the audience, and from Lincoln, demonstrated, on one level, hilarity at the neologism, and on a deeper level, approval of this declaration of independence from an aristocratically determined vocabulary and culture.[24] Lincoln had received his final lesson about republicanism in the Atlantic world.

Although the republican-minded Tom Taylor did not intend the following interpretation when he composed *Our American Cousin* in 1852, it is one that became evident as the American Civil War progressed. The tall, physically powerful, and virile Asa Trenchard recalls the popular image of Lincoln as the rail-splitter. Asa's good-hearted generosity toward the play's female characters, with the exception of Mrs. Mountchessington and her daughters, corresponds to the generous heart that Lincoln frequently showed. His fellow citizens knew that he had commuted the sentences of low-ranking soldiers discovered sleeping while on sentry duty, had visited hospitals in Washington and on battlefields to comfort the wounded, and had written grieving mothers. He had gained public approbation for his often reprinted letter consoling Mrs. Lydia Bixby on the death of her five sons with the thoughts that she had "the thanks of the Republic they died to save."[25]

Contrasted with the Lincoln-like hero are the effete-appearing and -sounding Lord Dundreary and Mrs. Mountchessington. With their polished manners, insincere words, and materialistic values sugar-coated with practiced gentility, they stand for an older Britain that reformers like John Bright were striving to end. As the end of the play suggested, the future did not reside with them. Additionally in the now re-United States, the surrender of General Lee signaled the imminent demise of a landed, slave-owning elite in the American South.

Robert E. Lee had derived his status partially from his lineage dating back to Virginia's first families of the colonial era. Having married Mary Custis, great-granddaughter of Martha Washington, and acceded to being master of Arlington House (known today as the Robert E. Lee Memorial), both the Lee family and the Trenchards had drawn their income from land, in one case an estate worked by tenant farmers, and in the other a plantation worked by slaves. With ratification of the Thirteenth Amendment in December 1865, free African-American laborers now populated Arlington. They had homes in the Freedman's Village, a settlement of contraband families on the former Lee property established in 1863, and the freed people retained for themselves the wages that they earned. In this sense, they now were no different from the former master of Arlington House. After the war, he would support his family by his own labor in an upper-middle-class professional position as president of Washington College (now Washington and Lee College) in Lexington, Virginia.[26]

At the same time that the battles of the Civil War were being fought, a cultural battlefront opened in playhouses on both sides of the Atlantic whenever theater troupes performed *Our American Cousin*. The popularity of the play during the 1860s shows that while the armies of the United States were triumphing on the battlefield, republican values and beliefs were campaigning for the popular mind in theaters as they taught republican lessons. Asa Trenchard's exclamation of sockdologizing signaled the moment of Lincoln's death. It also sounded the advent of a republican future – still little more than a hope in Great Britain, France, and the German states, but a future now closer to realization in the United States because of the leadership of Abraham Lincoln.

# Notes

## Introduction

1. Henry Clay, *The Life and Speeches of the Hon. Henry Clay*, edited by Daniel Mallory (New York: Robert P. Bixby & Co., 1843), 1:432, 439.
2. Douglas L. Wilson and Rodney O. Davis, eds., *Herndon's Informants: Letters, Interviews, and Statements about Abraham Lincoln* (Urbana: University of Illinois Press, 1998), 123.
3. Roy P. Basler, ed., *The Collected Works of Abraham Lincoln* (hereinafter *CW*) (New Brunswick, NJ: Rutgers University Press 1953), 2:116 for the quotation, and 2:62.
4. See Thomas Bender, *A Nation Among Nations: America's Place in World History* (New York: Hill and Wang, 2006). Also see Lynn Hunt, *Writing History in the Global Era* (New York: W. W. Norton, 2014), 44–45, for a graphic demonstration of the increase of books in English published in the United States and Great Britain with "Globalization" or "Globalisation" in their titles. After the composition of *Lincoln in the Atlantic World* was well under way, the first book to demonstrate Lincoln's legacy and memorialization around the world appeared. See Richard Carwardine and Jay Sexton, eds., *The Global Lincoln* (New York: Oxford University Press, 2011).
5. Michael B. Oren, *Power, Faith, and Fantasy: America in the Middle East, 1776 to the Present* (New York: W. W. Norton, 2007), 184–186, 181.
6. David Herbert Donald, *Lincoln* (New York: Simon & Schuster, 1995), 177. Historians now see the American colonies as situated in the Atlantic World, while American Studies scholars engage in a *transnational* understanding of the United States and its history. European, African, and colonial historians began to conceptualize their studies in terms of the Atlantic World in the late 1980s. For definitions and discussions of *Atlantic World* and *transnationalism*, see the articles in Lynn Dumenil and Paul Boyer, eds., *The Oxford Encyclopedia to American Social History*, either online or in print. For *transnationalism*, which gained currency in the first decade of the twenty-first century, also consult articles in *Encyclopedia of American Studies*, online at http://eas-ref.press.jhu.edu/index.html.

7. Frederic Bancroft et al., *The Reminiscences of Carl Schurz, 1852–1863* (New York: The McClure Company, 1907), 2:242–243; Donald, 321.

8. Amanda Foreman, *A World on Fire: Britain's Crucial Role in the American Civil War* (New York: Random House, 2010), 67; Michael Burlingame, *Abraham Lincoln: A Life* (Baltimore, MD: Johns Hopkins University Press, 2008), 2:119; Walter Stahr, *Seward: Lincoln's Indispensable Man* (New York: Simon & Schuster, 2012), 252–253.

9. Richard Carwardine, *Lincoln: A Life of Purpose and Power* (New York: Alfred A. Knopf, 2006), 181; Doris Kearns Goodwin, *Team of Rivals: The Political Genius of Abraham Lincoln* (New York: Simon & Schuster, 2005), 364.

10. Howard Jones, *Abraham Lincoln and The New Birth of Freedom: The Union and Slavery in the Diplomacy of the Civil War* (Lincoln: Nebraska University Press, 1999), 1; also idem, *Blue and Gray Diplomacy: A History of Union and Confederate Foreign Relations* (Chapel Hill: University of North Carolina Press, 2010); and Kevin Peraino, *Lincoln in the World: The Making of a Statesman and the Dawn of American Power* (New York: Crown Publishers, 2013).

11. Basler, *CW*, 4:426.

12. See Dorothy Ross, "Lincoln and the Ethics of Emancipation: Universalism, Nationalism, Exceptionalism," *Journal of American History* 96 (2009): 379–399 (hereinafter *JAH*).

13. An excellent, concise summary of Lincoln's ambition appears in Carwardine, *Lincoln*, 8–11. Daniel Walker Howe's discussion of Lincoln's self-transformation from Whig to Republican first directed my thinking along these lines. See his "Abraham Lincoln and the Transformation of American Whiggery," in his *The Political Culture of the American Whigs* (Chicago: University of Chicago Press, 1979), 263–298. Discussion of Lincoln's self-fashioning appears in chapter 1, chapter 3 for Kossuth's influence, and chapter 5 for Bright's influence.

14. "The Opening of Japan. City of Yedo," *Weekly Vincennes* (IN), *Gazette*, March 8, 1858, Library of Congress, Chronicling America: Historic American Newspapers Site at the Library of Congress (hereinafter Chronicling America). David Donald briefly refers to the origins of the Tycoon nickname in his *"We Are Lincoln Men": Abraham Lincoln and His Friends* (New York: Simon & Schuster, 2007), 186–187.

15. Dallas Finn, "The Guests of the Nation: Japanese Delegation to the Buchanan White House," online at http://www.whitehousehistory.org/history/documents/White-House-History-12-Finn-Japanese-Delegation.pdf. Also see Michael R. Auslin, *Pacific Cosmopolitans: A Cultural History of U.S.-Japan Relations* (Cambridge, MA: Harvard University Press, 2011), 50–52.

16. "The Politics of the Day," *New York Herald*, June 19, 1860, NewsBank/Readex.

17. "Visitors from Baltimore-Republican Ratification Meeting-the Japanese, & c," *The Sun* (Baltimore), May 29, 1860, NewsBank/Readex; see page 5 of *New York Herald*, February 12, 1861, NewsBank/Readex.

18. Reprinted from the *New York Spirit* in the *Anti-Slavery Bugle* New-Lisbon, Ohio), September 8, 1860, Chronicling America.
19. In John Hay, *Lincoln and the Civil War in the Diaries and Letters of John Hay*, ed. Tyler Dennett (New York: Dodd Mead, 1939), 5, the mention occurs on April 20, 1861. In John Hay, *Lincoln's Journalist: John Hay's Anonymous Writings for the Press, 1860–1864*, ed. Michael Burlingame (Carbondale: Southern Illinois University, 1998), 89, the mention occurs on August 5, 1861.
20. Advertisement, *New-York Tribune*, July 8, 1860, NewsBank/Readex; "National Cement," *Bobolink Minstrel, or Republican Songster for 1860*, ed. George W. Bungay (New York, O. Hutchinson Publisher, 1860), 39.
21. "Visit of the President and Mrs. Lincoln to the Patent Office," *New York Herald*, March 20, 1863, NewsBank/Readex; mention in the *Daily Picayune* (New Orleans), June 7, 1863, from "Another Iron-Clad," *Memphis Daily Appeal*, June 17, 1863, Chronicling America; Basler, *CW*, 6:95–96, 8:45.

### Chapter 1. The Second Shot Heard 'Round the World

1. Anthony S. Pitch, *"They Have Killed Papa Dead!": The Road to Ford's Theatre, Abraham Lincoln's Murder, and the Rage for Vengeance* (Hanover, NH: Steerforth, 2008), 113. Accounts of the assassination appear in most Lincoln biographies. Recent books that focus on the assassination are: James L. Swanson, *Manhunt: The Twelve-Day Chase for Lincoln's Killer* (New York: William Morrow, 2006), and Pitch, *They Have Killed Papa Dead*.
2. Lord Lyons to Earl John Russell, as quoted in Foreman, *World on Fire*, 53.
3. Queen Victoria to Mary Lincoln, April 29, 1865, Abraham Lincoln Papers at the Library of Congress (hereinafter ALP@LC). On April 28, 1865, Empress Eugénie of France wrote Mrs. Lincoln and the letter is included in a note in Justin G. Turner and Linda Levitt Turner, *Mary Todd Lincoln: Her Life and Letters* (New York: Alfred A. Knopf, 1972), n. 6, p. 355. The letter follows the formula for a basic condolence letter described below.
4. *Appendix to Diplomatic Correspondence of 1865: The Assassination of Abraham Lincoln, Late President of the United States of America,...* (Washington: GPO, 1866), 497 (hereinafter *ADC*).
5. *ADC*, 496–497. The volunteer numbers come from a speech by the German ambassador: Count Johann Bernstorff, "Abraham Lincoln as the Germans Regarded Him: Address delivered at Springfield, Ill., February 12, 1913." Albert Bernhardt Faust reports that 176,817 German Americans fought in the war; see his *The German Element in the United States with Special Reference to Its Political, Moral, Social, and Educational Influence*, vol. 1 of *The German Element in the United States* (New York: Houghton Mifflin, 1909), 523.
6. *Tribute to the Memory of Abraham Lincoln by the American Citizens Resident in Buenos Aires* (Buenos Aires: German Printing Office, 1865), 6.
7. *ADC*, 460–461 for Pisa, 437 for Canzo, Italy, and 441 for Chiavenna. Google maps now offers a map showing Lincoln's global influence by locating streets, squares, and monuments on every continent. See "Abraham

Lincoln's Global Legacy" at https://www.google.com/maps/d/u/o/viewer?
msa=0&mid=zLNT8RJQiGQk.kjp4Es16nkzE.

8. *Tributes to the Memory of Abraham Lincoln: Reproduction in Facsimile of
   Eighty-seven Memorials Addressed by Foreign Municipalities and Societies
   to the Government of the United States, Prepared under the Direction of
   the Secretary of State, in Accordance with a Joint Resolution of Congress,
   Approved Feb. 23, 1881* (Washington, DC: GPO, 1885), 14. Also see *Miscellaneous Documents of the House of Representatives, 1865–'66* (Washington,
   DC: GPO, 1866), 59–62.

9. *ADC*, 61 says silver; *The Assassination of Abraham Lincoln, Late President
   of the United States of America, and the Attempted Assassination of William
   H. Seward, Secretary of State, and Frederick W. Seward, Assistant Secretary,
   on the Evening of the 14th of April, 1865* (Washington, DC: GPO, 1867)
   says gold. The illustration in *Tributes to the Memory* (1885) shows gold
   stitching.

10. I have taken details of the subscription for the medal and its appearance
    from a variety of sources. Most important is Benjamin Gastineau, *Histoire
    de la Souscription Populaire à la Médaille Lincoln: La Médaille de la Lib-
    erté* (Paris, FR: c. 1866), passim. For invaluable assistance with the transla-
    tions, I am indebted to Liliane Saphier and my colleague Lisa Gasbarrone.
    The medal is also described in "To Sell Rare Lincoln Medal," *New York
    Times* (hereinafter *NYT*), January 31, 1909, at http://www.nytimes.com;
    and "Abraham Lincoln French Mourning Medal, 1865," in *American His-
    tory and Live Auction*, January 21, 2010, http://www.cowanauctions.com/
    past_sales_view_item.asp?itemid=73731. For the presentation to Mrs. Lin-
    coln in 1867 see *Diplomatic Correspondence of the United States*, 1868,
    216–218; and "Lincoln Medals," in *American Historical Record and Reper-
    tory of Notes and Queries*, ed. Benson J. Lossing (Philadelphia: Chase &
    Town, 1872), 534–535. Also see, Michael Vorenberg, "Liberté, Égalité, and
    Lincoln: French Readings of an American President," in Richard Carwardine
    and Jay Sexton, eds., *The Global Lincoln* (New York: Oxford University
    Press, 2011), 101–102.

11. French Medal Committee to Mrs. Lincoln, October 13, 1866, Series 4, Abra-
    ham Lincoln Papers, Manuscript Division, Library of Congress, reprinted in
    *Assassination of Abraham Lincoln* (1867), 88.

12. J.B.G., "A French Tribute to Lincoln: The Gold Medal Presented to his
    Widow in 1866," *Putnam's Magazine*, 7 (1909–1910): 671.

13. Dr. René Lefebvre (Edouard Laboulaye), *Paris in America*, trans. Mary
    L. Booth (New York: Charles Scribner, 1863), 74; Yasmin Sabina Khan,
    *Enlightening the World: The Creation of the Statue of Liberty* (Ithaca, NY:
    Cornell University Press, 2010), 15.

14. *ADC*, 67, and "Interesting from Paris," *New York Times*, May 16, 1865, at
    NYTimes.com (hereinafter *NYT*).

15. *ADC*, 108.

16. Benjamin Gastineau, *Histoire de la Souscription Populaire à la Médaille
    Lincoln: La Médaille de la Liberté* (Paris, FR: c. 1866), 16.

17. *Reproduction in Facsimile of Eighty-seven Memorials* (1885), n.p.

18. *Tributes to the Memory*, 87.
19. John Bigelow to William H. Seward, Communication 193, October 28, 1865, Records of Foreign Service Posts, Diplomatic Posts, France, Vol. 67, RG 59, 1756–1993, National Archives and Records Administration, College Park, MD (hereinafter NARA).
20. Post No. 940, April 28, 1865; Post No. 943, May 4, 1865; Post No. 948, May 11, 1865; Post No. 954, May 11, 1865; Post No. 974, June 2, 1865, Records of Foreign Service Posts, Diplomatic Posts, Great Britain, Vol. 25, RG 84, NARA.
21. Most of the original letters today reside at NARA. Reprinted, they appear in translation from the original language in a 717-page volume, an appendix to the 1865 *Foreign Relations of the United States*. The Department of State also published a revised version of this volume in 1867 as cited in note 9. I have taken all citations from *ADC*.
22. Official expressions of condolence upon the death of Abraham Lincoln, 1865, at Abraham Lincoln Presidential Library and Museum, Springfield, Illinois (hereinafter ALPLM). On line at: http://alplm-cdi.com/chroniclingillinois/items/browse?collection=219.
23. This description is based upon my own observation and an e-mail from James Cornelius, July 13, 2010. The Kettering letter is found in *ADC*, 245–246, and the signatures can be seen on the document at Folder 2–175, Box 2, Entry 177, RG 59, in Foreign Messages on the Death of Lincoln, 1865, General Records of the Department of State, Miscellaneous Correspondence, 1784–1906, at NARA.
24. Robert Lincoln to A. L. Mohler, April 24, 1905, at ALPLM.
25. E-mails from James Cornelius to the author, April 14 and July 13, 2010.
26. *ADC*, 500.
27. *ADC*, 238 for Dorset. Resolutions from Selby, Box 4, Entry 177, Record Group 59, in Foreign Messages on the Death of Lincoln.
28. *ADC*, 197. My thanks to Douglas Anthony for information on Cape Coast.
29. *ADC*, 273.
30. *ADC*, 430.
31. *ADC*, 60.
32. *ADC*, 281.
33. *ADC*, 50–51.
34. Cassius M. Clay to William Seward, No. 79, May 4, 1865, Records of Foreign Service Posts, Diplomatic Posts, [Union of Soviet Socialist Republics, Vol. 8, 1863–1870], RG 84.2, NARA; Clay to William Hunter, No. 81, May 16, 1865, ibid.
35. *ADC*, 471, 616.
36. *ADC*, 535.
37. *ADC*, 504.
38. *ADC*, 171, 322, 312, 163. For British and American Victorians, the condolences referred to in the second inaugural address, including its promise of conciliation and reference to divine punishment, possibly brought the brutal wartime deaths within the conventions of the "good death." See Drew Gilpin

Faust, *This Republic of Suffering: Death and the American Civil War* (New York: Random House, 2008), 6–17 and passim.

39. Basler, *CW*, 8:333.
40. ADC, 66, 283, 308.
41. Basler, *CW*, 8:333.
42. Passim in the several collections of condolence letters as well as in the manuscript collection at ALPLM.
43. *Assassination of Abraham Lincoln* (1867), 45, 167.
44. ADC, 34, 263, 267.
45. Howe, *Political Culture of the American Whigs*, 267.
46. ADC, 434.
47. On this transformation, see Howe, *American Whigs*, 266–267.
48. See the National Park Service website, "The Lincoln Home," at http://www .nps.gov/history/museum/exhibits/liho/rooms/frontParlor.html.
49. Benjamin Perley Poore, *Perley's Reminiscences of Sixty Years in the National Metropolis* (New York: Hubbard Brothers, 1885), 2:115–121; Catherine Clinton, *Mrs. Lincoln: A Life* (New York: Harper, 2008), 164–165.
50. Clinton, *Mrs. Lincoln*, 136; Jean H. Baker, *Mary Todd Lincoln: A Biography* (New York: W. W. Norton, 1987), 186–187. Also, e-mail from Susan Haake, curator, Lincoln Home National Historical Site, October 19, 2010, and "Furnishings Acquired by Mary Todd Lincoln," typescript obtained from William Allman, White House Curator, January 4, 2010.
51. ADC, 55.
52. ADC, 57.
53. ADC, 617, 167. Spelling conforms to the original document at the in Folder 48, E175, NARA.
54. ADC, 354, 560.
55. ADC, 577.
56. ADC, 434. Workingmen of Genoa shared this hope (ibid., 449).
57. ADC, 448.
58. *Diplomatic Correspondence*, 1862, 237; *Diplomatic Correspondence*, 1864, 308.
59. ADC, 257.
60. ADC, 400.
61. ADC, 227.
62. ADC, 291.
63. ADC, 538.
64. ADC, 498.


## Chapter 2. African Lessons

1. Roy P. Basler, "Introduction," to John Locke Scripps, *Life of Abraham Lincoln*, ed. Roy P. Basler and Lloyd A. Dunlap (1860; reprint, New York: Greenwood Press, 1961), 7.
2. Carwardine, *Lincoln*, 57.
3. See Scripps, *Life of Lincoln*, 35. Important twentieth-century Lincoln biographers do not mention his reading of Riley's *Narrative*, for instance,

Lord Charnwood (1917), Carl Sandburg (1926), James G. Randall (1945), David Herbert Donald (1995), Richard Carwardine (2003), Doris Kearns Goodwin (2005), and Ronald C. White (2009).

4. Michael Burlingame, a prominent Lincoln scholar, names more than these seven books as constituting his subject's youthful reading and says that he did not read *The Life of Franklin*. The inclusion of Franklin's *Life* in the Scripps biography underlines the intentional selectivity of Lincoln's choices. According to Burlingame a more complete list of his boyhood reading would include: Noah Webster's *American Spelling Book*, Asa Rhoads's *American Spelling Book*, *The Kentucky Preceptor*, James Barclay's English dictionary, Daniel Defoe's *Robinson Crusoe*, William Grimshaw's *History of the United States*, a biography of Henry Clay, and William Scott's *Lessons in Elocution*. See the online version of his *Abraham Lincoln: A Life*, chap. 2, 124–125, at www.knox.edu/academics/distinctive-programs/lincoln-studies-center/burlingame-abraham-lincoln-2-life.html.

5. Scripps tells Lincoln that he has included nothing that had been "not fully authorized." John L. Scripps to Abraham Lincoln, July 7, 1860, ALP@LC.

6. The definitive account of the popularity of the *Narrative* is Donald J. Ratcliffe, "Selling Captain Riley, 1816–1859: How Did His 'Narrative' Become So Well Known?" *Proceedings of the American Antiquarian Society* 117 (2007): 177–209. It corrects an earlier article by R. G. McMurtry, "The Influence of Riley's *Narrative* upon Abraham Lincoln," *Indiana Magazine of History* 30 (1934): 133–138. For additional information about Riley, I have relied on Dean King, *Skeletons on the Zahara: A True Story of Survival* (Boston, MA: Little, Brown, and Company, 2004).

7. Eric Foner, *Free Soil, Free Labor, Free Men: The Ideology of the Republican Party before the Civil War* (New York: Oxford University Press, 1970).

8. On Bacon, see Hugh Davis, *Leonard Bacon: New England Reformer and Antislavery Moderate* (Baton Rouge: Louisiana State University Press, 1998); Louise L. Stevenson, *Scholarly Means to Evangelical Ends: The New Haven Scholars and the Transformation of Higher Learning in America, 1830–1890* (Baltimore, MD: Johns Hopkins University Press, 1986), 22–26, 153; Burlingame, *Abraham Lincoln*, 377. Evidently, in 1861, Lincoln himself told Bacon of his influence and, in 1864, he mentioned it to Joseph Parrish Thompson, another Congregational minister. Nevertheless, it is true that Lincoln seems to have modified the antislavery formulation that Bacon made in his 1846 book in a letter to Albert Hodges in 1864. See Theodore Davenport Bacon, *Leonard Bacon: A Statesman in the Church* (New Haven, CT: Yale University Press, 1931), 271, 465. The origins of Lincoln's statement to Albert G. Hodges on April 4, 1864, "If slavery is not wrong, nothing is wrong," appear in Bacon's much lengthier quotation from *Slavery Discussed in Occasional Essays from 1833 to 1846* (New York: Baker and Scribner, 1846), x.

9. Michael Winship, "*Uncle Tom's Cabin*: History of the Book in the 19th-Century United States," at *Uncle Tom's Cabin and American Culture: A Multi-Media Archive* at http://utc.iath.virginia.edu/interpret/exhibits/winship/winship.html.

10. "Woman's True Mission," *Southern Literary Messenger* 19, no. 5 (1853): 305. For reception, also see Joan D. Hedrick, *Harriet Beecher Stowe: A Life* (New York: Oxford University Press, 1994), 222, 231–232.

11. Robert Bray, *Reading with Lincoln* (Carbondale: Southern Illinois University Press, 2010), 34.

12. Richard Lawrence Miller, *The Rise to National Prominence, 1843–1853*, vol. 3 of *Lincoln and His World* (Jefferson, NC: McFarland & Co., 2011), 153–154.

13. Ratcliffe, "Selling Captain Riley," 194–195; Donald Wayne Riddle, *Congressman Abraham Lincoln* (Urbana: University of Illinois Press, 1957), 8–9.

14. Ratcliffe, "Selling Captain Riley," 206–207.

15. (Samuel Griswold Goodrich), *The Tales of Peter Parley about Africa* (1831, rev. ed. Philadelphia: Desilver, Thomas, 1836), 81–96; (Samuel Griswold Goodrich), *The Story of Captain Riley and his Adventures in Africa* (Philadelphia: Henry F. Anners, 1841).

16. James Riley, *An Authentic Narrative... 1815* (New York: Leavitt and Allen, 1859).

17. *New Hampshire Sentinel*, April 15, 1840, NewsBank/Readex; "Maryland Institute Lectures," *The Sun* (Baltimore), January 3, 1856, NewsBank/Readex; "The Milliner's Apprentice; or, The False Teeth. A Story that Hath more Truth Than Fiction in It," *Godey's Lady's Book* (May, 1841); and Theodore Ledyard Cutler, "A Day at Lowell," ibid. (October, 1846).

18. William Willshire Riley, *Sequel to Riley's Narrative* (Columbus, OH: George Brewster, 1851), 384, 387.

19. For discussions of pro-slavery thought, see Drew Gilpin Faust, "Introduction," *The Ideology of Slavery: Proslavery Thought in the Antebellum South, 1830–1860* (Baton Rouge: Louisiana State University Press, 1981), 11, and "Thornton Stringfellow," ibid., 136–138. Quotations from Thornton Stringfellow, "A Brief Examination of Scripture Testimony on the Institution of Slavery," in *The Ideology of Slavery*, ed. Faust, 154, 165. Also see Paul Finkelman, *Defending Slavery: Proslavery Thought in the Old South: A Brief History with Documents* (New York: Bedford/St. Martin's, 2003), 31–33.

20. See E. N. Elliott, *Cotton Is King, and Pro-Slavery Arguments: Comprising the Writings of Hammond, Harper, Christy, Stringfellow, Hodge, Bledsoe, and Cartwright...* (Augusta, GA: Pritchard, Abbott & Loomis, 1860), 459–491; Faust, ed., *Ideology of Slavery*, 136–137.

21. Theodore Dwight Weld, *The Bible against Slavery: An Inquiry into the Patriarchal and Mosaic Systems on the Subject of Human Rights* (New York: American Anti-Slavery Society, 1837), 32.

22. Henry Ward Beecher, *Freedom and War: Discourses on Topics Suggested by the Times* (Boston, MA: Ticknor and Fields, 1863), 34.

23. Mark A. Noll, *The Civil War as a Theological Crisis* (Chapel Hill: University of North Carolina Press, 2006), 50.

24. Mason Locke Weems, *The Life of George Washington; with Curious Anecdotes, Equally Honorourable to Himself, and Exemplary to his Young Countrymen* (1800, Philadelphia: Joseph Allen, 1837), 211, 212.

25. Mason Locke Weems, ed., *The Life of Benjamin Franklin, Written Chiefly by Himself, with a Collection of His Best Essays* (1815, Philadelphia: M. Carey, 1817), 194.
26. Quoted in Matthew T. Mellon, *Early American Views on Negro Slavery* (New York: Bergman Publishers, 1963), 19. Also see Don B. Kates, Jr., "Abolition, Deportation, Integration: Attitudes toward Slavery in the Early Republic," *Journal of Negro History* 53 (1968): 41.
27. Thomas Dilworth, *A New Guide to the English Tongue* (New York: E. Duyckinck, D. D. Smith, W. B. Gilley, and G. Long, 1820), 128.
28. John Bunyan, *The Pilgrim's Progress from this World to that which is to Come* (1678; reprint, New York: John Tibout, 1804), 209.
29. Weems, *Washington*, 226, 67.
30. Martha Elena Rojas, "'Insults Unpunished': Barbary Captives, American Slaves, and the Negation of Liberty," *Early American Studies* 1 (Fall 2003): 169. Lynn Hunt might argue that the reading of eighteenth-century novels had prepared the reading public to empathize with the Barbary captives. See Lynn Hunt, *Inventing Human Rights: A History* (New York: W. W. Norton, 2007), chap. 1.
31. See Goodrich, *Lights and Shadows of African History* (Boston, MA: Bradbury, Soden, & Co., 1844), 235–249; *The Narratives of an Old Traveller* (Philadelphia: Willis P. Hazard, 1854), 86–124.
32. James Riley, *Sufferings in Africa: The Incredible True Story of a Shipwreck, Enslavement and Survival on the Sahara Narrative* (New York: Skyhorse Publishing, 2007), 34, 36. I have used this edition for quotations as readers can most easily access it in hardcopy. To make sure the quotations accurately reflect the content of editions that Lincoln might have read, I checked to ascertain that the quotation here and in the remainder of the chapter did appear in editions of the *Narrative* published between 1817 and 1860, with one exception explained later, in note 47.
33. Riley, *Narrative*, 34, 36.
34. Riley, *Narrative*, 90.
35. Riley, *Narrative*, 60–61.
36. In *Reading Fiction in Antebellum America: Informed Response and Reception Histories, 1820–1865* (Baltimore, MD: Johns Hopkins University Press, 2011), James L. Machor argues that "reviews enjoyed a publicly sanctioned authority buttressed by the institutional imprimatur of the publishing industry itself (31)." For a review, see "Riley's Narrative," *North American Review* 5 (1817): 389–409. My discussion of the Barbary narrative is drawn from Paul Baepler, "White Slaves, African Masters," *Annals of the AAPSS* 588 (July 2003): 90–107; idem, "The Barbary Captivity Narrative in American Culture," *Early American Literature* 39, no. 2 (2004): 217–246.
37. Discussion of the Barbary Wars is based on Oren, *Power, Faith, and Fantasy*, chaps. 1–3.
38. See Robert Battistini, "Glimpses of the Other before Orientalism: The Muslim World in Early American Periodicals, 1785–1800," *Early American Studies* 8 (2010): 446–474.
39. Oren, *Power, Faith, and Fantasy*, 75.

40. Martha Elena Rojas, "'Insults Unpunished': Barbary Captives, American Slaves, and the Negotiation of Liberty," *Early American Studies* 1 (2003): 165; Oren, *Power, Faith, and Fantasy*, 38.
41. Oren, *Power, Faith, and Fantasy*, 69–70.
42. Oren, *Power, Faith, and Fantasy*, 73–74.
43. Royall Tyler, *The Algerine Captive* (1816; reprint, Bedford, MA: Applewood Books, 2008), 240.
44. Oren, *Power, Faith, and Fantasy*, 77.
45. Oren, *Power, Faith, and Fantasy*, 78.
46. Peter Parley (Samuel Griswold Goodrich), *The Story of Captain Riley and his Adventures in Africa* (Philadelphia: Lippincott, Grambo & Co., 1854), 237.
47. Since modern editions of the *Narrative* omit Riley's antislavery statements, I am quoting from an earlier version that includes this text. See Riley, *An Authentic Narrative* ... (New York: Andrus and Judd, 1833), 260.
48. Ibid.
49. Ibid.
50. Eric Foner, *The Fiery Trial: Abraham Lincoln and American Slavery* (New York: W. W. Norton, 2010), 258–260. A debate about whether President Lincoln supported emancipation after January 1, 1863, prevails among Lincoln scholars. For a summary, see Phillip W. Magness and Sebastian N. Page, *Colonization after Emancipation: Lincoln and the Movement for Black Resettlement* (Columbia: University of Missouri Press, 2011), chs. 1 and 11.
51. Riley, *Narrative*, 259–260.
52. George Berkeley, *The Works of George Berkeley, D.D.*, ed. Alexander Campbell Frasier (Oxford: Clarendon Press, 1871), 3:232.
53. Riley, *Narrative*, 209.
54. Ibid.
55. Even the one exception usually cited does not qualify as an exception after closer examination. When the Haitian government had voted compensation to former slaves after that country's revolution from French control, it had done so in order to gain formal recognition from France for its independence. On compensated emancipation, see Stanley Engerman, "Slavery, Freedom, and Sen," in *Buying Freedom: The Ethics and Economics of Slave Redemption*, ed. Kwame Anthony Appiah and Martin Bunzl (Princeton, NJ: Princeton University Press, 2007), 86; Foner, *Fiery Trial*, 15.
56. Margaret M. R. Kellow, "Conflicting Imperatives: Black and White American Abolitionists Debate Slavery Redemption," in Appiah and Bunzl, eds., *Buying Freedom*, 200, 202, 205, 211.
57. John G. Nicolay and John Hay, *Abraham Lincoln: A History* (New York: The Century Co., 1890), 1:140–141; Burlingame, *Abraham Lincoln*, 1:122–123.
58. On the *Creole* rebellion, see Edward Bartlett Rugemer, *The Problem of Emancipation: The Caribbean Roots of the American Civil War* (Baton Rouge: Louisiana State University Press, 2009), 175–176. On the Somerset precedent, see Norman S. Poser, *Lord Mansfield: Justice in the Age of Reason* (Montreal: McGill-Queen's University Press, 2013), 292–298.

59. James Oakes, *Freedom National: The Destruction of Slavery in the United States, 1861–1865* (New York: W. W. Norton, 2013), 24–26, 35. George Washington Julian, *The Life of Joshua R. Giddings* (Chicago: A. C. McClurg and Company, 1892), 116–130; James Brewer Stewart, *Joshua R. Giddings and the Tactics of Radical Politics* (Cleveland, OH: Case Western Reserve University Press, 1970), 70–78.
60. Richard Lawrence Miller, *The Rise to National Prominence, 1843–1853*, vol. 3 of *Lincoln and His World* (Jefferson, NC: McFarland & Co., 2011), 157–159.
61. For the story of Wilson's abduction and release, see Kenneth J. Winkle, *Lincoln's Citadel: The Civil War in Washington, DC* (New York: W. W. Norton & Company, 2013), 28–33. See *Journal of the House of Representatives of the United States*, 1847–1848, January 17, 1848, p. 250, at A Century of Lawmaking for a New Nation: U.S. Congressional Documents and Debates, 1774–1875 (http://memory.loc.gov/ammem/amlaw/lawhome .html).
62. Julian, *Giddings*, 241–245; James K. Polk, *The Diary of James K. Polk during His Presidency* (Chicago: A. C. McClurg, 1910), 3:428–429. Both the kidnapping and *Pearl* incident are described in Miller, *Rise to National Prominence*, 177–180.
63. For disagreement between Giddings and Lincoln, see *Journal of the House of Representatives*, pp. 97, 107, and for agreement, pp. 105, 139, 208, 251, 326, 348, 454, and 1154.
64. Miller, *Rise to National Prominence*, 182.
65. Burlingame, *Abraham Lincoln*, 1:288–289.
66. Basler, CW, 2:20–22; Foner, *Fiery Trial*, 57–58.
67. *Journal of the House of Representatives*, p. 567, A Century of Lawmaking for a New Nation: U.S. Congressional Documents and Debates, 1774–1875, Statutes at Large, 31st Congress, 1st Session, pp. 462–465, at http://memory.loc.gov/cgi-bin/ampage?collId=llsl&fileName=009/llsl009 .db&recNum=489.
68. Foner, *Fiery Trial*, 258–260.

## Chapter 3. European Lessons

1. Benson J. Lossing, *Pictorial History of the Civil War in the United States of America* (Philadelphia: George W. Childs, 1866), 1:279–281. On Arnold, see James A. Rawley, "Isaac Newton Arnold, Lincoln's Friend and Biographer," *Journal of the Abraham Lincoln Association* 19 (Winter 1998): 39–56.
2. For mention of the first threats, see John George Nicolay to Therena Bates, October 16, 1860, Box 2, John G. Nicolay Papers, Library of Congress. Henry C. Whitney, *Life on the Circuit with Lincoln* (Boston, MA: Estes and Lauriat, 1892), 492–493; Carl Sandburg, *Lincoln Collector: The Story of Oliver R. Barrett's Great Private Collection* (New York: Harcourt, Brace, 1949), 57–67, and 65, for Pete Muggins to Old Abe Lincoln, November 25, 1860.

3. Mr. A. G. Frick to Mr Abe Lincoln, February 14, 1861, Chicago Historical Society, in Harold Holzer, ed., *Dear Mr. Lincoln: Letters to the President* (Boston, MA: Addison-Wesley, 1993), 341.

4. Lincoln to Major Hunter, January 26, 1861, Series II (Illinois Papers), www.papersofabrahamlincoln.org/images/newdocuments/239633-01.jpg.

5. Holzer, *Lincoln, President-Elect*, 389–390.

6. Michael Burlingame, ed., *Lincoln's Journalist: John Hay's Anonymous Writings for the Press, 1860–1864* (Carbondale: Southern Illinois University Press, 1998), 33–34; *Commercial Advertiser* (Buffalo), February 17, 1861.

7. Michael J. Kline, *The Baltimore Plot: The First Conspiracy to Assassinate Abraham Lincoln* (Yardley, PA: Westholme Publishing, 2008), 118–119.

8. Basler, CW, 4:240–241.

9. "Mr. Lincoln in Lancaster," *Lancaster Intelligencer*, February 26, 1861, http://digitalnewspapers.libraries.psu.edu/Default/Skins/civilwar/Client.asp?skin=civilwar; Burlingame, *Lincoln's Journalist*, 41; Basler, CW, 4:242.

10. "President Lincoln in Harrisburg," *Daily Patriot and Union* (Harrisburg), February 23, 1861 at http://digitalnewspapers.libraries.psu.edu/Default/Skins/civilwar/Client.asp?skin=civilwar; "The 22nd at Harrisburg," *Republican Compiler* (Gettysburg), February 25, 1861 at http://digitalnewspapers.libraries.psu.edu/Default/Skins/civilwar/Client.asp?skin=civilwar.

11. Lossing, *Pictorial History of the Civil War*, 1:280.

12. Lossing, *Pictorial History of the Civil War*, 1:281; Kline, *The Baltimore Plot*, 239, 258–259.

13. "Mr. Lincoln's Departure from Harrisburg," *Daily Patriot and Union* (Harrisburg), February 25, 1861, at http://digitalnewspapers.libraries.psu.edu/Default/Skins/civilwar/Client.asp?skin=civilwar.

14. "The National Crisis," *Daily Patriot and Union* (Harrisburg), February 26, 1861, at http://digitalnewspapers.libraries.psu.edu/Default/Skins/civilwar/Client.asp?skin=civilwar.

15. "Secret Departure of the President Elect from Harrisburgh," NYT, February 25, 1861.

16. Harold Holzer, "Like a Thief in the Night," NYT, February 22, 2011, http://opinionator.blogs.nytimes.com/2011/02/22/like-a-thief-in-the-night/.

17. For a popular retelling of Charles's disguises, see James Boswell, *The Journal of a Tour to the Hebrides with Samuel Johnson, L.L.D.* (London: Henry Baldwin, for Clark Dilly, 1785), 218–222. The first American edition appeared in 1810, and the volume was issued multiple times before 1860. My thanks to James Cornelius and my colleague Ben McRee for pointing out the connection. For a discussion of many of the cartoons, see Holzer, *Lincoln, President-Elect*, 397–403.

18. Zachary Taylor, Message to Congress, December 24, 1850, *Congressional Globe*, 13–14.

19. *Journal of the Senate of the United States of America*, March 3, 1851, p. 304; *Illinois Journal*, September 7, 1849, NewsBank/Readex; Basler, CW, 2:62.

20. Bills and Resolutions, Senate, 31st Congress, 2nd Session, February 17, 1851.

21. For the stud, see New Orleans *Times Picayune*, April 9, 1850; for the polka, see *The Sun* (Baltimore), January 7, 1850; and for the hats, ibid., May 4,

1850; for the march and Brougham's theater, see *New-York Daily Tribune*, November 15, 1851, all at NewsBank/Readex. Timothy Mason Roberts tells of the theatrical productions in *Distant Revolutions: 1848 and the Challenge to American Exceptionalism* (Charlottesville: University of Virginia Press, 2009), 149.

22. *Appleton's Cyclopaedia of American Biography* (1887), *s.v.* "Genin, John Nicholas"; "A Pebble Cast," *NYT*, March 4, 1852.
23. George Templeton Strong, *The Turbulent Fifties, 1850–1859*, vol. 2 of *Diary of George Templeton Strong*, 76. For these items, see the advertisement section in the *The Sun* (Baltimore), *Times-Picayune*, *Daily Ohio Statesman*, *Daily Alabama Journal*, *Barrie Gazette*, *Hartford Daily Courant*, and St. Louis *Sunday Morning Republican* from January 1850 through July 1852, all at NewsBank/Readex.
24. Henry W. De Puy, *Kossuth and his Generals: with a Brief History of Hungary* (Buffalo, NY: Phinney and Co., 1852), 353, 357.
25. *Kossuth in New England: A Full Account of the Hungarian Governor's Visit to Massachusetts* (Boston, MA: John P. Jewett & Co., 1852), 80.
26. De Puy, *Kossuth*, 343. For a report of this speech, see the *Daily Ohio Statesman*, October 28, 1851, NewsBank/Readex.
27. Eugene Davis, "Louis Kossuth," *Kate Field's Washington* 9 (April 4, 1894), 214.
28. *Weekly Herald* (New York), December 6, 1851, Newsbank/Readex.
29. Donald S. Spencer, *Louis Kossuth and Young America: A Study of Sectionalism and Foreign Policy, 1848–1852* (Columbia: University of Missouri Press, 1977), 12–13.
30. Alexander Buel in Part I of *Congressional Globe* (1850), 144.
31. Spencer, *Louis Kossuth*, 14.
32. Noah Porter, Jr., "The Youth of the Scholar," *Bibliotheca Sacra* 3 (1846): 99–100.
33. *Congressional Globe*, House of Representatives, 1st Session, 603–604.
34. Roberts, *Distant Revolutions*, 153. See Wendell Phillips, *Kossuth . . . Speech Delivered at the Antislavery Bazaar* (Boston, MA: 1852).
35. "The Kossuth Reception," *Daily Globe*, December 9, 1851, NewsBank/Readex; Esther C. Henck, *The Welcome of Louis Kossuth Governor of Hungary to Philadelphia by the Youth* (Philadelphia: P. H. Skinner, 1852), 30, ix, xvi.
36. John H. Komlos, *Louis Kossuth in America, 1851–1852* (Buffalo, NY: East European Institute, 1973), 84–85.
37. Komlos, *Kossuth in America*, 84–85.
38. Basler, *CW*, 2:115–116.
39. Robert V. Remini, *Henry Clay: Statesman for the Union* (New York: W. W. Norton, 1991), 222, 285.
40. David Stephen Heidler and Janice T. Heidler, *Henry Clay: The Essential American* (New York: Random House, 2010), 488; Remini, *Henry Clay*, 778; Kossuth as quoted in Carl Schurz, *Life of Henry Clay* (New York: Houghton, Mifflin, 1887), 2:395. The report of the visit appeared in the *NYT*, January 13, 1852.

41. Basler, CW, 2:116; Komlos, *Kossuth in America*, 118.
42. Roberts, *Distant Revolutions*, 162–163; Komlos, *Kossuth in America*, 127.
43. *Kossuth in New England*, 17.
44. Basler, CW, 2:115.
45. Basler, CW, 2:323, 3:222, 3:363.
46. Basler, CW, 3:151, 155, 4:426.
47. "Kossuth's Speech before the Legislature of Ohio," NYT, February 12, 1852.
48. Basler, CW, 4: 129, 130.
49. Basler, CW, 4:219.
50. Herman Melville, *Redburn: His First Voyage* (New York: Harper and Brothers, 1850), 222; idem, *Pierre; or the Ambiguities* (New York: Harper and Brothers, 1852), 328.
51. *Indiana State Journal*, March 12, 1852, as quoted in Roberts, *Distant Revolutions*, 160.
52. Advertisements in *New York Herald*, September 10, 1856, NewsBank/Readex.
53. In the vast collection of memoirs, diaries, and letters with Lincoln's presidency as their foci, I have found several instances of Lincoln wearing a Kossuth-type hat during his informal moments. Benjamin Brown French records that the president arrived at the White House on September 4, 1861, dressed unrecognizably "in gray woolen clothing, and had upon his head a most ordinary broad-brimmed slouch [hat]" in *Witness to the Young Republic: A Yankee's Journal, 1828–1870*, ed. Donald B. Cole and John J. McDonough (Hanover, NH: University Press of New England, 1989), 373. In *My Diary North and South* (Boston, MA: T. O. H. P. Burnham, 1863), William Howard Russell observes the president in a felt hat when rushing back to the White House and while sitting with some officers and telling "one of his jokes" (pp. 429, 523).
54. Harold Holzer, "Visualizing Lincoln: Abraham Lincoln as Student, Subject, and Patron of the Visual Arts," in Eric Foner, ed., *Our Lincoln: New Perspectives on Lincoln and His World* (New York: W. W. Norton, 2008), 83.

## Chapter 4. German Lessons

1. "How he Studied German," in Walter B. Stevens, *A Reporter's Lincoln* (Saint Louis: Missouri Historical Society, 1916), 91. With great thanks to my friend and colleague Cecile C. Zorach for providing the examples of the false cognates. Please compare the actual account published on this website (A.W.F.), "Statement: Mr. Lincoln studies German," Documents of Ida M. Tarbell, Allegheny College, https://dspace.allegheny.edu/bitstream/handle/10456/30699/17.3811.0005.pdf?sequence=1, with Ida M. Tarbell, *The Life of Abraham Lincoln* (New York: Doubleday & McClure Co., 1900), 1:239. Tarbell somewhat misrepresents what Lincoln's dentist actually wrote in this memo to her. Subsequent writers rely on Tarbell's published account, apparently not having consulted the original memo. See the following note and Wayne C. Temple, "A. W. French: Lincoln Family Dentist,"

*Lincoln Herald* 63 (Fall 1961): 151. The archivist at Allegheny College has also misread, I believe, the initials below the memo as *A.M.F.* The initials of Lincoln's dentist, who participated in the German lessons, are A.W.F.

2. Wayne C. Temple, "The Linguistic Lincolns: A New Lincoln Letter," *Lincoln Herald* 94 (Fall 1992), 110; Frank Baron, *Abraham Lincoln and the German Immigrants: Turners and Forty-Eighters* (Lawrence, KS: Society for German-American Studies, 2012), 146–47, 114 n. 20. With appreciation to Frank Baron for sending a copy of his publication.

3. Consular Report, December 12, 1864, in Consular Posts, Bremen, Germany, Vol. 179 at NARA, College Park.

4. Ella Lonn, *Foreigners in the Union Army and Navy* (Baton Rouge: Louisiana State University Press, 1951), 4; *Population of the United States in 1860* (Washington: GPO, 1864), pp. xxix–xxxi.

5. For the German immigration, I have relied on Baron, *Abraham Lincoln and the German Immigrants*, 1–9; Sabine Freitag and Steven W. Rowan (translator), *Friedrich Hecker: Two Lives for Liberty* (St. Louis, MO: St. Louis Mercantile Library, 2006), 128–29; Mischa Honeck, *We Are the Revolutionists: German-Speaking Immigrants and American Abolitionists after 1848* (Athens: University of Georgia Press, 2011), chap. 1; Lonn, *Foreigners in the Union Army and Navy*, 1–44.

6. See Carl J. Friedrich, "The European Background," in A. E. Zucker, ed., *The Forty-Eighters: Political Refugees of the German Revolution* (New York: Columbia University Press, 1950), 3–25.

7. Helen Nicolay, *Lincoln's Secretary, a Biography of John G. Nicolay* (New York: Longmans, Green, 1949), 5.

8. Nicolay, *Lincoln's Secretary*, 5–7, 10, 13, 19.

9. See the Lieber family correspondence in the Francis Lieber Collection, South Carolina University, Columbia.

10. See Oakes, *Freedom National*, chapter 1, for an extended discussion of slavery existing as a local institution in the United States.

11. Fred M. Schied, "Education and Working Class Culture: German Workers' Clubs in Nineteenth Century Chicago," http://www-distance.syr.edu/schied .html; Freitag, *Hecker*, 158. See Honeck, *We Are the Revolutionists*.

12. See *Hoffman v. Wernwag* at *The Law Practice of Abraham Lincoln*, http://www.lawpracticeofabrahamlincoln.org/Results.aspx.

13. Raymond Lohne, "Team of Friends: A New Lincoln Theory and Legacy," *Journal of the Illinois State Historical Society* 101 (2008), 292. Gustav Philipp Körner, *Memoirs of Gustave Koerner, 1809–1896: Life-sketches Written at the Suggestion of his Children* (Cedar Rapids: Torch Press, 1909), 1:443.

14. Freitag, *Hecker*, 141–42.

15. Körner, *Memoirs*, 1:581.

16. Lohne, "Team of Friends," 292.

17. Lincoln attended his first meeting to promote independence for Hungary on September 6, 1849. The meetings with regard to his visit to the United States occur in January 1852. Basler, CW, 2: 62, 115–116.

18. Basler, CW, 2:121–132; quote from ibid., 126.

19. *95 Years of Grace: A Brief Historical Sketch of Trinity Ev. Lutheran Church* (Springfield, IL, November 29, 1936), 3. For the population figures, see "Historical Census Browser," http://mapserver.lib.virginia.edu.
20. "Renewal of Slavery Agitation," *Trenton* (NJ) *State Gazette*, March 29, 1854, NewsBank/Readex.
21. Article from the *Chicago Tribune*, March 18, 1854, as quoted in Baron, *Abraham Lincoln and the German Immigrants*, 77–78.
22. Francis Lieber, *The Life and Letters of Francis Lieber*, ed. Thomas Sergeant Perry (Boston, MA: James R. Osgood and Company, 1882), 269.
23. Basler, CW, 4:67.
24. Basler, CW, 2:227.
25. Basler, CW, 2:284, and 284, n. 3.
26. Baron, *Abraham Lincoln and the German Immigrants*, 79.
27. Richard Lawrence Miller, *The Path to the Presidency*, vol. 4 of *Lincoln and His World* (Jefferson, NC: McFarland, 2012), 35–37.
28. David Herbert Donald, *Lincoln* (New York: Simon & Schuster, 1995), 173–178.
29. Horace White to Abraham Lincoln, October 25, 1854, ALP@LC.
30. John B. Jentz, "The 48ers and the Politics of the German Labor Movement in Chicago during the Civil War Era: Community Formation and the Rise of a Labor Press," in *The German-American Radical Press: The Shaping of a Left Political Culture, 1850–1940* (Urbana: Illinois University Press, 1992), 50; Baron, *Abraham Lincoln and the German Immigrants*, 70.
31. Tarbell, *Lincoln*, 290.
32. Baron, *Abraham Lincoln and the German Immigrants*, 83.
33. Miller, *Path to the Presidency*, 77.
34. As quoted in David C. Mearns, *The Lincoln Papers* (Garden City, NY: Doubleday, 1948), 1:189–190.
35. Basler, CW, 2:261.
36. Basler, CW, 2:266.
37. Basler, CW, 2:265.
38. Basler, CW, 2:268.
39. Basler, CW, 2:276. Knowing that Lincoln read the *New York Times*, I checked Lincoln's words beginning with "that the one retrograde institution in America" in the *New York Times* database and discovered that he was repeating words and phrases in the last paragraph of "Mr. Soule's 'Vulgar Turbulence' – George Sanders," that had appeared on September 29, 1854, as a reprinted editorial from the *London Daily News* of September 19. Further investigation revealed that Caleb McDaniel had made a similar discovery on his blog, *Offprints*. He suggested the Cuba reference; see "New Light on Lincoln Quote," at http://mcdaniel.blogs.rice.edu/?p=126.
40. Basler, CW, 2:323.
41. Helen Nicolay, *Lincoln's Secretary*, v, 20.
42. Burlingame, *Lincoln*, 1:412–413.
43. Basler, CW, 2:475.
44. Basler, CW, 2:499–500.
45. Basler, CW, 2:500.
46. Basler, CW, 2:502.

47. Basler, *CW*, 2:537; 3:79–80.
48. Basler, *CW*, 3:109, 115.
49. Basler, *CW*, 3:374–376, and ibid., 377, n. 1; Lohne, "Team of Friends," 36–37.
50. Basler, *CW*, 3:380, and n. 1, p. 381.
51. Basler, *CW*, 3:383. For an extended discussion of the deal, see Baron, *Abraham Lincoln and the German Immigrants*, 89–96.
52. Basler, *CW*, 3:391, and notes 1 and 2 on the same page. On the deal and the start of publication, see Harold Holzer, *Lincoln and the Power of the Press: The War for Public Opinion* (New York: Simon & Schuster, 2014), 190–192.
53. Basler, *CW*, 3:336, 2:410; Helen Nicolay, *Lincoln's Secretary*, 25–27.
54. John G. Nicolay, "All this is not the Result" (1858), Box 2, John G. Nicolay Papers, LC, and speech given to the "Capital Garde" and others by [?] Nicolay on July 4, 1859, Box 18, John G. Nicolay Papers, LC. Translation by Cecile C. Zorach.
55. See Helen Nicolay, *Lincoln's Secretary*, 28–30; and the clipping entitled "For President in 1860, Hon. Abraham Lincoln," scrapbook, p. 85, Nicolay Papers, LC.
56. Basler, *CW*, 1:112, 2:130, 4:240. Lord Charnwood was among the first historians to note the expanding application of the Declaration. See his *Abraham Lincoln* (New York: Henry Holt and Company, 1917), 184. For an excellent discussion of how German-American Republicans linked the Declaration, citizenship, and antislavery, see Alison Clark Efford, *German Immigrants, Race, and Citizenship in the Civil War Era* (Washington, DC: German Historical Insititute; Cambridge: Cambridge University Press, 2013), 1–85.

## Chapter 5. English Lessons

1. Hugh Sidey, "First Lady Brings History and Beauty to the White House," *Life*, September 1, 1961, 54–65.
2. "Bust of John Bright by John Warrington Wood," object 1866.1535.1, supplied by Office of the Curator, The White House, December 9, 2009.
3. "Britain's Prime Minister Hopes to Bolster U.S. Ties," *NYT*, March 3, 2009; "Barack Obama Sends Bust of Winston Churchill on Its Way Back to Britain," February 14, 2009, www.telegraph.co.uk; Ben Macintyre and Paul Orengoh, "Beatings and abuse made Barack Obama's grandfather loathe the British," *The Times* (London), December 3, 2008, http://www.timesonline.co .uk/tol/news/world/africa/article5276010.ece. *The Times* reporters say that the grandfather was tortured, although Barack Obama mentions only the imprisonment in his autobiography *Dreams from My Father: A Story of Race and Inheritance* (New York: Times Books, 1995), 419.
4. "Opinions of John Bright on the Re-election of President Lincoln," *Daily Evening Bulletin* (San Francisco), November 16, 1864.
5. James Edwin Thorold Rogers, ed., *Speeches on Questions of Public Policy: By the Right Honourable John Bright, M. P.* (London: Macmillan and Co., 1878), 300.

6. "Suffrage Reform in England," *The Weekly Wisconsin Patriot*, NewsBank/Readex, January 15, 1859. In England and Wales, the 1867 Reform Act enfranchised, in boroughs, all male householders and lodgers paying rent above a minimal level, and in the counties, landowners and tenants even of small holdings. For Bright's stand on the bill, see Robert Saunders, *Democracy and the Vote in British Politics, 1848–1867* (Burlington, VT: Ashgate Publishing Company, 2011), 34, 122, 231, 242.

7. Ibid., 301; "Compliment to our Country," *Emancipator and Republican* (Boston), August 29, 1850: "John Bright upon American Institutions – Speech at Manchester," *NYT*, December 29, 1858.

8. John Bright, Thursday, December 18, 1862 (Extract from Speech; extracted quotation in Abraham Lincoln's hand), ALP@LC.

9. Joseph C. Grubb to Abraham Lincoln, Sept. 3, 1863, ALP@LC. See "Barack Obama Sends Bust of Winston Churchill on its Way Back to Britain," February 14, 2009, www.telegraph.co.uk. Also, Mary Lincoln to Charles Sumner in Turner and Turner, *Mary Todd Lincoln*, 228, n. 8.

10. Basler, *CW*, 7:71; Charles Sumner to Abraham Lincoln, September 7, 1863, ALP@LC.

11. Discussion of the pocket contents may be found at the Library of Congress exhibit *American Treasures*, http://www.loc.gov/exhibits/treasures/trm012.html. An image of the Bright clipping appears there. In November 1864, numerous newspapers supporting Lincoln's candidacy reprinted Bright's letter.

12. See Mary Lincoln to Charles Sumner in Turner and Turner, *Mary Todd Lincoln*, 228, n. 8.

13. For a fuller discussion of the *Trent* Affair, see Foreman, *A World on Fire*, chap. 7. The British ambassador's reaction may be found in James J. Barnes, and Patience P. Barnes, *Private and Confidential: Letters from British Ministers in Washington to the Foreign Secretaries in London, 1844–67* (Selinsgrove, PA: Susquehanna University Press, 1993), 267–275.

14. Gordon H. Warren, *Fountain of Discontent: The Trent Affair and Freedom of the Seas* (Boston, MA: Northeastern University Press, 1981), chap. 1.

15. Warren, *Fountain of Discontent*, 27, and "Commodore Wilkes," *NYT*, December 5, 1861.

16. Jay Monaghan, *Diplomat in Carpet Slippers: Abraham Lincoln Deals with Foreign Affairs* (Indianapolis, IN: Bobbs-Merrill Company, 1945), 170.

17. *Congressional Globe*, House of Representatives, 37th Congress, 2nd Session, p. 5, at *A Century of Lawmaking for a New Nation: U.S. Congressional Documents and Debates, 1774–1875*, Library of Congress.

18. Charles Francis Adams's Diaries, 1823–1880, December 19 and 22, 1861, reel 76 of Adams Family Papers, microfilm edition. Foreman, *World on Fire*, 183, 839 n. 26; "Latest by the City of Washington," *NYT*, December 16, 1861; "The Situation," *New York Herald*, NewsBank/Readex, December 23, 1861; "Action of the British Government," *The Liberator*, December 20, 1861, Accessible Archives.

19. Foreman, *World on Fire*, 190.

20. Jay Sexton, *Debtor Diplomacy: Finance and American Foreign Relations in the Civil War Era 1837–1873* (Oxford: Clarendon Press, 2005), 137;

Howard Jones, *Abraham Lincoln and a New Birth of Freedom: The Union and Slavery in the Diplomacy of the Civil War* (Lincoln: University of Nebraska Press, 1999), 8–9.

21. John Bright to C. Dela Pryme, October 6, 1861, Bright Manuscripts, Friends Historical Library of Swarthmore College, Swarthmore, PA.

22. Edward Bates, *The Diary of Edward Bates, 1859–1866*, ed. Howard K. Beale (Washington, DC: GPO, 1933), 203; Titian J. Coffey, "Lincoln and the Cabinet," in Allen Thorndike Rice, ed., *Reminiscences of Abraham Lincoln by Distinguished Men of his Time*, 8th ed. (New York: North American Publishing Company, 1889), 245. The same point is repeated at the December 25 Cabinet meeting. See Bates, *Diary*, 212.

23. Burlingame, *Abraham Lincoln*, 2:226.

24. "Letters of John Bright, 1861–1862," *Proceedings of the Massachusetts Historical Society* (hereinafter *MHS*), 45 (1911–1912): 152, 148, 151.

25. "Letters of John Bright, 1861–1862," *MHS*, 45 (1911–1912): 154.

26. William Henry Seward and Frederick William Seward, *Seward at Washington as Senator and Secretary of State: A Memoir of His Life with Selections from his Letters* (New York: Derby and Miller, 1891), 28. See Weed's letters on pp. 22–32.

27. A thorough analysis of Bright's misrepresentations of British opinion appears in Duncan Andrew Campbell, *English Public Opinion and the American Civil War* (Suffolk, UK: The Boydell Press for the Royal Historical Society, 2003), 76–80.

28. Burlingame, *Abraham Lincoln*, 226.

29. Jacob William Schuckers, *The Life and Public Services of Salmon Portland Chase* (New York: D. Appleton and Company, 1874), 433.

30. James J. Barnes and Patience P. Barnes, *The American Civil War through British Eyes: Dispatches from British Diplomats* (Kent, OH: Kent State University Press, 2003), 1:259–260; Seward and Seward, *Seward at Washington*, 36; "Mason and Slidell Gone," *NYT*, January 3, 1862.

31. Seward and Seward, *Seward at Washington*, 35; "Passage of British Troops through the State of Maine," *Philadelphia Inquirer*, February 4, 1862, Newsbank/Readex.

32. For the postponement, *Congressional Globe*, Senate, 37th Congress, 2nd Session, p. 874, at *A Century of Lawmaking for a New Nation: U.S. Congressional Documents and Debates, 1774–1875*, Library of Congress.

33. "Bright-Sumner Letters, 1861–1872," *MHS* 46 (1912–1913): 103.

34. "Letters of John Bright, 1861–1862," *MHS*, 45: 157.

35. "Letters of John Bright, 1861–1862," *MHS*, 45: 158.

36. Foreman, *World on Fire*, 237–239.

37. Edward Bates, *Opinion of the Attorney General on Citizenship* (Washington: GPO, 1862), 26–27; "Foreign and Colonial News: America," *Illustrated London News* (hereinafter *ILN*), January 3, 1863, at http://beck.library.emory.edu/iln/. Also, Edward Bates, *The Diary of Edward Bates, 1859–1866*, ed. Howard K. Beale (Washington: GPO, 1933), 264, and 264, n. 60.

38. Burlingame, *Lincoln*, 351.

39. Seward to Adams, no. 187 *bis*, February 17, 1862, *FRUS* (1862), 137–138.

40. February 26, March 3 and 26, Consular Posts, Bremen, Germany, RG 84, vol. 179, NARA.

41. Oakes, *Freedom National*, 269, for the quotation, and 265–269, for discussion of the act. The act appears in *Statutes at Large*, 432.

42. Allen C. Guelzo, *Lincoln's Emancipation Proclamation: The End of Slavery in America* (New York: Simon & Schuster, 2004), 86.

43. Eric Foner, *Fiery Trial*, 199–201. See the description of the act and its transcription at: http://www.archives.gov/exhibits/featured_documents/dc_emancipation_act/transcription.html. The webpage reports this vote but the *Senate Journal* reports the Senate vote as 29 to 14 [U.S. Senate, *Senate Journal for the 2nd Session of the 37th Congress* (Washington DC: GPO, 1862), 1526], and the *House Journal* reports that vote as 92 to 39 [U.S. House of Representatives, *House Journal for the Second Session of the 37th Congress* (Washington DC: GPO, 1862), 539].

44. Foner, *Fiery Trial*, 195–198, quote from 213; Guelzo, *Emancipation Proclamation*, 92–96.

45. Foner, *Fiery Trial*, 219; Guelzo, *Emancipation Proclamation*, 123–124.

46. Guelzo, *Emancipation Proclamation*, 224–225.

47. Seward and Seward, *Seward at Washington*, 56–57.

48. Howard Jones, *Union in Peril: The Crisis over British Intervention in the Civil War* (Chapel Hill: University of North Carolina Press, 1992), 180.

49. Basler, *CW*, 5:434.

50. Stephen Rock, "Anglo-U.S. Relations, 1845–1930: Did Shared Liberal Values and Democratic Institutions Keep the Peace?" in Miriam Fendius Elman, ed., *Paths to Peace: Is Democracy the Answer?* (Cambridge, MA: MIT Press, 1997), 120; also see Foreman, *World on Fire*, 327.

51. Adams diary, April 24, 1862; Gladstone as quoted in Jones, *Union in Peril*, 182.

52. "Bright-Sumner Letters, 1861–1872," *MHS*, 46: 108.

53. H. W. Halleck to Major General W. S. Rosecrans, *Official Records of the Union and Confederate Armies* (Washington: GPO, 1887), Part 2, 20: 123.

54. "London; Saturday, January 24, 1863," *ILN*, January 24, 1863; Basler, *CW*, 6:424.

55. "Bright-Sumner Letters, 1861–1872," *MHS*, 46:112.

56. "Liberal Contributions in Money and Food," *NYT*, December 8, 1862. Also see Mark E. Neely, Jr., *The Boundaries of American Political Culture in the Civil War Era* (Chapel Hill: University of North Carolina Press, 2005), 81.

57. Thurlow Weed to Robert Minturn, December 4, 1862, reprinted in *NYT*, December 8, 1862.

58. "A Meeting Was Held at Rochdale," *ILN*, February 7, 1863; Seward and Seward, *Seward at Washington*, 68; Adams Diary, March 29, 1863.

59. Pike to Seward, no. 76, February 18, 1863, *FRUS* (1863), 885.

60. Adams to Seward, *FRUS* (1863), 5; *FRUS* (1863), 715.

61. R. J. M. Blackett, *Divided Hearts: Britain and the American Civil War* (Baton Rouge: Louisiana State University Press, 2001), 160.

62. James McPherson, *Battle Cry of Freedom: The Civil War Era* (New York: Oxford University Press, 1988), 550–551. Duncan Campbell argues that

historians have overstated the number of these meetings and their support for Lincoln. See his *English Public Opinion*, 215–26.

63. J. G. Randall, "Lincoln and John Bright," *Yale Review*, n.s. 34 (1944–1945): 303. Also see reports of the meetings in *FRUS* (1863).
64. McPherson, *Battle Cry of Freedom*, 558.
65. "Public Meeting on American Slavery," *The Scotsman*, February 20, 1863.
66. Basler, CW, 6: note 1, p. 65. Also see a record of the meeting from the *Manchester Guardian*, January 1, 1863, reprinted in F. Hourani, *Manchester and Abraham Lincoln: A Side-light on an Earlier Fight for Freedom* (Manchester: R. Aikman & Son, c. 1945).
67. Basler, CW, 6:64, 88–89.
68. Adams to Seward, March 2, 1863–March 26, 1863, *FRUS* (1863), 150–285.
69. "Autograph of President Lincoln," facsimile of original in George Macaulay Trevelyan, *The Life of John Bright* (Boston, MA: Houghton Mifflin, 1913), 303. Stephens's speech in Henry Cleveland, *Alexander H. Stephens in Public and Private*... (Philadelphia: National Publishing Company, 1866), 721.
70. Basler, CW, 6:176–177.
71. "Bright-Sumner Letters, 1861–1872," MHS, 46: 119.
72. "Denies Gotten up by Emancipation Society," *The Observer*, March 30, 1863, Proquest Historical Newspapers.
73. "Denies Gotten up by Emancipation Society," *The Observer*, March 30, 1863; "Mr. Bright and the American Minister," *Manchester Guardian*, May 5, 1863, Proquest Historical Newspapers.
74. Blackett, *Divided Hearts*, 164; "Mr. Bright and the American Minister," *Manchester Guardian*, May 5, 1863.
75. Adams to Seward, February 19, 1863, No. 327 in *FRUS* (1863), 136.
76. "Negro Emancipation: The Meeting in Exeter Hall," February 7, 1863, http://beck.library.emory.edu/iln/browse.php?id=iln42.1187.009& keyword=Exeter%20Hall.
77. Petition of the Workers of Birmingham, February 26, 1863, Entry 162: Proclamations Addressed to President Lincoln by Antislavery Societies, RG 59, NARA. My thanks to David Langbart in the Textual Records division of NARA for helping me locate and see the petition.
78. Adams Diary, February 27, 1863; "Deputation from Birmingham to the American Minister," undated newspaper clipping in the diary.
79. Seward to Adams, March 16, 1863, no. 512 in *FRUS* (1863), 168–169.
80. Adams to Seward, no. 359, March 28, 1863, *FRUS* (1863), 188; James S. Pike to Seward, no. 70, December 31, 1862, in *FRUS* (1863), 879.
81. Basler, CW, 4:438.
82. Ibid.
83. "American Topics Abroad: Mr. John Bright on our Troubles and the Cotton Question," NYT, August 15, 1861.
84. Although Churchill formally called for a "special relationship" between the two countries in his well-known speech in Fulton, Missouri, he had referenced the relationship earlier in parliamentary debate. See "Excerpts from Speeches of Churchill and Bevin to House of Commons," NYT,

November 8, 1945; "CHURCHILL SPEECH HAILED IN LONDON," *NYT*, March 6, 1946.
85. Basler, CW, 6:65.

## Chapter 6.  Lessons from International Law

1. Burlingame, *Lincoln's Journalist*, 334.
2. F. [Francis] B. [Bicknell] Carpenter, *Six Months at the White House with Abraham Lincoln: The Story of a Picture* (New York: Hurd and Houghton, 1867), 12, 11.
3. Carpenter, *Six Months at the White House*, 353.
4. My discussion of the painting draws on Harold Holzer, Gabor S. Boritt, Mark E. Neely, Jr., "Francis Bicknell Carpenter (1830–1900): Painter of Abraham Lincoln and His Circle," *American Art Journal* 16, no. 2 (Spring, 1984), 66–89.
5. Benjamin P. Thomas, *Abraham Lincoln: A Biography* (New York: Knopf, 1952), 457.
6. John G. Nicolay to Therena Bates, January 9, 1861, Box 1, John G. Nicolay Papers, Library of Congress.
7. I have drawn on Sean Wilentz's discussion of the Lincoln-Jackson connection. See his "Abraham Lincoln and Jacksonian Democracy," in *Our Lincoln*, 76.
8. Basler, CW, 4:341.
9. Basler, CW, 3:278.
10. "An Act to Confiscate Property used for Insurrectionary Purposes," *Statutes at Large, Treaties, and Proclamations*... (Boston, MA: Little, Brown and Company, 1863), 12:319, 591.
11. "Butler and Phelps," *The Liberator*, September 9, 1862, Accessible Archives. The correspondence between Butler and Phelps appeared in many newspapers; see "Bound to Arm the Negroes," *The Wisconsin Daily Patriot*, August 21, 1862, NewsBank/Readex.
12. Horace Greeley, *The American Conflict: A History of the Great Rebellion in the United States of America, 1860–'65* (Hartford, CT: O. D. Case, 1866), 2:249.
13. Basler, CW, 5:388.
14. Basler, CW, 4:263.
15. Basler, CW, 5:337.
16. For discussion of Story's and Whiting's books in another recent monograph, see Louis P. Masur, *Lincoln's Hundred Days: The Emancipation Proclamation and the War for the Union* (Cambridge, MA: Belknap Press of Harvard University Press, 2012), 243–44, 266–67.
17. I have chosen to use the 1858 edition as it might have included revisions influenced by events of the turbulent 1850s. I have not reviewed every edition from 1833 to trace those changes. See Joseph Story, *Commentaries on the Constitution of the United States*, 3rd ed. (Boston, MA: Little, Brown, 1858).
18. Story, *Commentaries* (1851) 1:440.
19. Story, *Commentaries* (1858) 2:100.

20. Story, *Commentaries* (1858) 2:607.
21. Story, *Commentaries* (1858) 2:611, n. 3.
22. See the text of *Prigg v. Pennsylvania* at http://caselaw.lp.findlaw.com/scripts/getcase.pl?navby=CASE&court=US&vol=41&page=539.
23. Story, *Commentaries* (1858) 2:611, n. 3.
24. See William Whiting, *The War Powers of the President, and the Legislative Powers of Congress in Relation to Rebellion, Treason and Slavery*, 2nd ed. (Boston, MA: John L. Shorey, 1863), i. The most complete discussion linking Story to Adams to Whiting to Lincoln appears in Burrus M. Carnahan, *Act of Justice: Lincoln's Emancipation Proclamation and the Law of War* (Lexington: University Press of Kentucky, 2007). I am indebted to his findings, although I find my own path.
25. On Vattel, see Carnahan, *Act of Justice*, 22.
26. Carnahan, *Act of Justice*, 38, 48.
27. Whiting, *War Powers*, 76–82; quote from 79.
28. Charles Sumner, *Charles Sumner: His Complete Works* (Boston, MA: Lee and Shepard, 1872), 7:260–64.
29. "Payment for Slaves. Speech of Mr. Giddings, of Ohio," *The National Era* (January 18, 1849), Accessible Archives.
30. Burlingame, *Abraham Lincoln*, 1:260.
31. I have reviewed articles from 1836 through 1859 in *The Liberator, National Era*, and *The North Star*.
32. Sumner, *Works*, 6:30–31. David Herbert Donald drew on Ellis Yarnall's memoirs (1899), which repeat a conversation between Yarnall and Sumner in 1863, to modify the conversation that Sumner reported in the collected *Works* (1877) for which he supervised publication. Yarnall says that Sumner recalled telling Lincoln, "that under the war power the right had come to him to emancipate the slaves." See Donald, *Charles Sumner and the Coming of the Civil War* (New York: Knopf, 1960), 388. Observe the considerable difference between Sumner's own account and the one that Yarnall wrote twenty years later: Yarnall, *Wordsworth and the Coleridges, with other Memories, Literary and Political* (New York: Macmillan, 1899), 385.
33. For further information, see John Lockwood and Charles Lockwood, *The Siege of Washington: The Untold Story of the Twelve Days that Shook the Union* (New York: Oxford University Press, 2011), 182–239.
34. Edward Lillie Pierce, *Enfranchisement and Citizenship: Addresses and Papers* (Boston: Roberts Brothers, 1896), 22. Pierce was a lowly soldier under Butler's command with passionate antislavery feelings. He wrote an account of his experiences at Fort Monroe in the *Atlantic Monthly* 8 (November 1861), 626–40. Adam Goodheart provides an excellent secondary account in *1861: The Civil War Awakening* (New York: Knopf, 2011), 297–298, 432–33, notes 7–9.
35. Goodheart, *1861*, 297.
36. Basler, *CW*, 4:263.
37. Benjamin Butler, *Autobiography and Personal Reminiscences of Major-General Benjamin F. Butler: Butler's Book* (Boston, MA: A. M. Thayer, 1892), 256–257.

38. Edward E. Dunbar, *The Mexican Papers, Containing the Rise and Decline of Commercial Slavery in America* (New York: Rudd & Carleton, 1861), 196; *Accounts and Papers of the House of Commons* 64 (1861), 125.
39. For example, see "Seizure of Powder and Contraband Goods," *Philadelphia Inquirer*, April 27, 1861, NewsBank/Readex; "From Norfolk and Portsmouth," *The Sun* (Baltimore), April 29, 1861, NewsBank/Readex.
    If Butler had consulted the foremost textbook on military science that many volunteer commanders consulted, he would have received no advice on how to deal with the fugitives. The most widely read text, Henry Halleck's *Elements of Military Art and Science* (1846, 1860), contains no mention of how to treat enemy property. Halleck's *International Law; or, Rules Regulating the Intercourse of States in Peace and War* was published in 1861 just after the Fort Monroe incident. While Halleck does discuss contraband property in chapter 24, he does not discuss fugitive slaves as contraband.
40. Butler to Lieutenant-General Winfield Scott, 24 May 1861, in *Operations in Maryland, Pennsylvania, Virginia, and West Virginia* (Washington: GPO, 1880), 648–51, vol. 2 of *War of the Rebellion*; Butler, *Butler's Book*, 258, and as confirmed by the major on p. 263.
41. Butler, *Butler's Book*, 259.
42. *War of the Rebellion*, 2:652.
43. Butler, *Butler's Book*, 259.
44. "General Butler on the Fugitive Slave Law from a Military Point of View," *New York Herald*, May 28, 1861, NewsBank/Readex.
45. "The '*Contraband Goods*' at Fortress Monroe," *Douglass' Monthly*, July 1861, Accessible Archives.
46. "The Fugitives at Our Strongholds. At Fortress Monroe," *Douglass' Monthly*, August 1861, Accessible Archives.
47. See Kate Masur, "'A Rare Phenomenon of Philological Vegetation': The Word 'Contraband' and the Meanings of Emancipation in the United States," *JAH* 93 (2007): 1050–1052.
48. All these images may be found at Civil War Treasures from the New-York Historical Society, http://memory.loc.gov/ammem/ndlpcoop/nhihtml/cwnyhshome.html. Discussion of the envelopes appears in Steven R. Boyd, *Patriotic Envelopes of the Civil War: The Iconography of Union and Confederate Covers* (Baton Rouge: Louisiana State University Press, 2010), 2–4, 74–76.
49. "Song of the Contrabands" (New York: Horace Waters, 1861), 7, at Performing Arts Encyclopedia, Library of Congress.
50. "Ole Shady, or the Song of the Contraband by the author of Darling Nelly Gray" (Boston, MA: Oliver Ditson & Co., 1861), 2. Ibid.
51. "Letters from Camp," *The Ladies Repository* 30 (1861): 284; Anon., *The Adventures of G. Whillikens, C.S.A. . . . by a Citizen of the Cotton Country* (Philadelphia, 1861), 76.
52. See, for example, "The War Power over Slavery," *The Liberator*, June 7, 1861, and "Speech of Hon. Chas. Sumner," *The Liberator*, October 4, 1861; "The War. Lecture by Wendell Phillips, Esq. at the Cooper Institute, New York," *The Liberator*, December 27, 1861, all at Accessible Archives.

53. See Whiting, *War Powers of the President*, 2nd ed. (1863), i; *Memoir of the Hon. William Whiting, LL.D.* (Boston, MA: D. Clapp and Son, 1874), 7, 8; also see Benson J. Lossing, *Pictorial History of the Civil War in the United States of America* (Hartford, CT: T. Belknap, 1868), 2:558, n. 3.
54. See Whiting, *War Powers of the President* (1862), 82, 83.
55. Whiting, *War Powers of the President* (1862), 39.
56. See the Library of Congress catalogue for William Whiting, *The War Powers of the President*.
57. Whiting, *War Powers of the President* (1862), 38–39; and see the text of the decision at http://supreme.justia.com/cases/federal/us/67/635/case.html. For a discussion of the Prize Cases, see Allen C. Guelzo, *Fateful Lightning: A New History of the Civil War and Reconstruction* (New York: Oxford University Press, 2012), 224–25; James F. Simon, *Lincoln and Chief Justice Taney: Slavery, Secession, and the President's War Powers* (New York: Simon & Schuster, 2007), 223–31; Jeffrey L. Amestoy, "The Supreme Court Argument that Saved the Union Richard Henry Dana, Jr., and the Prize Cases," *Journal of Supreme Court History* 35 (2010): 10–24.
58. Whiting, *War Powers of the President* (1862), 69, and chapter 3 passim.
59. Basler, CW, 5:530.

### Chapter 7. German Lessons for Reelection

1. John G. Nicolay to John Hay, August 25, 1864, and Nicolay to Therena Bates, August 28, 1864, in Michael Burlingame, ed., *With Lincoln in the White House: Letters, Memoranda, and other Writings of John G. Nicolay, 1860–1865* (Carbondale: Southern Illinois University Press, 2000), 152, 153.
2. Elizabeth Keckley, *Behind the Scenes, or Thirty Years a Slave, and Four Years in the White House* (New York: G. W. Carleton, 1868), 133–134.
3. John F. Marszalek, *Commander of All Lincoln's Armies: A Life of Henry W. Halleck* (Cambridge, MA: Belknap Press of Harvard University Press, 2004), 208–209; French, *Witness to the Young Republic*, 453; Matthew Pinsker, *Lincoln's Sanctuary: Abraham Lincoln and the Soldiers' Home* (New York: Oxford University Press, 2003), 134, 143–144. Pinsker gives a full account of the engagement on pp. 135–142.
4. Lieber, *Life and Letters*, 343–344.
5. Lieber, *Life and Letters*, 350–351.
6. "The German Press," *Daily Ohio Statesman*, July 18, 1864, NewsBank/Readex; *Westliche Post* as quoted in Bates, *Diary*, 404.
7. Burlingame, ed., *With Lincoln*, 151; Basler, CW, 7:514–515.
8. Oscar Lieber to Matilda Lieber, October 1860, South Carolinian Library, University of South Carolina, Columbia, SC; Frank Freidel, *Francis Lieber: Nineteenth-Century Liberal* (Baton Rouge: Louisiana State University Press, 1947), 300.
9. Frank Burt Freidel, "The Life of Francis Lieber" (PhD diss., University of Wisconsin Madison, 1941), 586.
10. Lieber, *Life and Letters of Francis Lieber*, 313.

11. James O. Breeden, "Oscar Lieber: Southern Scientist, Southern Patriot," *Civil War History* 36 (1990): 238–248; quote from 248.
12. "Republican Party Platform of 1860," at http://www.presidency.ucsb.edu/ws/index.php?pid=29620.
13. An explication of the slogan appears in Eric Foner's *Free Soil, Free Labor, Free Men*, which does not discuss the slogan's coded meaning.
14. See the essays in Frederick C. Luebke, ed., *Ethnic Voters and the Election of Lincoln* (Lincoln: University of Nebraska Press, 1971), and Baron's discussion in *Abraham Lincoln and the German Immigrants*, 148–151.
15. "Movements of the President Elect: Reply to an Address from the Germans," *The Sun* (Baltimore), February 15, 1861, NewsBank/Readex; Cincinnati German Workingmen to Abraham Lincoln, February 1861, at ALP@LC; Basler, *CW*, 4:202–203.
16. Basler, *CW*, 4:292–293.
17. Consular Reports, Bremen, 1862–1863, Consular Posts, vol. 178; Department of State Circular, Number 19, August 8, 1862.
18. Circular No. 32, February 8, 1863, in *FRUS* (1863), 1388–1389.
19. Consular Reports, Bremen, September 10, 1862–October 15, 1862, November 10, 1862, March 30, 1863, in Consular Posts, Bremen, Germany; William W. Murphy to Abraham Lincoln, June 2, 1863, ALP@LC; Herman Kreismann to William Seward, December 26, 1863, *FRUS* (1864), 196–197; Amos Perry to Seward, May 2, 1863, *FRUS* (1863), 1319.
20. Consular Reports, Bremen, November 5, 1862, March 30, 1863, in Consular Posts, Bremen, Germany; Bigelow to Seward, September 19, 1862, in *FRUS* (1863), 1353.
21. Basler, *CW*, 7:40; Act of July 4, 1864, *Statutes at Large*, 13: 385–387.
22. Lieber to Matilda Lieber as quoted in Freidel, *Life of Francis Lieber*, 601–602.
23. For a discussion of Fort Monroe and General Butler, see Chapter 6, and for McClellan, see Stephen W. Sears, *George B. McClellan: The Young Napoleon* (Boston, MA: Ticknor and Fields, 1988), 79–80. Matthew Mancini corrects previous narratives of the genesis of the Lieber Code in "Francis Lieber, Slavery, and the 'Genesis' of the Laws of War," *Journal of Southern History* 77 (2011): 325–348. With thanks to Professor Mancini for his help with interpreting the Lieber Code.
24. Lieber, *Life and Letters of Francis Lieber*, 322.
25. F.L. [Francis Lieber], "The Disposal of Prisoners," *NYT*, August 19, 1861.
26. "Dr. Lieber's Lectures on the Laws and Usages of War," in *NYT*, November 1, 1861; January 13, 19; February 4, 10, 16; and March 4, 7, 17, 1862.
27. Marszalek, *Commander of All Lincoln's Armies*, 167; Freidel, *Lieber*, 324.
28. Major-General H. W. Halleck to Francis Lieber, August 6, 1862, in Francis Lieber, *Guerilla Parties Considered with Reference to the Laws and Usages of War* (New York: D. Van Nostrand, 1862); Gideon M. Hart, "Military Commissions and the Lieber Code: Toward a New Understanding of the Jurisdictional Foundations of Military Commissions," *Military Law Review* 203 (Spring 2010): 17. For a discussion of *Guerilla Parties*, see Paul J. Springer

and Glenn Robins, *Transforming Civil War Prisons: Lincoln, Lieber, and the Politics of Captivity* (New York: Routledge, 2015), 17–18.

29. Lieber, *Guerilla Parties*, 22; Halleck to Lieber, August 20, 1862, in *Lieber's Code and the Law of War*, 78.

30. Marszalek, *Commander of all Lincoln's Armies*, 178; Francis Lieber, *Instructions for the Government of Armies of the United States in the Field* (New York: D. Van Nostrand, 1863). The full text of the code may be found at http://avalon.law.yale.edu/19th_century/lieber.asp.

31. Lieber, *Life and Letters of Francis Lieber*, 334.

32. Burrus M. Carnahan, *Act of Justice: Lincoln's Emancipation Proclamation and the Law of War* (Lexington: University Press of Kentucky, 2007), 132; Springer and Robins, *Transforming Civil War Prisons*, 19.

33. Lieber, *Instructions*, Article 152, p. 34.

34. Lieber, *Instructions*, Article 43, p. 13. The political scientist did not consider the experience of enslavement in the African slave trade. Definitions of slavery and freedom among East African peoples differed from those prevailing in Europe and the Americas.

35. Constitution of the United States, Art. 1, Sec. 2, Para. 3, and Art. 4, Sec. 2, Para. 3. For a discussion of slavery as established by the Constitution as a local institution, see James Oakes, *Freedom National: The Destruction of Slavery in the United States, 1861–1865* (New York: W. W. Norton, 2013), chap. 1.

36. Lieber, *Instructions*, Article 43, p. 13; Lieber to Benson Lossing, January 21, 1866, in Francis Lieber Papers, LC. With thanks to Matthew Mancini for bringing this letter to my attention.

37. In *Act of Justice*, 137, Carnahan argues a similar point about Lincoln's concession to pro-slavery theorists.

38. Lieber, *Life and Letters of Francis Lieber*, 340.

39. Carnahan, *Act of Justice*, 106–109, 78. I qualify Carnahan on a small point. With regard to confiscation of property during wartime, William Whiting did draw on Jean Jacques Burlamaqui, the French theorist, and Francis Lieber did not draw on his treatise. James Oakes argues that Lieber's Code implied his support of the Emancipation Proclamation. Admittedly the logic of the Code followed the Somerset precedent and endorsed emancipation when enslaved people fled into Union lines or occupied territory in the seceded states. This endorsement does not imply his endorsement of the Proclamation as constitutional because he refused to consider that the enslaved people were anything but people. See Oakes, *Freedom National*, 350–352.

40. "Miscellaneous News Items, Resisting the Enrollment," *Philadelphia Inquirer*, September 9, 1862, NewsBank/Readex; "Revolt in Schuylkill County," *Philadelphia Inquirer*, September 1, 1862, NewsBank/Readex; "Draft Riots in Wisconsin," *Weekly Patriot and Union* (Harrisburg, PA), November 27, 1862, NewsBank/Readex; "Resistance to the draft in Wisconsin," unknown newspaper title from Milwaukee, Wisconsin, November 12, 1862, available at http://www.wisconsinhistory.org/wlhba/articleView.asp?pg=1&id=6958&key=draft&cy=.

41. Lieber to Halleck as quoted in Marszalek, *Commander of All Lincoln's Armies*, 182–183.

42. Act of July 17, 1862, *Statutes at Large*, 12: 597.

43. For numerous reports of Prussian impressment, see posts from Berlin in *FRUS* for 1863 as well as consular reports from Bremen.

44. "The Diffusion of Political Knowledge," *Wisconsin Daily Patriot*, February 20, 1863, NewsBank/Readex; "Professor Morse's Letter," *Weekly Patriot and Union* (Harrisburg, PA), April 9, 1863, NewsBank/Readex.

45. *Proceedings at the First Anniversary Meeting of the Loyal Publication Society, Feb. 13, 1864* (New York: Loyal Publication Society, 1864), 4, 20. A comprehensive history of the society appears in Frank Freidel, "The Loyal Publication Society: A Pro-Union Propaganda Agency," *Mississippi Valley Historical Review* 26 (1939): 359–376.

46. "Monster Mass Meeting," *NYT*, March 7, 1863. Text from the *Tribune* and *Herald* as quoted in *The Great Mass Meeting of Loyal Citizens* (New York: Loyal Publication Society, 1863), 1.

47. Francis Lieber, *Lincoln or McClellan?: An Appeal to the Germans in America* (New York: Loyal Publication Society, 1864), 7–8.

48. *The New International Encyclopedia* (1905), *s.v.* Lieber, Guido Norman.

49. Schurz spoke on September 16 in Philadelphia, October 7 in Brooklyn, and October 28 in Milwaukee. For these speeches, see *Speeches of Carl Schurz* (Philadelphia: J. B. Lippincott & Co., 1865).

50. Francis Lieber, *Amendments of the Constitution* (New York: Loyal Publication Society, 1865), 21; "Philosophy of the Chicago Platform," *NYT*, September 13, 1864.

51. Lieber, *Lincoln or McClellan*, 5.

52. See Hermann Raster, *Einheit und Freiheit* (New York: Loyal Publication Society, 1863).

53. "The German Press," *Daily Constitutional Union* (Philadelphia), October 14, 1864, NewsBank/Readex.

54. Figures taken from http://uselectionatlas.org/RESULTS/. Lieber to Sumner, November 10, 1864, as quoted in Freidel, *Francis Lieber*, 353.

55. Henry Boernstein to William Seward, Consular Reports, November 21, 1864, November 29, 1864, in Consular Posts, Bremen, Germany; "The German Press on American Politics," *Philadelphia Inquirer*, December 31, 1864, NewsBank/Readex.

56. "European News," *NYT*, December 26, 1864.

57. Basler, *CW*, 8:150.

### Chapter 8. The Last Lesson

1. General Roeliff Brinkerhoff, *Recollections of a Lifetime* (Cincinnati, OH: Robert Clarke Company, 1900), 164.

2. Basler, *CW*, 8: 399, 403.

3. Roger Meersman and Robert Beyer, "The National Theatre in Washington: Buildings and Audiences, 1835–1972," *Records of the Columbia Historical Society, Washington D.C.* 71/72 1973, 237.

4. Details of the national and Washington celebrations are taken from the *National Republican*, April 6–14, 1865, Chronicling America.

5. Basler, *CW*, 8:333. The insightful George Templeton Strong records similar thoughts in his diary, July 31, 1864. See Allan Nevins and Milton Halsey Thomas, eds., *The Civil War, 1860–1865*, vol. 3 of *The Diary of George Templeton Strong* (New York: Macmillan Co., 1952), 468–469.

6. See Bray, "What Abraham Lincoln Read: An Evaluative and Annotated List"; Don E. Fehrenbacher and Virginia Fehrenbacher, eds., *Recollected Words of Abraham Lincoln* (Stanford, CA: Stanford University Press, 1996), 19, 521, 477, 417, 18.

7. http://www.thelincolnlog.org/ and John J. Pullen, *Comic Relief: The Life and Laughter of Artemus Ward, 1834–1867* (Hamden, CT: Archon Books, 1983), 2–3.

8. Charles Farrar Browne, *Artemus Ward: His Book* (New York: Carleton, Publisher, 1862), 34–35.

9. Petroleum V. Nasby (David Ross Locke), *The Nasby Papers: Letters and Sermons* (Indianapolis, IN: C. O. Perrine, 1864), ii, 26.

10. Mary Lincoln's rendition of her husband's words during their carriage ride and his desire to visit the Holy Land was popularized in public talks in 1881 and 1882 given by the Reverend Noyes W. Miner, who had lived near the Lincolns in the 1850s and whose sister corresponded with Mary. Since Miner was a clergyman, I discount his memories as he may have been trying to redeem the president and Mary from his audiences' disapproval. It might have been evoked by the purportedly impious behavior of the Lincolns on the day commemorating the Christian God's crucifixion. Instead of devoting themselves to religious thoughts, they watched a comedy in a theater, a venue the minister considered undignified. By portraying the couple as sharing religious thoughts and seeking privacy away from crowds at Ford's Theatre, either Mary or the minister repeating her words adjusted the president's last wishes and demise to comport with prevailing conventions of a good death. For Miner's speeches, see SC 1052, Noyes W. Miner, folder 2, at ALPLM, and for description of the good death, see Faust, *Republic of Suffering*, 6–11.

11. "Law Reports: 'OUR AMERICAN COUSIN IN COURT'," *NYT*, October 22, 1865.

12. Advertisement, *New York Herald*, December 29, 1859, NewsBank/Readex; "Operatic and Dramatic Matter," *New York Herald*, December 19, 1859, NewsBank/Readex; Advertisement, *San Francisco Bulletin*, December 15, 1864, NewsBank/Readex; George Clinton Densmore Odell, *Annals of the New York Stage* (New York: Columbia University Press, 1927–1949), 7:355; Rebecca Lea Ray, "A Stage History of Tom Taylor's Our American Cousin" (Ph.D. diss., School of Philosophy, New York University, 1985), 126, 267. For the sheet music, see images at http://levysheetmusic.mse.jhu.edu/catalog/levy:167.026 and http://digitalcollections.baylor.edu/cdm/compoundobject/collection/fa-spnc/id/15029/show/15024.

13. Winton Tolles, *Tom Taylor and the Victorian Drama* (New York: Columbia University Press, 1940), 197. See the http://www.thelincolnlog.org for January 23, 1864.

14. Ray, "Stage History," 50.
15. Ray, "Stage History," 47, 51.
16. T. Allston Brown, *A History of the New York Stage: From the First Performance in 1732 to 1901* (New York: Dodd, Mead and Company, 1903), 2:134.
17. Nevins and Halsey, *Diary*, 300.
18. Welford Dunaway Taylor, ed., *Our American Cousin: The Play that Changed History* (Washington, DC: Beacham Publishing, 1990), 39, 45.
19. Taylor, ed., *Our American Cousin*, 46, 45, 49.
20. Taylor, ed., *Our American Cousin*, 68.
21. Taylor, ed., *Our American Cousin*, 82.
22. John Russell Bartlett, *Dictionary of Americanisms: A Glossary of Words and Phrases usually Regarded as Peculiar to the United States* (New York: Bartlett and Welford, 1848), 121, 319–320.
23. Bruce McConachie, "American Theatre in Context, from the Beginnings to 1870," in *Beginnings to 1870*, vol. 1 of *The Cambridge History of American Theatre*, eds. Don B. Wilmeth and Christopher Bigsby (Cambridge: Cambridge University Press, 1998), 160.
24. I have drawn from Richard W. Bailey, "American English Abroad," in *English in North America*, vol. 6 of *Cambridge History of the English Language*, ed. John Algeo (Cambridge: Cambridge University Press, 2001), 457–458.
25. Basler, CW, 8: 116–117. Little matter that subsequent research revealed that only two of her sons had died and that John Hay wrote the letter.
26. Roberta Schildt, "Freedman's Village: Arlington, Virginia, 1863–1900," *Arlington Historical Magazine* 7, no. 4 (1984): 11–21.

# Selected Bibliography

## Manuscript Collections

Abraham Lincoln Papers, Library of Congress at http://memory.loc.gov/ammem/alhtml/malhome.html.

Bright Manuscripts, Friends Historical Library of Swarthmore College, Swarthmore, PA.

Charles Francis Adams's Diaries, 1823–1880 (microfilm edition). Adams Family Papers. Massachusetts Historical Society, Boston, MA.

Consular Posts, Bremen, Germany, RG 84, Vol. 179. National Archives and Records Administration, College Park, MD (hereinafter NARA).

Foreign Messages on the Death of Lincoln, 1865, General Records of the Department of State, Miscellaneous Correspondence, 1784–1906. NARA.

James Riley, Riley's Narrative: Manuscript, 1817, Mss. Collection, New-York Historical Society, New York, NY.

John G. Nicolay Papers, Manuscript Division, Library of Congress.

Law Practice of Abraham Lincoln at http://www.lawpracticeofabrahamlincoln.org/Results.aspx.

Proclamations Addressed to President Lincoln by Antislavery Societies, RG 59, NARA.

Records of Foreign Service Posts, Diplomatic Posts, 1756–1993. NARA.
  France, Vol. 67, RG 59.
  Great Britain, Vol. 25, RG 84.
  Union of Soviet Socialist Republics, Vol. 8, 1863–1870, RG 84.2.

## Government Documents and Websites

*Appendix to Diplomatic Correspondence of 1865: The Assassination of Abraham Lincoln, Late President of the United States of America*.... Washington: GPO, 1866.

Bates, Edward. *Opinion of the Attorney General on Citizenship*. Washington, DC: GPO, 1862.

*Congressional Globe: Debates and Proceedings, 1833–1873,* on line at http://memory.loc.gov/ammem/amlaw/lwcglink.html#anchor29.

*Journal of the House of Representatives of the United States,* 1847–1848 at *A Century of Lawmaking for a New Nation: U.S. Congressional Documents and Debates, 1774–1875* (http://memory.loc.gov/ammem/amlaw/lawhome.html).

*Miscellaneous Documents of the House of Representatives, 1865–'66.* Washington, DC: GPO, 1866.

*Tributes to the Memory of Abraham Lincoln: Reproduction in Facsimile of Eighty-seven Memorials Addressed by Foreign Municipalities and Societies to the Government of the United States, Prepared under the Direction of the Secretary of State, in Accordance with a Joint Resolution of Congress, Approved Feb. 23, 1881.* Washington, DC: GPO, 1885.

United States, State Department. *Foreign Relations of the United States.* Washington, DC: GPO, 1861–1865. Also at http://digital.library.wisc.edu/1711.dl/ FRUS.

### Published Primary Sources, Including Diaries, Letters, and Memoirs

Bancroft, Frederic, et al. *The Reminiscences of Carl Schurz, 1852–1863.* New York: The McClure Company, 1907.

Barnes, James J. and Patience P. Barnes. *The American Civil War through British Eyes: Dispatches from British Diplomats.* Kent, OH: Kent State University Press, 2003.

———. *Private and Confidential: Letters from British Ministers in Washington to the Foreign Secretaries in London, 1844–67.* Selinsgrove, PA: Susquehanna University Press, 1993.

Basler, Roy P. ed. *The Collected Works of Abraham Lincoln,* 8 vols. New Brunswick, NJ: Rutgers University Press, 1953.

Bates, Edward. *The Diary of Edward Bates, 1859–1866,* edited by Howard K. Beale. Washington, DC: GPO, 1933.

Beecher, Henry Ward. *Freedom and War: Discourses on Topics Suggested by the Times.* Boston, MA: Ticknor and Fields, 1863.

Boernstein, Henry. *Memoirs of a Nobody: The Missouri Years of an Austrian Radical, 1849–1866,* translated and edited by Steven Rowan. St. Louis: Missouri Historical Society Press, 1997.

Boswell, James. *The Journal of a Tour to the Hebrides with Samuel Johnson, L.L.D.* London: Henry Baldwin, for Clarke Dilly, 1785.

Bright, John. "Letters of John Bright, 1861–1862." *Proceedings of the Massachusetts Historical Society* 45 (1911–1912): 148–165.

———. "Bright-Sumner Letters, 1861–1872." *Proceedings of the Massachusetts Historical Society* 46 (1912–1913): 93–164.

Brinkerhoff, Roeliff. *Recollections of a Lifetime.* Cincinnati, OH: Robert Clarke Company, 1904.

Bunyan, John. *The Pilgrim's Progress from this World to that which is to Come.* 1678. Reprint, New York: John Tibout, 1804.

Burlingame, Michael, ed. *Lincoln's Journalist: John Hay's Anonymous Writings for the Press, 1860–1864.* Carbondale: Southern Illinois University Press, 1998.

————. *With Lincoln in the White House: Letters, Memoranda, and other Writings of John G. Nicolay, 1860–1865.* Carbondale: Southern Illinois University Press, 2000.

Butler, Benjamin F. *Autobiography and Personal Reminiscences of Major-General Benjamin F. Butler: Butler's Book.* Boston, MA: A. M. Thayer, 1892.

Carpenter, Francis Bicknell. *Six Months at the White House with Abraham Lincoln: The Story of a Picture.* New York: Hurdand Houghton, 1867.

Clay, Henry. *The Life and Speeches of the Hon. Henry Clay,* edited by Daniel Mallory. 2 vols. New York: Robert P. Bixby & Co., 1843.

D'Orleans de Paris, Phillippe Louis. *Voyage en Amérique, 1861–1862: Un Prince Français dans la Guerre de Sécession.* Paris: Perrin, 2011.

Dahlgren, Madeleine Vinton. *Memoirs of John A. Dahlgren, Rear-Admiral United States Navy.* New York: Charles L. Webster & Co., 1891.

Dilworth, Thomas. *A New Guide to the English Tongue.* New York: E. Duyckinck, D. D. Smith, W. B. Gilley, and G. Long, 1820.

Dunbar, Edward E. *The Mexican Papers, Containing the Rise and Decline of Commercial Slavery in America.* New York: Rudd & Carleton, 1861.

Elliott, E. N. *Cotton Is King, and Pro-Slavery Arguments: Comprising the Writings of Hammond, Harper, Christy, Stringfellow, Hodge, Bledsoe, and Cartwright....* Augusta, GA: Pritchard, Abbott & Loomis, 1860.

Fehrenbacher, Don E. and Virginia eds. *Recollected Words of Abraham Lincoln.* Stanford, CA: Stanford University Press, 1996.

French, Benjamin Brown. *Witness to the Young Republic: A Yankee's Journal, 1828–1870,* edited by Donald B. Cole and John J. McDonough. Hanover, NH: University Press of New England, 1989.

Gastineau, Benjamin. *Histoire de la Souscription Populaire à la Médaille Lincoln: La Médaille de la Liberté.* Paris: c. 1866.

Goodrich, Samuel Griswold. *The Story of Captain Riley and his Adventures in Africa.* Philadelphia: Henry F. Anners, 1841.

————. *The Tales of Peter Parley about Africa.* 1831, rev. ed. Philadelphia: Desilver, Thomas, 1836.

Greeley, Horace. *The American Conflict: A History of the Great Rebellion in the United States of America, 1860–'65.* Hartford: O. D. Case, 1866.

Hay, John. *Lincoln's Journalist: John Hay's Anonymous Writings for the Press, 1860–1864,* edited by Michael Burlingame. Carbondale: Southern Illinois University, 1998.

Henck, Esther C. *The Welcome of Louis Kossuth, Governor of Hungary to Philadelphia by the Youth.* Philadelphia: P. H. Skinner, 1852.

Holzer, Harold, ed. *Dear Mr. Lincoln: Letters to the President.* Boston, MA: Addison-Wesley, 1993.

Keckley, Elizabeth. *Behind the Scenes, or Thirty Years a Slave, and Four Years in the White House.* New York: G. W. Carleton, 1868.

Körner, Gustav Philipp. *Memoirs of Gustave Koerner, 1809–1896: Life-Sketches Written at the Suggestion of His Children.* Cedar Rapids, IA: Torch Press, 1909.

Lieber, Francis. *Amendments of the Constitution.* New York: Loyal Publication Society, 1865.

———. *Guerilla Parties Considered with Reference to the Laws and Usages of War*. New York: D. Van Nostrand, 1862.

———. *Instructions for the Government of Armies of the United States in the Field*. New York: D. Van Nostrand, 1863.

———. *The Life and Letters of Francis Lieber*, edited by Thomas Sergeant Perry. Boston, MA: James R. Osgood and Company, 1882.

———. *Lincoln or McClellan?: Appeal to the Germans in America*. New York: Loyal Publication Society, 1864.

Lossing, Benson J. *Pictorial History of the Civil War in the United States*. New York: G. W. Childs, 1866.

———. *Pictorial History of the Civil War in the United States of America*. Hartford, CT: T. Belknap, 1868.

Mearns, David C. *The Lincoln Papers*. Garden City: Doubleday, 1948.

Melville, Herman. *Redburn: His First Voyage*. New York: Harper and Brothers, 1850.

*Memoir of the Hon. William Whiting, LL.D.* Boston, MA: D. Clapp and Son, 1874.

Perry, Thomas Sergeant, ed. *Life and Letters of Francis Lieber*. Boston, MA: James R. Osgood, 1882.

Pierce, Edward Lillie. *Enfranchisement and Citizenship: Addresses and Papers*. Boston, MA: Roberts Brothers, 1896.

Polk, James K. *The Diary of James K. Polk during His Presidency*. Chicago: A. C. McClurg, 1910.

Raster, Hermann. *Einheit und Freiheit*. New York: Loyal Publication Society, 1863.

Rice, Allen Thorndike, ed. *Reminiscences of Abraham Lincoln by Distinguished Men of his Time*. 8th ed. New York: North American Publishing Company, 1899.

Riley, James. *Sufferings in Africa: The Incredible True Story of a Shipwreck, Enslavement and Survival on the Sahara Narrative*. 1817. Reprint, New York: Skyhorse Publishing, 2007.

Riley, William Willshire. *Sequel to Riley's Narrative*. Columbus, OH: George Brewster, 1851.

Rogers, James Edwin Thorold, ed. *Speeches on Questions of Public Policy: By the Right Honourable John Bright, M. P.* London: Macmillan and Co., 1878.

Russell, William Howard. *My Diary North and South*. Boston, MA: T.O. H. P. Burnham, 1863.

Scripps, John Locke. *Life of Abraham Lincoln*, edited by Roy P. Basler and Lloyd A. Dunlap. 1860. Reprint, New York: Greenwood Press, 1961.

Seward, William Henry and Frederick William Seward. *Seward at Washington as Senator and Secretary of State: A Memoir of His Life with Selections from his Letters*. New York: Derby and Miller, 1891.

Story, Joseph. *Commentaries on the Constitution of the United States*, 3 vols. 3rd ed. Boston, MA: Little, Brown, 1858.

Strong, George Templeton. *Diary of George Templeton Strong*, edited by Allan Nevins and Milton Halsey Thomas. 3 vols. New York: Macmillan, 1952.

Sumner, Charles. *Charles Sumner: His Complete Works*. Boston, MA: Lee and Shepard, 1872.

Turner, Justin G. and Linda Levitt Turner. *Mary Todd Lincoln: Her Life and Letters*. New York: Alfred A. Knopf, 1972.

Tyler, Royall. *The Algerine Captive*. 1816. Reprint, Bedford, MA: Applewood-Books, 2008.

Villard, Henry. *Lincoln on the Eve of '61: A Journalist's Story*, edited by Harold G. and Oswald Garrison Villard. New York: Alfred A. Knopf, 1941.

Walker, David. *Walker's Appeal with a Brief Sketch of His Life*. New York: J. H. Tobitt, 1848.

Weems, Mason Locke, ed. *The Life of Benjamin Franklin, Written Chiefly by Himself, with a Collection of His Best Essays*. Philadelphia: M. Carey, 1817.

Weems, Mason Locke, ed. *The Life of George Washington; with Curious Anecdotes, Equally Honorourable to Himself, and Exemplary to his Young Countrymen*. Philadelphia: Joseph Allen, 1837.

Weld, Theodore Dwight. *The Bible against Slavery: An Inquiry into the Patriarchal and Mosaic Systems on the Subject of Human Rights*. New York: American Anti-Slavery Society, 1837.

Whiting, William. *The War Powers of the President, and the Legislative Powers of Congress in Relation to Rebellion, Treason and Slavery*, 2nd ed. Boston, MA: John L. Shorey, 1863.

Whitney, Henry C. *Life on the Circuit with Lincoln*. Boston, MA: Estes and Lauriat, 1892.

Wilson, Douglas L., and Rodney O. Davis. *Herndon's Informants: Letters, Interviews, and Statements about Abraham Lincoln*. Urbana: University of Illinois Press, 1998.

Yarnall, Ellis. *Wordsworth and the Coleridges, with other Memories, Literary and Political*. New York: Macmillan, 1899.

## Secondary Works

### Books

Auslin Michael R. *Pacific Cosmopolitans: A Cultural History of U.S.-Japan Relations*. Cambridge, MA: Harvard University Press, 2011.

Bacon, Theodore Davenport. *Leonard Bacon: A Statesman in the Church*. New Haven, CT: Yale University Press, 1931.

Baker, Jean. *Mary Todd Lincoln: A Biography*. New York: W. W. Norton, 1987.

Baron, Frank. *Abraham Lincoln and the German Immigrants: Turners and Forty-Eighters*. Lawrence, KS: Society for German-American Studies, 2012.

Bender, Thomas. *A Nation among Nations: America's Place in World History*. New York: Hill and Wang, 2006.

Blackett, R. J. M. *Divided Hearts: Britain and the American Civil War*. Baton Rouge: Louisiana State University Press, 2001.

Boyd, Steven R. *Patriotic Envelopes of the Civil War: The Iconography of Union and Confederate Covers.* Baton Rouge: Louisiana State University Press, 2010.

Bray, Robert. *Reading with Lincoln.* Carbondale: Southern Illinois University Press, 2010.

Brown, T. Allston. *A History of the New York Stage: From the First Performance in 1732 to 1901.* New York: Dodd, Mead and Company, 1903.

Burlingame, Michael. *Abraham Lincoln: A Life.* Baltimore, MD: Johns Hopkins University Press, 2008.

Campbell, Andrew. *English Public Opinion and the American Civil War.* Suffolk, UK: The Boydell Press for the Royal Historical Society, 2003.

Carnahan, Burrus M. *Act of Justice: Lincoln's Emancipation Proclamation and the Law of War.* Lexington: University Press of Kentucky, 2007.

Carwardine, Richard. *Lincoln: A Life of Purpose and Power.* New York: Alfred A. Knopf, 2006.

Carwardine, Richard and Jay Sexton, eds. *The Global Lincoln.* New York: Oxford University Press, 2011.

Clinton, Catherine. *Mrs. Lincoln: A Life.* New York: Harper Collins, 2008.

Davis, Hugh. *Leonard Bacon: New England Reformer and Antislavery Moderate.* Baton Rouge: Louisiana State University Press, 1998.

De Puy, Henry W. *Kossuth and His Generals, with a Brief History of Hungary.* Buffalo, NY: Phinney and Co., 1852.

Donald, David Herbert. *Charles Sumner and the Coming of the Civil War.* New York: Alfred A. Knopf, 1960.

———. *Lincoln.* New York: Simon & Schuster, 1995.

———. *"We Are Lincoln Men": Abraham Lincoln and His Friends.* New York: Simon & Schuster, 2007.

Efford, Alison Clark. *German Immigrants, Race, and Citizenship in the Civil War Era.* Washington, D.C.: German Historical Insititute; Cambridge: Cambridge University Press, 2013.

Faust, Albert Bernhardt. *The German Element in the United States with Special Reference to Its Political, Moral, Social, and Educational Influence.* Boston: Houghton Mifflin, 1909.

Faust, Drew Gilpin. *The Ideology of Slavery: Proslavery Thought in the Antebellum South, 1830–1860.* Baton Rouge: Louisiana State University Press, 1981.

———. *This Republic of Suffering: Death and the American Civil War.* New York: Alfred A. Knopf, 2008.

Finkelman, Paul. *Defending Slavery: Proslavery Thought in the Old South: A Brief History with Documents.* New York: Bedford/St. Martins, 2003.

Foner, Eric. *The Fiery Trial: Abraham Lincoln and American Slavery.* New York: W. W. Norton, 2010.

———. *Free Soil, Free Labor, Free Men: The Ideology of the Republican Party before the Civil War.* New York: Oxford University Press, 1970.

Foreman, Amanda. *A World on Fire: Britain's Crucial Role in the American Civil War.* New York: Random House, 2010.

Freidel, Frank. *Francis Lieber: Nineteenth-Century Liberal.* Baton Rouge: Louisiana State University Press, 1947.

Freitag, Sabine. *Friedrich Hecker: Two Lives for Liberty.* Translated by Steven W. Rowan. St. Louis, MO: St. Louis Mercantile Library, 2006.

Goodheart, Adam. *1861: The Civil War Awakening*. New York: Knopf, 2011.

Goodwin, Doris Kearns. *Team of Rivals: The Political Genius of Abraham Lincoln*. New York: Simon & Schuster, 2005.

Guelzo, Allen C. *Lincoln's Emancipation Proclamation: The End of Slavery in America*. New York: Simon & Schuster, 2004.

Hedrick, Joan D. *Harriet Beecher Stowe: A Life*. New York: Oxford University Press, 1994.

Heidler, David Stephen and Janice T. Heidler. *Henry Clay: The Essential American*. New York: Random House, 2010.

Hodes, Martha. *Mourning Lincoln*. New Haven: Yale University Press, 2015.

Holzer, Harold. *Lincoln and New York*. New York: New-York Historical Society, 2009.

———. *Lincoln and the Power of the Press: The War for Public Opinion*. New York: Simon & Schuster, 2014.

———. *Lincoln, President-Elect: Abraham Lincoln and the Great Secession Winter*. New York: Simon & Schuster, 2008.

Honeck, Mischa. *We Are the Revolutionists: German-Speaking Immigrants and American Abolitionists after 1848*. Athens: University of Georgia Press, 2011.

Howe, Daniel Walker. *The Political Culture of the American Whigs*. Chicago: University of Chicago Press, 1979.

Jones, Howard. *Abraham Lincoln and a New Birth of Freedom: The Union and Slavery in the Diplomacy of the Civil War*. Lincoln: University of Nebraska Press, 1999.

———. *Union in Peril: The Crisis over British Intervention in the Civil War*. Chapel Hill: University of North Carolina Press, 1992.

Julian, George Washington. *The Life of Joshua R. Giddings*. Chicago: A. C. McClurg and Company, 1892.

Khan, Yasmin Sabina. *Enlightening the World: The Creation of the Statue of Liberty*. Ithaca, NY: Cornell University Press, 2010.

King, Dean. *Skeletons on the Zahara: A True Story of Survival*. Boston, MA: Little, Brown, and Company, 2004.

Kline, Michael J. *The Baltimore Plot: The First Conspiracy to Assassinate Abraham Lincoln*. Yardley, PA: Westholme Publishing, 2008.

Komlos, John H. *Louis Kossuth in America, 1851–1852*. Buffalo, NY: East European Institute, 1973.

Lehrman, Lewis E. *Lincoln at Peoria: The Turning Point: Getting Right with the Declaration of Independence*. Mechanicsburg, PA: Stackpole Books, 2008.

Lockwood, John and Charles Lockwood. *The Siege of Washington: The Untold Story of the Twelve Days that Shook the Union*. New York: Oxford University Press, 2011.

Lonn, Ella. *Foreigners in the Union Army and Navy*. Baton Rouge: Louisiana State University Press, 1951.

Luebke, Frederick C., ed. *Ethnic Voters and the Election of Lincoln*. Lincoln: University of Nebraska Press, 1971.

Machor, James L. *Reading Fiction in Antebellum America: Informed Response and Reception Histories, 1820–1865*. Baltimore, MD: Johns Hopkins University Press, 2011.

Marszalek, John F. *Commander of All Lincoln's Armies: A Life of Henry W. Halleck*. Cambridge, MA: Belknap Press of Harvard University Press, 2004.

Magness, Phillip W. and Sebastian N. Page. *Colonization after Emancipation: Lincoln and the Movement for Black Resettlement*. Columbia: University of Missouri Press, 2011.

Masur, Louis P. *Lincoln's Hundred Days: The Emancipation Proclamation and the War for the Union*. Cambridge, MA: Belknap Press of Harvard University Press, 2012.

McPherson, James. *Battle Cry of Freedom: The Civil War Era*. New York: Oxford University Press, 1988.

Mellon, Matthew T. *Early American Views on Negro Slavery*. New York: Bergman Publishers, 1969.

Miller, Richard Lawrence. *The Path to the Presidency*, vol. 4 of *Lincoln and His World*. Jefferson, NC: McFarland, 2012.

———. *The Rise to National Prominence, 1843–1853*, vol. 3 of *Lincoln and His World*. Jefferson, NC: McFarland & Co., 2011.

Monaghan, Jay. *Diplomat in Carpet Slippers: Abraham Lincoln Deals with Foreign Affairs*. Indianapolis, IN: Bobbs-Merrill Company, 1945.

Neely, Mark E., Jr. *The Boundaries of American Political Culture in the Civil War*. Chapel Hill: University of North Carolina Press, 2005.

Nicolay, Helen. *Lincoln's Secretary, a Biography of John G. Nicolay*. New York: Longmans, Green, 1949.

Nicolay John G. and John Hay. *Abraham Lincoln: A History*, 10 vols. New York: The Century Co., 1890.

Noll, Mark A. *The Civil War as a Theological Crisis*. Chapel Hill: University of North Carolina Press, 2006.

Oakes, James. *Freedom National: The Destruction of Slavery in the United States, 1861–1865*. New York: W. W. Norton, 2013.

Odell, George Clinton Densmore. *Annals of the New York Stage*. New York: Columbia University Press, 1927–1949.

Oren, Michael B. *Power, Faith, and Fantasy: America in the Middle East, 1776 to the Present*. New York: W. W. Norton, 2007.

Peraino, Kevin. *Lincoln in the World: The Making of a Statesman and the Dawn of American Power*. New York: Crown Publishers, 2013.

Pinsker, Matthew. *Lincoln's Sanctuary: Abraham Lincoln and the Soldiers' Home*. New York: Oxford University Press, 2003.

Pitch, Anthony S. *"They Have Killed Papa Dead!": The Road to Ford's Theatre, Abraham Lincoln's Murder, and the Rage for Vengeance*. Hanover, NH: Steerforth, 2008.

Poser, Norman S. *Lord Mansfield: Justice in the Age of Reason*. Montreal: McGill-Queen's University Press, 2013.

Pullen, John J. *Comic Relief: The Life and Laughter of Artemus Ward, 1834–1867*. Hamden, CT: Archon Books, 1983.

Roberts, Timothy Mason. *Distant Revolutions: 1848 and the Challenge to American Exceptionalism*. Charlottesville: University of Virginia Press, 2009.

Sandburg, Carl. *Lincoln Collector: The Story of Oliver R. Barrett's Great Private Collection*. New York: Harcourt, Brace, 1949.

Schuckers, Jacob William. *The Life and Public Services of Salmon Portland Chase*. New York: D. Appleton and Company, 1874.

Sears, Stephen W. *George B. McClellan: The Young Napoleon*. Boston, MA: Ticknor and Fields, 1988.

Sexton, Jay. *Debtor Diplomacy: Finance and American Foreign Relations in the Civil War Era 1837–1873*. Oxford: Clarendon Press, 2005.

Spencer, Donald S. *Louis Kossuth and Young America: A Study of Sectionalism and Foreign Policy, 1848–1852*. Columbia: University of Missouri Press, 1977.

Springer, Paul J. and Glenn Robins. *Transforming Civil War Prisons: Lincoln, Lieber, and the Politics of Captivity*. New York: Routledge, 2015.

Stahr, Walter. *Seward: Lincoln's Indispensable Man*. New York: Simon & Schuster, 2012.

Stevens, Walter B. *A Reporter's Lincoln*, 2 vols. Saint Louis: Missouri Historical Society, 1916.

Stewart, James Brewer. *Joshua R. Giddings and the Tactics of Radical Politics*. Cleveland, OH: Case Western Reserve University Press, 1970.

Swanson, James L. *Manhunt: The Twelve-Day Chase for Lincoln's Killer*. New York: William Morrow, 2006.

Taliaferro, John. *All the Great Prizes: The Life of John Hay, from Lincoln to Roosevelt*. New York: Simon & Schuster, 2014.

Tarbell, Ida M. *The Life of Abraham Lincoln*. New York: Doubleday & McClure Co., 1900.

Taylor, Welford Dunaway, ed. *Our American Cousin: The Play that Changed History*. Washington, DC: Beacham Publishing, 1990.

Thomas, Benjamin P. *Abraham Lincoln: A Biography*. New York: Knopf, 1952.

Tolles, Winton. *Tom Taylor and the Victorian Drama*. New York: Columbia University Press, 1940.

Trevelyan, George Macaulay. *The Life of John Bright*. Boston, MA: Houghton Mifflin, 1913.

Vorenberg, Michael. *Final Freedom: The Civil War, the Abolition of Slavery, and the Thirteenth Amendment*. New York: Cambridge University Press, 2001.

Warren, Gordon H. *Fountain of Discontent: The Trent Affair and Freedom of the Seas*. Boston, MA: Northeastern University Press, 1981.

Winkle, Kenneth J. *Lincoln's Citadel: The Civil War in Washington, DC*. New York: W. W. Norton & Company, 2013.

Witt, John Fabian. *Lincoln's Code: The Laws of War in American History*. New York: Free Press, 2012.

### Articles in Journals and Anthologies

Baepler, Paul. "The Barbary Captivity Narrative in American Culture." *Early American Literature* 39 (2004): 217–246.

———. "White Slaves, African Masters." *Annals of the AAPSS* 588 (2003): 90–104.

Battistini, Robert. "Glimpses of the Other before Orientalism: The Muslim World in Early American Periodicals, 1785–1800." *Early American Studies* 8 (2010): 446–474.

Bray, Robert. "What Abraham Lincoln Read: An Evaluative and Annotated List." *Journal of the Abraham Lincoln Association* 28, no. 2 (2007): 28–81.

Breeden, James O. "Oscar Lieber: Southern Scientist, Southern Patriot." *Civil War History* 36 (1990): 226–249.

Engerman, Stanley. "Slavery, Freedom, and Sen," in *Buying Freedom: The Ethics and Economics of Slave Redemption*, edited by Kwame Anthony Appiah and Martin Bunzl, 77–107. Princeton, NJ: Princeton University Press, 2007.

Freidel, Frank. "The Loyal Publication Society: A Pro-Union Propaganda Agency." *Mississippi Valley Historical Review* 26 (1939): 359–376.

Friedrich, Carl J. "The European Background," in *The Forty-Eighters: Political Refugees of the German Revolution*, edited by A. E. Zucker, 3–25. New York: New York University Press, 1950.

Hart, Gideon M. "Military Commissions and the Lieber Code: Toward a New Understanding of the Jurisdictional Foundations of Military Commissions." *Military Law Review* 203 (2010): 1–77.

Holzer, Harold. "Like a Thief in the Night," *New York Times*, February 22, 2011.

———. "Visualizing Lincoln: Abraham Lincoln as Student, Subject, and Patron of the Visual Arts," in *Our Lincoln: New Perspectives on Lincoln and His World*, edited by Eric Foner, 80–108. New York: W. W. Norton, 2008.

Holzer, Harold H., Gabor S. Boritt, and Mark E. Neely, Jr., "Francis Bicknell Carpenter (1830–1900): Painter of Abraham Lincoln and His Circle." *American Art Journal* 16, no. 2 (1984): 66–89.

Jentz, John B. "The 48ers and the Politics of the German Labor Movement in Chicago during the Civil War Era: Community Formation and the Rise of a Labor Press," in *The German-American Radical Press: The Shaping of a Left Political Culture, 1850–1940*, edited by Elliot Shore, Ken Fones-Wolf, and James P. Danky, 49–62. Urbana: Illinois University Press, 1992.

Kates, Don B., Jr. "Abolition, Deportation, Integration: Attitudes toward Slavery in the Early Republic." *Journal of Negro History* 53 (1968): 33–47.

Kellow, Margaret M. R. "Conflicting Imperatives: Black and White American Abolitionists Debate Slavery Redemption," in *Buying Freedom: The Ethics and Economics of Slave Redemption*, edited by Kwame Anthony Appiah and Martin Bunzl, 200–213. Princeton, NJ: Princeton University Press, 2007.

Lohne, Raymond. "Team of Friends: A New Lincoln Theory and Legacy." *Journal of the Illinois State Historical Society* 101 (2008): 285–314.

McConachie, Bruce. "American Theatre in Context, from the Beginnings to 1870," in *Beginnings to 1870*. Vol. 1 of *The Cambridge History of American Theatre*, edited by Don B. Wilmeth and Christopher Bigsby. Cambridge: Cambridge University Press, 1998.

Mancini, Matthew. "Francis Lieber, Slavery, and the 'Genesis' of the Laws of War." *Journal of Southern History* 77 (2011): 325–348.

Masur, Kate. "'A Rare Phenomenon of Philological Vegetation': The Word 'Contraband' and the Meanings of Emancipation in the United States." *Journal of American History* 93 (2007): 1050–1084.

McMurtry, R. G. "The Influence of Riley's Narrative upon Abraham Lincoln." *Indiana Magazine of History* 30 (1934): 133–138.

Meersman, Roger and Robert Beyer. "The National Theatre in Washington: Buildings and Audiences, 1835–1972." *Records of the Columbia Historical Society, Washington D.C.* 71/72 (1973), 190–242.

Randall, J. G. "Lincoln and John Bright." *Yale Review*, n.s. 34 (1944–1945): 292–304.

Ratcliffe, Donald J. "Selling Captain Riley, 1816–1859: How Did His 'Narrative' Become So Well Known?" *Proceedings of the American Antiquarian Society* 117 (2007): 177–209.

Rawley, James A. "Isaac Newton Arnold, Lincoln's Friend and Biographer." *Journal of the Abraham Lincoln Association* 19, no. 1 (1998): 39–56.

Rock, Stephen. "Anglo-U.S. Relations, 1845–1930: Did Shared Liberal Values and Democratic Institutions Keep the Peace?" in *Paths to Peace: Is Democracy the Answer?*, edited by Miriam Fendius Elman, 101–149. Cambridge, MA: MIT Press, 1997.

Rojas, Martha Elena. "'Insults Unpunished': Barbary Captives, American Slaves, and the Negation of Liberty." *Early American Studies* 1 (2003): 159–186.

Ross, Dorothy. "Lincoln and the Ethics of Emancipation: Universalism, Nationalism, Exceptionalism." *Journal of American History* 96 (2009): 379–399.

Schied, Fred M. "Education and Working Class Culture: German Workers' Clubs in Nineteenth Century Chicago," http://www-distance.syr.edu/schied.html.

Schildt, Roberta. "Freedman's Village: Arlington, Virginia, 1863–1900," *Arlington Historical Magazine* 7, no. 4 (1984): 11–21.

Temple, Wayne C. "A. W. French: Lincoln Family Dentist." *Lincoln Herald* 63 (Fall 1961): 151–154.

———. "The Linguistic Lincolns: A New Lincoln Letter." *Lincoln Herald* 94 (Fall 1992): 108–114.

Vorenberg, Michael. "Liberté, Égalité, and Lincoln: French Readings of an American President," in *The Global Lincoln*, edited by Richard Carwardine and Jay Sexton, 95–106. New York: Oxford University Press, 2011.

Wilentz, Sean. "Abraham Lincoln and Jacksonian Democracy," in *Our Lincoln: New Perspectives on Lincoln and His World*, edited by Eric Foner. New York: W. W. Norton, 2008.

Winship, Michael. "*Uncle Tom's Cabin*: History of the Book in the 19th-Century United States," at *Uncle Tom's Cabin and American Culture: A Multi-Media Archive* at http://utc.iath.virginia.edu/interpret/exhibits/winship/winship.html.

### Dissertations

Freidel, Frank Burt. "The Life of Francis Lieber." PhD diss., University of Wisconsin–Madison, 1941.

Ray, Rebecca Lea. "A Stage History of Tom Taylor's *Our American Cousin*." PhD diss., School of Philosophy, New York University, 1985.

# Index

For EU product safety concerns, contact us at Calle de José Abascal, 56–1°,
28003 Madrid, Spain or eugpsr@cambridge.org.